Soul

Also by Phil Cousineau

Deadlines: A Rhapsody on a Theme of Famous and Infamous Last Words

Also edited by Phil Cousineau

The Hero's Journey: Joseph Campbell on His Life and Work
The Soul of the World (with photographs by Eric Lawton)

SOUL

An Archaeology

Readings from
Socrates to Ray Charles

Compiled and with Commentary
by Phil Cousineau

HarperSanFrancisco
A Division of HarperCollins*Publishers*

HarperSanFrancisco and the author, in association with the Rainforest Action Network, will facilitate the planting of two trees for every one tree used in the manufacture of this book.

Permissions credits begin on page 237.

FIRST EDITION

Text design by Margery Cantor
Art by Ginger Beringer

Library of Congress Cataloging-in-Publication Data

Soul : an archaeology : readings from Socrates to Ray Charles /
    compiled and with commentary by Phil Cousineau. — 1st ed.
        p.   cm.
    Includes bibliographical references and index.
    ISBN 0–06–250239–5 (alk. paper)
    ISBN 0–06–250243–3 (pbk.)
    1. Soul.   I. Cousineau, Phil.
BL290.S68   1994
128'.1—dc20   93–30040
                                                          CIP

94 95 96 97 98 ❖ HAD 10 9 8 7 6 5 4 3 2 1

To the memory of David Cousineau,
my uncle, my mentor, my friend.

CONTENTS

PART TWO

THE SEAT OF THE SOUL

PART FIVE
SOUL WORK

Contents xi

PART SIX
THE WORLD SOUL

PART SEVEN

SOUL AND DESTINY

You could not discover the frontiers of soul, even if you traveled every road to do so; such is the depth of its meaning.

Heraclitus of Ephesus

The soul is a fire that darts its rays through all the senses; it is in this fire that existence consists; all the observations and all the efforts of the philosophers ought to turn towards this, the center and moving power of our sentiments and our ideas.

Madame de Staël

It's eternity in a person that turns the crank handle.

Franz Kafka

Acknowledgments

No one can plunge deeply into the underworld of soul without wise guides. Although years of lone wolf exploration of philosophy, mythology, religion, poetry, literature, art, and music went into the creation of this volume, it was through invaluable crossroad conversations with many soulful friends, teachers, mentors, and family that this anthology took on its protean form. To all those who have graced this project with their blue pencils, arcane references, and soul talk, I am grateful.

Most of all, I want to express my hearty thanks to those who answered when the call went out, "Can I Get a Witness?" and volunteered to "Stand By Me" through the book shape-shifting sessions "In the Midnight Hour," especially: Huston Smith for sharing a lifetime of wisdom about the notion of soul among world religions, and his invaluable comments on the manuscript; Brian Swimme for his soaring cosmological views on the depths of the soul in the universe; James Hillman for his trailblazing work in bringing soul back into psychology; Robert Johnson for his animated encouragement about my work and his illuminations about eros and psyche; Valerie Andrews for her Aretha-worthy "respect" for the presence of soul in the natural world; Brother David Steindl-Rast for generously sharing his thoughts with me on the role of soul in the contemplative life; Jamake Highwater for our provocative discussions on the difference between personal and communal soul; Jay Fikes for his scholarly leads on soul belief in Native culture; and to the late Reuben Snake for his wise counsel on the meaning of soul journeys for Native Americans; and the late Joseph Campbell for his trickster advice on my pursuit of the "soul's high adventure."

I also want to remember David Darling for the amazing grace of his bluesy cello music that accompanied many of my all-night sessions; Richard Beban for years of caffeinated talks from Paris to North Beach on that eternal question of whether or not there's any cure for the summertime blues; Keith Thompson for our marathon round table talks on the astonishment of it all; Eric Lawton for shining light on the soul power of images with his photography during our years of collaboration; Lynne Kaufman for her dramatic thoughts on the soul of the writing life; Bruce Bochte for embodying the soulful side of sports; Michael Guillen for being my guide through the maze of Mesoamerican concepts on soul; Mort Rosenblum and Jeannette Hermann for sharing the soul of the road; David Whyte for his uncanny ability to bridge soul and business, poetry, and memory; Joyce Jenkins for turning the pages of so much new poetry for me and for her passionate conviction of how interanimated the soul of the world is with the poetry of the world; my nephew Adam Balcerek, whose courage in starting life over has helped revive my faith in the soul of the future; and to my late Uncle Dave Cousineau whose passing on has provoked me to contemplate more than ever the mystery of the destiny of the soul.

For his original enthusiasm and confidence in my "taking it to the streets" approach for an anthology on soul, I want to thank my publisher, Tom Grady at HarperSanFrancisco. Thanks, too, to my editor, Caroline Pincus, whose deft touch and care of the soul of the project coaxed it home after its long journey; Kevin Bentley for his stalwart support; Hilary Vartanian for her sage advice about the anthology steeplechase that had to be run; and to Jo Beaton who has shown a "heart full of soul" with her selfless attention to the myriad details surrounding this book, which, in the long view, is as fine as any definition you'll find for soul work.

Finally, I would like to spin a record of thanks to all those at Motown, Memphis, and Muscle Shoals for the soul music soundtrack that's had me singin' in the shower and dancin' in the street since I first made the soul connection between philosophy and music, basketball and poetry, Socrates and Ray Charles. "Tell me what I'd say. . . ."

PHIL COUSINEAU
San Francisco
Indian Summer, 1993

Prologue

I

The philosophy of six thousand years has not searched the chambers and magazines of the soul.

—Ralph Waldo Emerson

To fathom the unfathomable soul we immediately plunge into mystery. To probe the images of the soul as the vital force, the source of consciousness, the persistence of things, the core of individuality, the depth dimension, the raw, blue rhythm of life, is to suddenly, with Lear, "take upon us the mystery of things, as if we were God's spies."

The mystery has to do with how something outside of the world rushes in—a sulfurous mixture that ignites the spark of life where there was none before and carves out a cavernous inner dimension unique to all things. It has to do with the imperceptible forces that echo whenever the slow combustion of eternity is evoked. It taps into the conjunction of energies that are strangely impersonal, yet far nearer to our essential selves than the fleeting consciousness that streams through our minds.

If we're not bewildered by the mysteries of the soul, we're not thinking clearly, to paraphrase the scrawling on subway walls. For the soul's mysteries compress the most profound mythic questions that have always intrigued human beings: Where do we come from? Why are here? Where do we go when we die?

But there is some consolation built into consternation, as the Sufi mystic Mevlana Rumi knew when he wrote seven centuries ago that "Bewilderment is intuition." From pharaonic Egypt to Delta blues clubs, from the marble-marveled agora of classical Athens to the vast white tundra of Arctic hunters, belief in an uncanny force at the heart of things has been intuited, a sleep-strange feeling rooted in a *presence* of tremendous impact that circulates through and animates all of nature.

Uncanny, strange, unsettling, but not ineffable. Every known culture has taken upon itself the naming of this force, usually after the words for wind, shadow, movement, smoke, strength.

According to the Greek philosopher Diogenes, it was Xenophanes who first equated breath with soul, using the word *psyche* with its colorful associations of coolness, bellows, and butterfly. Twenty-three centuries later, in 1828, Charles Nodier wrote in Paris, "The different names for the soul, among nearly all peoples are just so many breath variations, and onomatopoeic expressions for breathing."

Psyche, anima, atman, savira, semangat, nephesh, otachuk, loákal, tunzi, prana, duk, and *geist* are sacred words used by primal peoples the world over for the surge of life itself, linguistic cousins of what was called *sawol* in Old English, *sawal* by the Anglo-Saxons, *sala* by the Icelandic folk, and eventually, as if stone-polished by the ages, what we now call *soul.* A persistent presence not conjured up as a mystical hoax or priestly dogma, but keenly recognized as the influence of breath upon birth and death, or profoundly experienced in transportive dream or deep trance. In these soul moments are the flash points of eternity.

As the "life-giving principle," in Aristotle's classic definition, soul has bountiful associations: fire and warmth, sexual fertility and inspiration, ecstasy and fantasy, love and madness. As a far-ranging inner landscape, it shares many frontiers, including the realms of dream, imagination, poetry, religion, mythology, death and the underworld. As the parallax point of our individuality, it is where we converge into world. Rich in allusions, but poor in definitions, soul eludes reductionism and embraces elaboration.

In the phenomenology of the soul the image of something immaterial and incorruptible that survives after death as ghost or spirit is found throughout history. Of the ancient view, religious historian Mircea Eliade mused in his journals in January 1964, "in postulating the autonomy of the soul and its survival post-mortem, man opened to himself an unlimited perspective, thanks to which a whole 'phenomenology of the Spirit' became possible." But with the advent of scientific reductionism and empirical psychology at the end of the often spiritually chloroformed nineteenth century, metaphysical beliefs were scoffed at for being unverifiable, or worse, irrational. Though the "soul" was exiled from so-called rational discourse, even considered a four-letter word in some hermetically sealed circles, the presence is still there, as evident by the curious sense of *being lived by* psychic forces—emotions, dreams, desires—far beyond the realm of rational explanation, but well within the physics of the soul, the realm of unlimited mythological perspectives.

In our own time, some still hold on to the traditional view of an immortal and divine soul, but the ancient Greek idea of soul being more like the slippery shape-shifter god Proteus than a single static image has been vindicated by the modern many-masked role it now plays: life force, immortality symbol, the bold standard for quality, charisma, character. We are no less in awe of the mystery power that vivifies our lives—the unknown factor—but more than ever regard the soul as a vigorous symbol for what lurks behind the flux of the mind, beyond the changes of any individual life, below the ordinary senses. For many, soul is the constellating image for the paradox of *unchanging depths in an ever-changing universe.* In a postmodern world of instantaneous revisionism of all we hold sacred, soul is an existential anchor for the drifting ship of awareness.

Peculiarly enough, though, the reality of the soul has also long been expressed by terrified references to its loss, the fear of its *absence* as much as its presence. Like an artist's way of seeing the things of the world by the *outlines formed by negative space,* soul is often visualized by references to what it *isn't;* that is, in the harrowing suspicion that a piece of ourselves is "missing," or in the sudden losses of our personal lives, the disturbing disappearance of beauty in our city architecture, the sacrifice of quality to the cult of mediocrity in culture, the vanishing of vitality in business and politics, the trivialization of contemporary life.

This "psychic numbing," as Robert J. Lifton has called it, the existential crunch of the day, is the "disease of our times," a glossy way of naming what the ancients simply called "soul loss." As far back as the grievous days after World War II, author Wallace Stegner was saying, "The sickness of our times is not a political sickness; it's a soul sickness." A more familiar litany of descriptions of our fragmented world from any contemporary morning newspaper or evening notebook of a therapist, teacher, or priest would include: a sense of alienation, rootlessness, apathy, burnout, torpor, anxiety, cynicism, the fear of leading an inauthentic life. Every illness has its symptoms, and ours is betrayed by our obsessions, addictions, and violence; our corrosive loneliness, vague purposelessness, and hall-of-mirrors narcissism. Soulless times are often marked by black humor reveling in the self-doubt that our lives are mere movie scripts or, worse, that we're tourists rather than travelers on this road of life. Our passive responses to a world drained of soul by the spiritual vampires of corporate Transylvania, our numb acceptance of a world of gleaming surfaces, is encouraged by the basilisk stare of the threshold guardians at the gates to the depths, those who insist there is nothing below and beyond what is immediately apparent—so we might as well turn back. These scoundrels are soul-catchers in the wry. Their emblem is snide irony, like the madhatter movie critic who concluded his review of the cyber-souled *Blade Runner,* "With all this style, who needs substance?"

Novelist Walker Percy said just before he died, "Something has gone wrong with the postmodern world—to the core of meaning itself." And yet, the paradox—one of many surrounding soul—is that these "pathologies," as depth psychologist James Hillman describes them, that entangle us may be the most vivid ways for us to *"realize the soul as real."* Our bittersweet destiny just may unfold for us out of our most tightly folded experiences: death, lunacy, depression, fantasy, what William Blake called the "soul-shuddering vacuum." Out of this contorting and twisting, what the Russians call *ostranenie,* the "making strange," the deliberate defamiliarization of the too-familiar, soul can reappear where it once was lost.

Together, these images outline as if in dark charcoal the meaningfull shape of soul. Identifying what we've tragically lost, sold to the devil, or had violently seized from us can help us recognize why soul describes the elusive element that infuses existence with meaning, vitality, authenticity, beauty, deep desire, real character. Soul is that unmistakable fire that infuses all truly creative endeavors and sends the shiver up the spine, telling us we're in the presence of *lived truth.*

Not a thing but a perspective, not substance but symbol, not dogma but touchstone, the test word for gold in the depths of our lives. From Socrates, the insatiable seeker after truth, to Ray Charles, the incendiary genius of soul music, the soul-navigating Siberian shamans to Carl Jung in his dream-roving tower at Bollingen, rogue philosophers have observed that the only universe as vast as the one outside is the one inside—one consisting of galaxies of images that have accumulated for billions of years and condensed like stardust in our imaginations. Contemplating the night sky of the soul might remind us of the poetic comforts of the old alchemical truth, "As above, so below," but its sheer elusiveness can also intensify our grave doubts about the truth of our insights about the accumulated images hovering there in the "inscapes."

So why bother? Why ponder the imponderable? Speak of the ineffable? Because something undeniable presses in on us: beauty, time, death, the holiness of the world, a "nostalgia for the universal," as the painter Piet Mondrian saw it. And out of the reeling vertigo that comes from looking into the black hole at the center of ourselves and being able to only conjure up "uncertainty principles" comparable to the ever-shifting conclusions of physicists comes what religious historian Huston Smith has called the profound need of people "to believe that the truth they perceive is rooted in the unchanging depths of the universe; for were it not, could the truth be really important?"

Soul, the strange weave of light, shadow, flame, and breath, is rooted there, in the spontaneous creating of continuous images and ideas about the unknown continuity of things.

II

What ghost is this that walks with me;
always in darkness walks with me?

—Conrad Aiken

For as long as I can remember I've been confounded by these mysteries of the soul's dark beauty. My *Soul* anthology has shape-shifted out of this lifelong fascination for the mystifying connections around the world between the language, lore, and imagery of the soul. During my research for an earlier book I created with the photographer Eric Lawton, *The Soul of the World: A Modern Book of Hours,* I was rather startled to discover that I couldn't find any collection of writing on soul. I explored the central sources, the ambrosial work of Plato and Aristotle, Thomas Aquinas, Saint Teresa of Avila, and Marsilio Ficino, Sigmund Freud, Carl Jung, and James Hillman, who all use soul as a kind of lodestone to keep their work pointing to magnetic north. Much to my surprise, though, no compilation existed of the classical references, myths, legends, literature, poetry, or contemplations that might give a panoramic view of the imperative territory of the soul.

So when my enthusiasm for collecting soulful quotes for our Book of Hours far exceeded what was needed, I decided to "keep on keepin' on," as soul singers scat, despite Saint Augustine's curiosity-killing riddle: "What did God do before he made heaven and earth?" ("He was preparing hell for pryers into the mysteries.") But after gathering the most compelling passages from thousands of books, articles, and essays, and plundering my own cache of notebooks from my previous work in mythology, poetry, and film-making, I found myself, if not exactly in Augustine's hell, at least in Homer's underworld.

Wrestling with the slippery material about the soul has reminded me of the marooned Greek warriors in the *Odyssey* wrestling with the sea god Proteus. They held on for dear life, with hopes of tricking him into revealing his secrets, while he transmogrified from beast to beast. Like Menelaus and his men, I've been constantly astonished by the "protean" forms, the convolutions of the soul for anyone trying to pin it down. But I've learned that frustration, uncertainty, confusion, and fear of drowning in the depths is at least a sign that we have our hands on it. The best any of us can do is to hold on long enough for soul to speak for itself, so we may finally learn, like Menelaus and his restless men, the secret only Proteus knew—the way home across the winedark sea.

In the following pages soul speaks for itself through the per-sonae—the masks—of more than 130 voices from around the world, revealing in its own time clues about the depths. The selections come from all five continents and range from an Egyptian Gnostic origin myth of the soul from late antiquity to Emily Dickinson's poetry about the "soul's distinct connection to immortality," Socrates's deathbed thoughts on cultivating the soul to Alice Walker's "Dear Joanna," a searing imaginary letter about soul loss in women.

Still, no anthology can be comprehensive. The best an anthologist can hope for is to be representative, which I hope I've done, for the sake of both rarely voiced cultures and the general reader. To my mind, the advantage of this ecumenical approach is that the only consensus offered here will be the one formed in the imaginations of those who follow the motile soul on its meandering travels along the river of history.

Otherwise, those fascinated with a deeper encounter will only be stuck once again with more "unintelligible answers to insoluble questions," as Henry Adams defined the philosophical spirit, rather than being intrigued with the soul-satisfying passion of their inquiry.

Not to worry. "There is no understanding of soul," anyway, as Thomas Moore reminds us, only cultivation, contemplation, or care. Because soul defies definition like Søren ("If you define me you negate me") Kierkegaard, it is revealed here quality by quality, through selections and excerpts from letters, journal entries, myths, legends and fairy tales, song lyrics, literature, poetry, and essays that describe the soul's meanderings and tone feelings. More than a lust for seductive definitions, what's needed is a genuine "love of the conundrums of the soul," as Hillman refers to the encounter; what's called for is a bold acceptance of the postmodern challenge to become one's own sphinx and be defiant enough to answer one's own riddles with more riddles.

Besides collecting some of history's most influential ideas and memorable descriptions on soul, there has been another reason for me to "press on, regardless," in this exasperating task of trying to get a grip on the squirming question of soul. Frankly, I'm haunted by the vexing questions: Why do I hear Gregorian chant, hell-for-leather sermons, and the whiskey-and-smoke voice of Ray Charles whenever I hear the very word *soul?* What is this "ghost that walks with me"? Why does this cavernous universe within me resound like a cathedral organ reverberating with Bach, the three-tone chords of Tibetan monks, and sometimes, in the heat of the night, the chilling opening chords of Percy Sledge's soul-piercing "When a Man Loves a Woman"?

I suspect I'm not alone when I hear whole worlds in the word. For a long time it's been a keystone in my overarching belief system, an alternately philosophical and funky synonym for depth, character, profundity, rhythm, warmth, flow, even "*It,*" in the patois of my Breton brother, Beat writer Jack Kerouac, who discovered a firestorm in John Coltrane's soaring saxophone, then lit up his own writing with its bebop rhythms.

My almost anachronistic use of the word goes all the way back to my soul-riddled youth. Growing up French Catholic in the suburbs outside Detroit in the volatile sixties meant two things to me. First was being subjected to apoplectic sermons obsessed with saving my woebegone soul at Latin mass every morning before classes in the hallowed halls of old redbricked Wayne St. Mary's. Second was listening to WCHB, "The Motor City's Sound of Soul," after school while playing basketball with the brothers in nearby tough black neighborhoods. The irony of hearing the combustible word evoked by priests at mass and nuns at school, then by Aretha Franklin's ecstatic gospel-inspired soul songs and B. B. King's gut-bucket blues on the crackling transistor radios that the sisters danced to alongside the asphalt courts, wasn't lost on me.

Rather than the vague and somber definition of soul described in the Baltimore Catechism (a hovering chalkboard I imagined, terribly darkened by every sin of the flesh and even imagination—but miraculously washed clean by confession!), I was keen on my own self-fused image from mythology, theology, and the "musicology" of hometown soul music. The sheer idea that ancient philosophers and my homeboy soul singers alike were describing soul as *a mysterious inner movement* had a fine kind of funky poetic justice to it.

Not unlike the way the Greeks had opened the possibility of spiritual perspective with the notion of soul, as Eliade conjectured, Otis, Smokey, Barbara Lewis, and other soul singers confirmed the spiritual perspective of ordinary life by bringing sacred gospel music down into the profane streets. "Music might not heal you, baby, but it'll help your soul," moaned soul deejay Frank Cocker, The Love Man, of WWRL, "Reach out and touch the radio one time—" And with a turn of the radio dial, the pulsing *presence* of soul, for centuries confined to the head and confused with *mind,* could suddenly . . . sensually . . . be back in the rest of the body. Suddenly we were "dancin' in the streets" with Martha and the Vandellas, to the "sweet soul music" of Arthur Conley, and the "some kinda wonderful" feeling of the Soul Brothers Six:

When she wraps her lovin' arms around me
She sets my soul on fire.
Oh, when my baby kiss me
My heart becomes filled with desire.

With background music like this how could I help but notice
soul everywhere? From blues concerts at Detroit's infamous
Keyboard Lounge to the sports pages that gushed purple ink about
the "soulful moves" of Dave Bing, Elgin Baylor, or O. J. Simpson,
workshops like "How to Stay in Business and Not Lose Your Soul,"
and hilarious immortality routines by comedians like Woody Allen
and unintentionally comedic routines on the transmigration of
souls by channel-hopping New Age channelers, how could I help
but wonder what the connections might be between the ancient
and the modern? *Does* Socrates have anything in common with Ray
Charles? Sappho with Aretha? Chartres Cathedral with Fenway
Park? Is there a link between Thales who believed that gods lived in
all things, the Polynesians with their belief in the force of *mana,*
and the animating principles of *mgembe* and *ntum* of African
tribes? Or is it just a coincidence of language? An aberration of
analogy? A charm of words? If Blake was right, that "Everything
that lives is holy," does it follow that everything that lives or even
exists has soul? If not, why not?

To listen to everyday conversation or read a daily newspaper in
this light is to quickly learn to appreciate how the word has persisted despite the awkwardness of trying to describe it. We still
constantly stretch to capture her gypsy heart with proverbs, para-
bles, similes, metaphors, folk sayings, and song lyrics, expressions
that plumb the depths of language when we describe how we
search our soul or lose it; how eyes are windows of the soul, or why
harmonious architecture is full of soul and concrete jungles are
soulless; how carefully handicrafted works are soulful and assem-
bly line goods devoid of it, or how we give our souls up to God and
sell them to the devil; how we break our hearts but lose our souls,
have mortal bodies but immortal souls, seek out food for the soul
and devour soul food; how soul mates long to live together, and
soul brothers share soul handshakes; how we do soul work, suffer
soul loss and drift like lost souls, study soul theft and soul retrieval
in anthropology studies, play duets of "Heart and Soul" on the
piano and select "Soul and Inspiration" on the jukebox, earnestly
try to harmonize mind, body, and soul in therapy, or just plain
describe folks as hearty souls, troubled souls, gentle souls, old
souls.

More than a collection of poetic soul entries to be preserved in amber or a museum of philosophical artifacts, this anthology hopes to provoke the active imagination of readers into wondering what images express their own ideas of the soul. Is it the news of an impending birth and the speculation about where life comes from? An illness in the family that forces us to imagine where life goes after death? The sheer beauty of the prose of the King James version of the Bible or the mystical love poetry of the Sufi mystic Rumi? Or is it the distant gaze in the bronze eyes of the Delphi Charioteer? The soft blue eyes of the children staring lovingly at their mother in Mary Cassatt's luminous paintings? The battle-carved faces of Civil War soldiers dreaming of their young wives they know they'll never see again? The call of Sunday church bell chimes in a remote Devon village? The slow amblin', train-whistle moanin' blues of Alberta Hunter? The streaking flames of the quetzal's feathers in a Guatemalan rain forest?

These soul-evoking images arise spontaneously for me when I ponder my own epiphanies about soul. None are as close to home as the faraway look I remember in my own grandfather's eyes in his old scrapbook photos that show him working the rails in Saskatchewan in 1915. In that fathoms-deep gaze of Grampa Horace Cousineau, which appears again in family photos of him with my own father in the family Model T in Detroit in the 1930s, again while he's standing with his hand on the shoulder of my dying Uncle Roland fifty years later, and again as he walks the lakes around Orlando, Florida, in reluctant retirement, is something I can only call the *persistence of things*. Something that apparently has not changed despite all the other worldly changes around him.

Should we bring it closer? "Bring it on home," as the Muscle Shoals session players sang in soul-soothing lowdown voices. How about as close as my own thousand-yard stare in the family scrapbook photos of my youth that is still there every morning in my shower-fogged bathroom mirror?

Peering closely reveals something quicksilver behind all the rippling traits of my "self" that pass for "me." It is the irreducible "I-in-the-eye," the core element, the blue flame that makes me feel distinct from anyone else who has ever lived.

For me, the "mystery of all things" that tortured Lear is just this persistence. However antiquated the "intimations of immortality" may seem to our postmodern minds, there remains in the fogged-up mirror that we have to wipe clean each morning the question of our own strange persistent gleam and the need to explain it at least to ourselves.

III

Do not seek answers;
live the questions.

—Rainer Maria Rilke

To paraphrase Somerset Maugham's thoughts on the novel, there are three rules for writing about the soul. Unfortunately, nobody knows what they are.

So after scouring the wisdom literature of the world are we only left with Ogden Nashian metaphysics like: "Well, I have learned that life is something which you can't conclude anything except it is full of vicissitudes/ and when you expect logic you only come across eccentricitudes"?

Only if by eccentric we just mean "wandering off center," which is exactly what is supposed to happen with any "brave disputation," as Ambrose Bierce defined the vaporings about soul in his delightfully irreverent *Devil's Dictionary.* So chastened by Maugham's walk on the razor's edge of language; forewarned by Heraclitus's thoughts on the boundless frontiers of the soul; chastened by Louis Armstrong's warning about the dangers of explaining away the soul of jazz, this anthology won't risk the wrath of the gods by explaining away the mystery. For overexplanation, as the surrealist playwright Eugène Ionesco pointed out, "separates us from astonishment." But allusion maintains mystery, as Emily Dickinson knew when she wrote of the phantom that walked beside her, "I cannot see my soul, but know 'tis there."

While some of the entries in the following pages attempt to set steel-jawed beartraps of definition, most approach the subject stealthily, allusively, carefully describing, literally "encircling" the soul. I make no claims to these selections being the "best" of anything except my own collection. Since I first began copying down favorite quotes and sometimes entire pages of ecstatic prose in the back pages of my travel journals twenty years ago, I've simply been impassioned by immortalizing lines and ideas and lyrics about soul. So, like autumn leaves under a Michigan maple tree, the pages have accumulated for the last few years. But the harder I tried to rake it all into one pile the harder the wind blew. The more I attempted to organize the book the faster the ideas flew away.

Finally, all that was left to do for anything resembling a structure for an anthology was "loafe and invite [the] soul," in the spirit of the exultant Walt Whitman. Letting go, themes emerged. Eventually they developed into what might be called fractal patterns of the literature of the soul. More than idealized shapes, a certain disorderly order emerged beneath the chaos of the volatile debates down through the centuries; a collage of subatomic particle word traces of the soul's movement through us and through the world.

After reviewing the selections for patterns and perspectives in the traditions, they devolved into seven stages of the spiraling path of the soul that became the seven sections of the book: The Fall of Soul into Time, The Seat of the Soul, Heart and Soul, Soul Crisis, Soul Work, The World Soul, and Soul and Destiny. Each section became a fugue of voices chosen from history's long bookshelf of myths, fables, biographies, poetry. Each is anchored by historically significant passages such as Plato's description of the "chariot of the soul," Saint Teresa's vision of the "interior castle" of the soul, or Wassily Kandinsky's sublime essay "On the Spiritual in Art." Contrasting the classics are counterpoint pieces that should help trigger a few new synapses of thought on the ways soul has been expressed through the ages. To bypass theology's territorial claims, philosophy's stratospheric readouts, and psychology's too-often self-canceling lack of soul, I've included such passages as an anonymous sixteenth-century Mesoamerican song of lamentation over lost souls, the legend of bluesman Robert Johnson's pact with the devil at the "crossroads" to play soul-searing guitar, A. Bartlett Giamatti's nostalgic look at the soul of a rookie baseball player at play in the fields of the "green cathedral," and Swedish poet Tomas Transtromer's meditation on how soul pours into the world like the black liquid mystery of "Espresso."

Other passages are included simply because I appreciate the leaps of imagination, like Chet Raymo's essay on the "Soul of the Night"; the soul-shaking power of their disturbing truths, like Viktor Frankl's gripping account of the life-saving power of the memory of his wife's love while he was imprisoned at Auschwitz; or for their sheer astonishing imagery, such as Robert Bly's translation of Antonio Machado's poem "The wind, one brilliant day, called."

Within each chapter, whenever possible, I've also contrasted familiar points of view, such as the Hebrew story of Genesis with the unfamiliar, such as the Stone Age Tasaday belief in the transparent edge between dream, death, and soul, a story so otherworldly it borders on fable. Occasionally I've taken a familiar mythologem, or archetypal theme, like the Eros and Psyche myth by the Roman writer Apuleius, and chosen a contemporary version instead, such as the gorgeous retelling by storyteller Diane Wolkstein.

If an anthology brazenly combining the soul writing of Aquinas and Jack Kerouac, Hildegard of Bingen, and Mary Shelley surprises some readers, my response is that if a world without soul is a wasteland, then a study or contemplation of soul without vigorously updated examples of the way soul is now vitally expressed in the world only contributes to the drought.

The soul journey as traced in this anthology begins in Part 1, "The Fall of Soul into Time," with a few of our oldest known stories about the origins of the soul including a Stone Age tribe in the Philippines, the Egyptian Gnostics, and several Native American nations. In the interest of illustrating early on in the book the often serious implications of interpretations of the soul I've included an excerpt from the work of the German theologian Uta Ranke-Heinemann on the politics surrounding the beliefs of the moment of conception. Since word origins can often illuminate the dark caves of meaning, I've chosen an excerpt from Swedish anthropologist Åke Hultkrantz's brilliant study of religion among North American Indians for a fascinating etymology on soul. Concluding the chapter is an excerpt from *Brother Ray,* Ray Charles's silhouette memory of the bluesy origins of a "righteous roots music" that takes you down, takes you back, takes you into the raw truth with soul-scorching music wrung from a hardscrabble life. Of such fire came the birth of soul music.

What happens after the soul tumbles into time and world? What form does it take? What does it consist of? Where does it manifest in the body? In Part 2, "The Seat of the Soul," a phrase borrowed from the hymns of the German Romantic poet Novalis, we explore what he called "the points of overlap" in the body and images conjured up by writers on soul through the ages. Selections about the nature of the soul include the serene metaphysics of the Upanishads, the alchemical vantage point of Paracelsus, the mystical experience of being "oned" with the universe of Julian of Norwich, the mechanistic perspective of Descartes, the poetic visions of Longfellow, Blake, and Whitman, and a piece I might have subtitled *Hillman's Razor,* a critically cutting essay on the distinction between soul and spirit.

After soul manifests in the body, a common belief holds that it can be "drawn out" by Eros, symbolized by the drawn bow and arrows of the god of love. From the purely psychological view this is anima leading the soul deeper into consciousness, or "love quickening the soul," in the marvelous phrasing of the medieval ages. Part 3, "Heart and Soul," follows the traditional pairing of Eros and Psyche and ranges from the sublime letters of the tragically fated twelfth-century lovers, Heloise to Abelard, to Christine Downing's deeply moving meditation on the "otherness" of other women in an excerpt from her book *Psyche's Sisters,* a piece I've called "The Significance of Soul for Women."

The American psychologist Rollo May wrote in *The Cry for Myth,* "To live is to war with trolls in heart and soul." Sages have long advised that attachment is soon followed by the inevitable agony of loss. Part 4, "Soul Crisis," explores the lost world of the soul, the grit in the oyster shell, the dark grime on the walls of the labyrinth, the soul's theft, its madness, the numerous menaces to a life of the soul. From Africa I've chosen a fable about "soul-taking," from Germany Goethe's epic soul struggle in *Faust,* the prototype for the Robert Johnson legend. Out of Gothic literature, a veritable gold mine of soul crisis material, I've chosen the final frisson-filled pages from Robert Louis Stevenson's tale of Dr. Jekyll and Mr. Hyde.

Contemporary examples of soul desolation include Sue Nathanson-Elkin's brutally honest account of her abortion and Susan Griffin's gripping essay on the politics, mythology, and street reality of rape. Concluding the section is Greil Marcus's haunting riff on the crossroad crisis of blues genius Robert Johnson.

If soul can be lost, can it be rediscovered? Is there a hidden desire to be torn apart, to struggle, to die as to be reborn? Can soul be consciously re-created? Part 5, "Soul Work," moves from the Apollonian theater of ancient Athens to the Apollo Theater in Harlem. In its wake are passages that range from Psalm 23 and the exalted *Enneads* of Plotinus, to Francis Yates on art and the soul of memory, May Sarton on the poetics of solitude, and Wassily Kandinsky on the soul-stirring alchemy of color and light.

One of the perennial philosophical traditions is that the world is alive. "For many people," as nature writer Barry Lopez has described elsewhere, "the individual self does not end at the skin, but continues with the reach of the senses out onto the land. Not everybody believes that the soul stops at the skin." In other words, there is soul and spirit and a "pervasive energy" outside of us as well as inside; people everywhere have conceived of soul as being active, activating, animating in the world. Part 6 of the anthology segues from a focus on individual soul to "The World Soul," with representative passages describing the vale where mythic soul making takes place, as well as the task to recognize and honor the spirit and genius in the world, and respond to poet Machado's startling question, "What have you done with the garden entrusted to you?"

Among my selections to illustrate these themes are the gently jolting twelfth-century verse of the Indian poet and mystic Kabir, a turn-of-the-century Eskimo hunting prayer, and a clarion call from Eliezer Shore for "The Soul of Community." Other too often overlooked aspects of soul in the world are embraced with a delicious introduction to soul food by former soul singer Sheila Ferguson, a nostalgic view of the soul of childhood by Valerie Andrews, and Keith Thompson's elegiac meditation on the soul of animals.

What is the soul's fate once it has infused the natural world and people? Tradition has long held that the wheel of fate keeps turning, sending it on its long journey homeward. In Part 7, "Soul and

Destiny," the journey of the wayward soul is timelessly evoked in the immortal words of Socrates in his last hours, the thunderous final battle of Beowulf, a rare Welsh poem attributed to Taliesin, a Sufi poem, and illustrative selections from Siberia, Australia, and the Amazon, among other sources.

Bearing in my mind what the great Greek translator and master of Balliol College at Oxford, Benjamin Jowett, once said, "We have sought truth, and sometimes perhaps found it. But have we had any fun?" I've also searched the far side of soul for a few offbeat selections. What I found was an oddly elevating example of magical realism from the Dominican Republic writer Juan Bosch in a story innocently called "The Beautiful Soul of Don Damian," which is told from the point of view of the dearly departed's soul as it flutters away—uncertain about its departure, and an excerpt from a science fiction yarn by Alan Brennert, named after a line in a W. B. Yeats poem, "Her Pilgrim Soul."

These images of soul are the gods and goddesses of our own inner mythology. All told there may not be the definitions still yearned for by many, but at least we'll have tried in the spirit of the Hollywood wag, Samuel Goldwyn, who asked his screenwriters to "Be obscure clearly."

Looking through this long exhibition hall of a book, with its masks and mirrors of soul, is it possible to find any constant themes from our search for constants "drawn from the soul's bottomless well" as Kathleen Raine calls it? Only that we must take the plunge into the depths—or else. The blue flame of secret desire forges us there where every idea about soul is a ripple to eternity.

The first step was to lose the way, the second to pay keen attention to find our way back, a lifelong task, as poet Mary Oliver reminds us:

This is the earnest work.
We're only given so many mornings to do it—
to look around and love the oily fur of our lives,
hoof and grass-stained muzzle. . . .

What are all these cartographers of the inner seas in this anthology telling us? That a deep awareness of soul points us toward the need to "love life more than the meaning of life," as Dostoyevsky concluded after his relentless exploration of the depths of the human condition. That the myths, images, philosophies of soul remind us of the *long story,* the eternal aspect of ourselves. That there is no last word on the soul, only the long slow incantations, the lion-hearted voices, the deep *yarrrgh* of spellbinding bards, like the Irish bluesman Van Morrison who, late one night under a splintered moon over the Berkeley hills, cried out in that turn-your-bones-blue voice, "I wanna know, did ye get the feelin'? Did ye get it deep down in your soul?" And in that moment the hard shell of modern life is ripped off in an impassioned cry for genuine, gutsy soul-searching.

Down deep in your soul where infinity is echoing. Deep down where the backbeat of eternity resounds, the deep bass line underneath the melody of all things. Soul, nothing but infinity closing, constantly.

I am haunted by soul.

PART ONE

THE
FALL
OF
SOUL
INTO
TIME

For the soul is the beginning of all things.
It is the soul that lends all things movement.
                                        —Plotinus

"But here" Patu murmured, grazing at her fingers, "here in the skin of
our fingertips we see the trail of the wind." And then she made a circular
motion to indicate the whirlwind that had left its imprint in the whorl at
the tips of the human finger. "It shows where the wind blew life into my
ancestors when they were first made. It was in the legend days when these
lines happened. It was in the legend days when the first people were given
the breath of life."
                                        —Jamake Highwater

Some people tell me I'd invented the sounds they called soul—but
I can't take any credit. Soul is just the way black folk sing when they
leave themselves alone.
                                        —Ray Charles

Introduction

As much a source of awe and astonishment as the apparition of a sudden snow crystal appearing out of mere vapor in the night sky, subatomic particles darting in and out of the void, or the sudden surges of evolution cryptically evident in bedrock fossil, the soul appears as if from the "mysterious shadow world beyond nature," as naturalist Loren Eisley describes the dark source of "men and catfish and green leaves."

Soul is the reconciling image for these silent origins of life, breath, movement. William Wordsworth imagined it as:

The Soul that rises with us, our life's Star,
Hath had elsewhere its setting
And Cometh from afar.

"Naturally, one does not know how it happened until it is well over beginning happening," as the circumlocutive Gertrude Stein wrote about curious origins. Her odd rhythms playfully circle around, rather than solemnly attack, the core of mystery, as do most myths, legends, folktales, and philosophical musings of the origin of soul. In their world-bridging images and ideas can be felt what Elie Wiesel has called the "divine beauty of learning" that life didn't begin with our birth alone, that other people, other souls, have been here before us.

Our cycle of soul writing begins with an origin myth of the soul of no known origins, dating back, as far as scholars can tell, to the period of late antiquity in Hellenized Egypt. In the Egyptian Gnostic Myth, as discovered by Marie-Louise von Franz in a papyrus collection in Paris, the world came into existence through seven laughs of the God. With the first loud laugh came light, then water, Hermes, the god of the psyche, (the fourth laugh is missing), Moira, the goddess of fate, Chronos, god of time and power, and finally the soul, born in the combustible moment when the God was laughing and crying at the same time. The centuries-old command to the soul, "Thou shalt move everything. . . ." reveals an archaic desire to resolve the mysterious relationship between breath and movement, and the ecstasy and agony of existence.

Many centuries later, in the book of Genesis, similar themes emerge when on the seventh day the breath of God produces human beings, "the clay that speaks"—"the living soul." Further parallels are found in the Arabian Creation Myth where "seven handfuls of clay" are animated and "embued with an intelligent soul," and in June Singer's beautiful retelling of an old Jewish legend of God calling upon the seventh angel to "fetch a certain soul" and bring it down to the world below, the fall into time. In the references to the number seven, regarded as holy since antiquity, is the alchemical correspondence, "As above so below." If there are seven planets above, ancient sages observed that there must be a ruling seven somewhere below.

With the Greek philosophers, soul is identified with the life principle itself, and again, the source and motivation of movement. What moves lives; what lives moves. For Aristotle, we learn from a passage from *De Anima*, soul was the "essential whatness," or "essential character." Analogously, among traditional people soul is commonly regarded as the fundamental sacred essence, that wellspring of the eternal element in human beings. From John Nance's book *The Gentle Tasaday*, we find the central image of the soul as the conscious part of the *dreaming* that is at the heart of life. Åke Hultkrantz's seminal work on soul belief among North American Indian tribes reveals a colorful range of origin metaphors any North Beach poet would envy, including a "cold puff of wind" of the Tanaina, or the delivery of the soul by the sacred manitou of the Ojibway. In contrast is the "no soul doctrine" of the Buddha. As religious historian Huston Smith points out in an excerpt from his classic work, *The World's Religions*, Buddha rebelled at the notion of an eternal spiritual substance. Instead, he sought to free his hearers from all illusions of a permanent soul and convince them of *im*permanence, the ultimate transitory nature of existence.

To German theologian Rudolf Otto, the argument of a substantial soul is far less important to a deeply religious life than the recognition of "the feeling of the uncanny," the presence that releases feelings of "mystery and marvel," and so reveals what rational speculation conceals: the numinous, the divine spark of all life.

For an incisive view of the political implications of theological disputes over the origins of the soul I've included alternating passages from a contemporary German theologian and a French scientist. Uta Ranke-Heinemann, in her worldwide best-selling book on the politics of sexuality and the Roman Catholic church, writes of the differing doctrines of "animation" of male and female fetuses. Deciding on different lengths of *time* for the *quickening* of the body by the soul, she argues, inevitably led to a perceived difference in the *quality* between women and men. Etienne-Emile Baulieu, inventor of the controversial RU-486, writes, with Mort Rosenblum, of the tangled roots of religious, philosophical, and legal opposition to his abortion pill.

From William Irwin Thompson's brilliant *The Time Falling Bodies Take to Light*, I've selected a passage on the soul as the cosmic egg of Humpty Dumpty who sat on a wall and fell into time, history, and memory. For Thompson, nursery rhymes are language cribs for raising mythic consciousness, the origins of awareness.

From Ralph Waldo Emerson's ever-replenishing essay "The Over-Soul," I've chosen a long excerpt that explores how time and space are inverse measures of the soul's energies. For Emerson the origin of the soul is ultimately unknowable. "Man is a stream whose source is hidden. Our being is descending into us from we know not where."

Finally, for those with the mythic slant on life, the passage from *Brother Ray*, the autobiography of Ray Charles and birth of soul music, has marvelously familiar elements found in origin myths: a sense of sacred time (midnight), sacred space (a blues club), sacred energy ("I love the feeling of the two streams of voice and piano flowing together"), alchemy (a mad mix of down-n-dirty rhythm and blues and sacred gospel music). "*Uhh-huhh,*" the soul man moaned over the wild controversies surrounding his ecstatic music during the often dry-souled fifties. "If you can't figure out 'What I'd Say,' then something's wrong. Either that, or you're not accustomed to the sweet sounds of love."

An Egyptian Gnostic Creation Myth
Late Antiquity

And God said, Thou shalt move everything, and everything will be made happier through you.

And the God laughed seven times. The God laughed seven times: Ha-Ha-Ha-Ha-Ha-Ha-Ha. God laughed, and from these seven laughs seven Gods sprang up which embraced the whole universe; those were the first Gods.

When he first laughed, light appeared and its splendor shone through the whole universe. The God of the cosmos and of the fire. Then: BESSEN BERITHEN BERIO, which are magic words.

He laughed for the second time and everything was water; the earth heard the sound and saw the light and was astonished and moved, and so the moisture was divided into three and the God of the abyss appeared. The name is ESCHAKLEO: you are the OE, you are the eternal BETHELLE!

When the God wanted to laugh for the third time, bitterness came up in his mind and in his heart and it was called Hermes, through whom the whole universe is made manifest. But the one, the other Hermes, through whom the universe is ordered, remains within. He was called SEMESILAMP. The first part of the name has to do with Shemesh, the sun, but the rest of the word is not explained.

Then the God laughed for the fifth time and while he was laughing he became sad and Moira (fate) appeared, holding the scales in her hand, showing that in her was justice. So you see justice comes from a state between laughing and sadness. But Hermes fought with Moira and said, "I am the just one!" While they were quarreling, God said to them, "Out of both of you justice will appear, everything should be submitted to you."

When the God laughed for the sixth time, he was terribly pleased and Chronos appeared with his scepter, the sign of power, and God said to him that he should have the glory and the light, the scepter of the ruler, and that everything present and future, would be submitted to him.

Then he laughed for the seventh time, drawing breath, and *while he was laughing he cried, and thus the soul came into being.* And God said, "Thou shalt move everything, and everything will be made happier through you. Hermes will lead you." When God said this, everything was set in motion and filled with breath.

When he saw the soul he bent down to the earth and whistled mightily and hearing this, the earth opened and gave birth to a being of herself. She gave birth to a being of her own, the Pythic dragon, [that is the dragon buried under the Delphic oracle] who knew everything ahead through the sound of the Godhead. And God called him ILLILU ILLILU ILLILU ITHOR, the shining one, PHOCHOPHOBOCH. When he appeared, the earth swelled up and the pole stood still and wished to explode. And God saw the dragon and was afraid and through his fright there came out Phobos (terror), full of weapons and so on.

from *Patterns of Creativity Mirrored in Creation Myths,*
by Marie-Louise von Franz, pp. 135–37.

Genesis 2:2–7

And on the seventh day God ended his work which he had made; and he rested on the seventh day from all his work which he had made.

And God blessed the seventh day, and sanctified it; because that in it he had rested from all his work which God created and made.

These *are* the generations of the heavens and of the earth when they were created, in the day that the LORD God made the earth and the heavens,

And every plant of the field before it was in the earth, and every herb of the field before it grew: for the LORD God had not caused it to rain upon the earth, and there was not a man to till the ground.

But there went up a mist from the earth, and watered the whole face of the ground.

And the LORD God formed man *of* the dust of the ground, and breathed into his nostrils the breath of life; and man became a living soul.

King James Version

The Angel and the Unborn Soul
An Old Jewish Legend
June Singer, American psychoanalyst and author

The angel goes to the seventh heaven as he is bidden and invites the soul to come along to the world below.

An old Jewish legend speaks to this knowing and forgetting that we know. It is told that when the soul of Adam was created, the souls of all the generations were created and stored in a promptuary in the seventh heaven. When a child is conceived, God decrees what manner of human being it shall become—male or female, strong or weak, beautiful or ugly, short or tall, fat or thin. Piety and wickedness alone are left to the determination of the person. Then God calls upon the angel appointed to souls, to fetch a certain soul that is hidden in the seventh heaven and carry it to the womb of its mother. The angel goes to the seventh heaven as he is bidden and invites the soul to come along to the world below. The soul opens her mouth and pleads, "Do not take me from this place. I am well pleased with where I am." The angel replies, "The world to which I will bring you is better than this one, and besides, it is for this purpose that God created you." So the soul is dragged away and forcibly placed in the womb of the mother. Two angels are set to watch that the soul does not escape.

In the morning, the first angel returns and takes the soul on a trip to Paradise, and shows her the righteous who sit there in glory with crowns upon their heads. "Do you know who these are?" the angel asks. When the soul replies that she does not, the angel says, "These were formed like you in the wombs of their mothers, and when they came into the world they observed God's commandments. When they departed that world they became partakers in the happiness that you now see. Know that you, too, if you observe God's commandments, will be found worthy of sitting among these when your life on earth is over. But if you do not, you will be doomed to the other place." So saying, he returns the soul to the mother's womb. The next morning the angel comes again, and this time he takes the soul to Hell, and points out the sinners who are being smitten with fiery scourges by the angels of destruction, and who cry, "Woe, woe is me!" The angel tells the soul that these, too, were created like herself, but that when they were put into the world they did not observe God's commandments, and for that reason they came to this sorry state. "Know then that your destiny is also to depart the world. Be just therefore, and not wicked, that you may not come to such an end as this." On the third day, the angel returns and carries the soul around and shows her where she will live and where she will die, whom she will marry and where she will be buried, and many other things. Then he replaces the soul in the womb, to remain there for nine months.

When it is time for the child to emerge from the womb, the angel returns and tells the soul, "The time has come for you to go forth into the world." The soul objects strenuously, saying, "No, I like it here. Why should I go forth into the world?" The angel replies, "As you were formed against your will, so you shall be born against your will and you shall die against your will." The soul continues to resist mightily, until the angel strikes the babe on the nose, extinguishes the light at its head, and brings it forth into the world against its will. Immediately the child forgets all it has learned and comes into the world kicking and screaming.

from *Seeing Through the Visible World*, pp. 7–8.

The Arabian Creation Myth
The Animation of Adam and Eve

The angels Gabriel, Michael, and Israfil were sent by God, one after another, to fetch for that purpose seven handfuls of earth from different depths, and of different colors; but the Earth being apprehensive of the consequence, and desiring them to represent her fear to God that the creature He designed to form would rebel against Him, and draw down His curse upon her, they returned without performing God's command; whereupon He sent Azrael on the same errand, who executed his commission without remorse, for which reason God appointed that angel to separate the souls from the bodies, being therefore called *the angel of death.*

The earth he had taken was carried into Arabia, to a place between Mecca and Tayef, where, being first kneaded by the angels,
it was afterward fashioned by God himself into a human form, and
left to dry for the space of forty days, or, as others say, as many
years, the angels in the meantime often visiting it, and Eblis (then
one of the angels who are nearest to God's presence, afterward the
devil) among the rest; but he, not contented with looking on it,
kicked it with his foot till it rang, and knowing God designed that
creature to be his superior, took a secret resolution never to acknowledge him as such. After this, God animated the figure of clay
and endued it with an intelligent soul, and when He had placed
him in paradise, formed Eve out of his left side.

from *Sun Songs: Creation Myths from Around the World,* edited,
introduced, and with commentaries by Raymond Van Over, p. 186.

The Tasaday Soul

John Nance, American journalist

The soul may be the part of you that sees the dream.

Balayam was just a boy when his father died. "He had a very
painful chest while he was gathering food in the forest. And he
died there." The body was left in the forest. If someone died in the
cave, the body was taken into the forest; but there was not one
general burial place, nor were the spots marked in any way. The
body was merely covered with leaves.

"What about the soul of a dead person? What happens to it?"

Balayam did not answer—perhaps he had not understood the
question or did not want to understand it. Talking about his parents' death had made him uneasy. And it was always especially difficult to translate abstract ideas like soul.

So Mai asked if the Tasaday had dreams. Balayam said yes and
then apparently saw the connection between that question and the
previous—or it may have been suggested by Mai or Igna—because
he added: "The soul may be the part of you that sees the dream."
He said the dream (or the seer of dreams) was called *lomogul.* "I
dream," he said, "but I don't know where it ends or starts."

from *The Gentle Tasaday,* p. 118.

Conceptions of the Soul Among North American Indians

Åke Hultkrantz, Swedish anthropologist

Four nights before I was born I knew that I would be born. My mind was as clear when I was born as it is now. I saw my father and my mother, and I knew who they were. I knew the things an Indian uses, their names and what they were good for. . . .

The supernatural origin of the human soul finds particularly clear expression in the idea of pre-existence. Here we are not referring to the pre-existence that a reincarnated individual has had in a previous earthly life as man or animal: We are referring to the pre-incarnative existence, man's life before he is incarnated on earth. "Man" stands here for the individual reality, which from the psychological viewpoint is the extra-physical soul, the free-soul, and which consequently represents man's ego in the pre-incarnative state. . . .

Where the prenatal original home does not coincide with the realm of the dead it is nevertheless localized to places that remind one of the abode of the dead. The Ingalik believe that "there is a place filled with the spirits of little children, all impatient to be 'called,' i.e., born into this life." In the depths of the forest there is according to Kwakiutl belief a mysterious house. "Since one of the performances held in this house was that of giving birth, it was probably believed that from this house all generation of men, animals, and plants, took place." The Indians in the northwesternmost U.S.A. have a "babyland" where the unborn children live and play before they come to the earth. The Chinook children lived "a quite definite existence" before birth, in the sun, the daylight. The Montagnais tradition to the effect that children come from the clouds, on the other hand, is evidently only a pedagogical fiction. According to the Eastern Shawnee, unborn children live on the little stars of the Milky Way. But we also find the belief that they live together with the creator, "Our Grandmother.". . .

Some Eskimo imagine that children, like eggs, live in the snow and creep into the womb. The Mackenzie Eskimo have many mutually incompatible notions concerning incarnation. One believes that the soul (*nappan*) comes with the water when the mother drinks, or from the ground when she urinates. Another believes that the child gets a soul at the same time as it is born. And a third believes that the soul comes at some time during the pregnancy, "how or when she does not know." The breath of a child to be enters a Tanaina woman like a cold puff of wind. The (free-) soul of a Tlingit Indian is not reincarnated until the body with which it is to be united has been born. The soul of the Hisla Indian is often the spirit of an uncle, which takes possession of his body even before the birth of the individual. The unitary soul among the Sanpoil appears already in the embryo. Among the Plains Cree the free-soul takes up its abode in the body at birth. The Naskapi Indian receives his "Great Man" during the embryonic stage. According to the Shawnee, "a soul goes to earth and jumps through the mother's vagina and into the body of the child through the fontanelle just before birth." Jones writes that according to the belief of the Ojibway "the manitou on the other side of the world" delivers their souls to the people before their birth. The Fox imagine that the life-soul is with the human embryo during the embryonic development, while the free-soul remains outside the mother during this period, and does not enter the child's body until its birth. . . .

Evidence that the child is believed to have soul-activity during the embryonic stage is afforded in the Indian notion of the foetal consciousness: the child feels and thinks during the time it spends in the mother's body. Sometimes this consciousness is intensified to the point of precognition, prophetic clairvoyance.

A Bella Coola child that cries in the womb is believed to have an excellent intellect. A shaman from the Great Bear Lake district declared that before his birth he had seen a star, which revealed to him all the medicines that have power over man. The Chipewyan embryo warns its mother if she is approached by an evil spirit. The unborn Lummi Indian hears what his future relatives are saying and knows what they are thinking; if they have evil thought in their mind he leaves them before his birth. A sagacious Lenape declared that he had acquired supernatural knowledge even before his birth. . . . The Saulteaux relate that in former times the Indians had consciousness during the embryonic stage, and in this connection also certainty concerning the content of earthly life, a prophetic capacity that was one of the signs of magic power. Such things are now rare. A Saulteaux did, however, tell Hallowell the following: "Four nights before I was born I knew that I would be born. My mind was as clear when I was born as it is now. I saw my father and my mother, and I knew who they were. I knew the things an Indian uses, their names and what they were good for. . . ." Such certainty is said to be founded on the fact that the person in question had earlier lived a life among human beings.

The unborn Fox child understands what its mother is saying, and abandons her if she proves to be quarrelsome. The Winnebago medicine-man, who is sent down to a woman's womb from his pre-existence, retains his consciousness both at the conception and during the entire embryonic period. The Wahpeton shamans know everything about their future existence before their birth. . . .

The events after the incarnation, and especially at the actual moment of birth, have been dramatically described by a reincarnated Winnebago shaman: "Then I was brought down to earth. I did not enter a woman's womb, but I was taken into a room. There I remained, conscious at all times. One day I heard the noise of little children outside and some other sounds, so I thought I would go outside. Then it seemed to me that I went through a door, but I was really being born again from a woman's womb. As I walked out I was struck with the sudden rush of cold air and I began to cry."

from *Essential Sacred Writings from Around the World,*
edited by Mircea Eliade, pp. 189–93.

The Essential Whatness
Aristotle, Greek philosopher, 384–322 B.C.E.

Moreover, since the possession of knowledge must precede its exercise, the soul may be defined as *the initial actuality of a natural body endowed with the capacity of life.*

This definition of soul is applicable to whatever body possesses organs. The term organs is here extended to include the parts of plants; for these, in spite of their rudimentary structure, exhibit certain analogies to animal organs: the leaf, for instance, serves as protective covering for the pericarp, and the pericarp for the fruit; while again, the roots are analogous to mouths, since like them they digest food. Hence if we require a general definition applicable to every type of soul, we may define the soul as *the initial actuality of a natural body possessing organs.* The question whether soul and body are identical, therefore, is as superfluous as to ask whether wax and the shape imprinted on it are identical, or, in general whether the material of a thing is identical with the thing of which it is the material. "Is" and "one" have various meanings, but in their most legitimate meaning they connote the fully actual character of a thing.

We have now stated in a broad way what soul is: it is the "essential whatness" (*ousia*) of a thing in the sense of its "definitive meaning" (*logos*); the "essential and enduring character" (*ti en enai*) of a body possessing the capacity of life. Suppose, for example, that an instrument such as an axe were a natural body. Its character of being an axe would then be its "whatness, or essential thinghood" (*ousia*), and therefore its "soul"; if this were taken away it would no longer be an axe except in name. But in point of fact the axe is merely a manmade instrument, not the kind of body whose definitive nature may be called a soul; for soul is ascribed only to a particular kind of natural body which has within itself the "power of producing" (*arche*) movement and rest.

We must further consider our definition of soul with reference to the parts of the living body. If the eye were an independent organism, sight would be its soul, for it is in terms of sight that the essential whatness of the eye must be defined. The eye is the "material condition" (*hyle*) of seeing, and if its power of sight were removed it would no longer be an eye—except in name, like an eye carved in stone or sketched. What is thus true of a bodily organ must be no less true of the whole organism; for a particular mode of perceptual awareness stands in the same relation to its particular organs as our whole conscious life stands to the whole sentient body as such . . .

from *Aristotle: The Way of Philosophy*,
selected and translated by Philip Ellis Wheelwright, pp. 126–27.

The Etymology of Soul
Sir Edward Burnett Tylor, British anthropologist, 1832–1917

The act of breathing, so characteristic of the higher animals during life, and coinciding so closely with life in its departure, has been repeatedly and naturally identified with the life or soul itself. . . .

To understand the popular conceptions of the human soul or spirit, it is instructive to notice the words which have been found suitable to express it. The ghost or phantasm seen by the dreamer or the visionary is in unsubstantial form, like a shadow or reflection, and thus the familiar term of the *shade* comes in to express the soul. Thus the Tasmanian word for the shadow is also that for the spirit, the Algonquins describe a man's soul as *otahchuk*, "his shadow"; the Quiche language uses *natub* for "shadow, soul"; the Arawak *ueja* means "shadow, soul, image"; and Abipones made the one word *loákal* serve for shadow, soul, echo, image." The Zulus not only use the *tunzi* for "shadow, spirit, ghost," but they consider that at death the shadow of a man will in some way depart from the corpse, to become an ancestral spirit. The Basutos not only call the spirit remaining after death the *seriti* or "shadow," but they think that if a man walks on the river bank, a crocodile may seize his shadow in the water and draw him in; while in Old Calabar there is found the same identification of the spirit with the *ukpon* or "shadow," for a man to lose which is fatal. There are thus found among the lower races not only the types of those familiar classic terms, the *skia* and *umbra*, but also what seems the fundamental thought of the stories of shadowless men still current in the folklore of Europe, and familiar to modern readers in Chamisso's tale of Peter Schlemihl. Thus the dead in Purgatory knew that Dante was alive when they saw that, unlike theirs, his figure cast a shadow on the ground. Other attributes are taken into the notion of soul or spirit, with especial regard to its being the cause of life. Thus the Caribs, connecting the pulses with spiritual beings, and especially considering that in the heart dwells man's chief soul, destined to a future heavenly life, could reasonably use the word *iouanni* for "soul, life, heart." The Tongans supposed the soul to exist throughout the whole extension of the body, but particularly in the heart. . . .

The act of breathing, so characteristic of the higher animals during life, and coinciding so closely with life in its departure, has been repeatedly and naturally identified with the life or soul itself. . . . It is thus that West Australians used one word *waug* for "breath, spirit, soul"; that certain Greenlanders reckoned two souls to man, namely his shadow and his breath, and in Java use the same word *nawa* for "breath, life, soul." How the notions of life, heart, breath, and phantom unite in the one conception of a soul or spirit, and at the same time how loose and vague such ideas are among barbaric races, is well brought into view in the answers to a religious inquest held in 1528 among the natives of Nicaragua. "When they die, there comes out of their mouth something that resembles a person and is called *julio* [Aztec *yuli* = to live]. This being goes to the place where the man and woman are. It is like a person, but does not die, and the body remains here."

. . . The conception of the soul as breath may be followed up through Semitic and Aryan etymology, and thus into the main streams of the philosophy of the world. Hebrew shows *nephesh*, "breath," passing into all the meanings of "life, soul, mind, animal," while *ruach* and *neshamah* make the like transition from "breath" to "spirit"; and to these the Arabic *nefs* and *ruh* correspond. The same is the history of Sanskrit *atman* and *prana*, of

Greek *psyche* and *pneuma*, of Latin *animus, anima, spiritus.* So Slavonic *duch* has developed the meaning of "breath" into that of soul or spirit: and the dialects of the Gypsies have this word *duk* with the meaning of "breath, spirit, ghost," whether these pariahs brought the word from India as part of their inheritance of Aryan speech, or whether they adopted it in their migration across Slavonic lands. German *geist* and English *ghost,* too, may possibly have the same original sense of breath. And if any should think such expressions due to mere metaphor, they may judge the strength of the implied connection between breath and spirit by cases of most unequivocal significance. Among the Seminoles of Florida, when a woman died in childbirth, the infant was held over her face to receive her parting spirit, and thus acquire the strength and knowledge for its future use. These Indians could have well understood why at the death-bed of an ancient Roman, the nearest kinsman leant over to inhale the last breath of the departing (*et excipes hanc animam ore pio*). Their state of mind is kept up to this day among Tyrolese peasants who can still fancy a good man's soul to issue from his mouth at death like a white cloud.

from *Essential Sacred Writings from Around the World,*
edited by Mircea Eliade, pp. 177–79.

The Origin of the Numinous
Rudolf Otto, German theologian, 1869–1937

Soul or Atman is properly the thing of marvel and stupefaction quite undefinable outsoaring all conceptions.

The non-rational which we were looking for in the idea of the divine was found in the numinous, and in our recognition of this we came to see that rationalistic speculation tends to conceal the divine in God, and that before God becomes for us rationality, absolute reason, a personality, a moral will, He is the wholly non-rational and "other," the being of sheer mystery and marvel. We had to turn to the feelings of horror and shudder and spectral haunting in order, by means of these caricatures of the authentic numinous emotions, to break through the hard crust of rationalism and bring into play the feelings buried deep down in our religious consciousness.

Now what is true of our apprehension of the divine is true also of its counterpart in the creature—soul and spirit. Gregory of

Nyssa well says: "Since one of the signs of the Divine Nature is its essential incomprehensibility, in this also must the copy be like the original. For were the nature of the copy comprehended, when the original was above comprehension, the copy would be a mistaken one. But, inasmuch as the nature of our spirit is above our understanding, it has here an exact resemblance the incomprehensible Being of God." Here, too, we need to break up anew our hardened and crusted feelings and to withstand the intellectualizing tendency to which we are so prone in our doctrine of the soul and its creation in God's image. For this divine image in man also does not merely consist in the fact that he is reasonable, moral, intelligent, and a person, but primarily in the fact that in its profoundest depths his being is indeed for religious self-consciousness something numinous—that the soul is mystery and marvel. This is how mysticism apprehends it, and we can understand at once why this is so from our definition of mysticism as the tendency to stress up to an extreme and exaggerated point the non-rational aspect of religion. And what was already stirring in crude fashion at the earliest and lowest stage of numinous feeling recurs at the most exalted level of mysticism with after-effects that colour the whole experience. In the mystic's praise of the soul, and in that "*fundus animae*" of which he tells the mysteries, there echoes the "stupor" before the "wholly other" that characterized the primitive belief in souls and even primitive feeling of the presence of ghosts.

We said above . . . that the most interesting point in the primitive idea of the soul is not the form given to it in fantasy, multifarious in its variations, but the element of feeling—*stupor*—which it liberates, and the character of "mystery" and "wholly otherness" which surrounds it. This fact is obscured in the measure in which the "soul" becomes later the subject of myth, fairy story, and narrative, speculation and doctrine, and finally of psychological investigation. It then becomes more and more something entirely rational; its origin in magic and mystery becomes overlaid with concepts, scholastic terms, and classifications. The Doctrine of souls, or *Atman* of the Indian *Sankhya* system is the best example of this. But even this cannot entirely conceal the fact that "Soul" or *Atman* is *properly* the thing of marvel and stupefaction, quite undefinable, outsoaring all conceptions, "wholly alien" to our understanding.

from *The Idea of the Holy,*
translated by John W. Harvey, pp. 193–95.

The Origin of the Buddha's No Soul Doctrine
Huston Smith, American philosopher

The most startling thing Buddha said about the human self is that it has no soul. This *anatta* (no soul) doctrine has caused Buddhism to seem religiously peculiar, but the word must be examined. What was the *atta* (Pali for the Sanskrit *Atman* or soul) that the Buddha denied? At the time it had come to signify (a) a spiritual substance that, in keeping with the dualistic position in Hinduism, (b) retains its separate identity forever.

Buddha denied both these features. His denial of spiritual substance—the soul as homunculus, a ghostly wraith within the body that animates the body and outlasts it—appears to have been the chief point that distinguished his concept of transmigration from prevailing Hindu interpretations. Authentic child of India, the Buddha did not doubt that reincarnation was in some sense a fact, but he was openly critical of the way his *Brahmanic* contemporaries were interpreting the concept. The crux of his criticism may be gathered from the clearest description he gave of his own view on the subject. He used the image of a flame being passed from candle to candle. As it is difficult to think of the flame on the final candle as being the original flame, the connection would seem instead to be a casual one, in which influence was transmitted by chain reaction but without a perduring substance . . .

This denial of spiritual substance was only an aspect of Buddha's wider denial of substance of every sort. Substance carries both a general and a specific connotation. Generally, it refers to something relatively permanent that underlies surface changes in the thing in question; specifically, this more basic something is thought to be matter. The psychologist in Buddha rebelled against the latter notion, for to him mind was more basic than matter. The empiricist in him, for its part, challenged the implications of a generalized notion of substance. It is impossible to read much Buddhist literature without catching its sense of the transitoriness (*anicca*) of everything finite, its recognition of the perpetual perishing of every natural object. It is this that gives Buddhist descriptions of the natural world their poignancy. "The waves follow one after another in an eternal pursuit."

So struck was Buddha with impermanence that he listed it as the first of his Three Signs of Being, or characteristics that apply to everything in the natural order, the other two being suffering and the absence of a permanent soul. Nothing in nature is identical with what it was the moment before; in this Buddha was close to modern science which has discovered the problem of identity to be one of the most puzzling. Buddha was concerned to emphasize the ephemeral character of human life that his hearers might be freed from all illusions on this score. So he called the forces holding life together *skandas*—skeins that hang together as loosely as yarn. The body, for its part, was a "heap," its elements no more permanently gathered than the grains of a sandpile. Froth, too, seemed an apposite metaphor, and there were others:

> —*a phantom, dew, a bubble,*
> *A dream, a flash of lightning, and a cloud:*
> *Thus we should look upon all that was made.*

from *The World's Religions*, pp. 115–17.

When Are We Ensouled?
Uta Ranke-Heinemann, German theologian

Up till the end of the nineteenth century the doctrine of successive anima-tion had prevailed in theology. This, we recall, maintained that the male embryo received a soul on or about the fortieth day, the female embryo on or about the eightieth.

The prevailing view in Antiquity was Aristotle's notion that the ani-mation of the masculine fetus did not take place until forty days after conception, while the female fetus acquired a human soul only ninety days after conception. Before then the fetus had been first a vegetable, then an animal soul (*On the History of Animals* 7, 3, 583b). This temporal difference in the genesis of the soul in men and women would not have been simply a matter of time, but of human quality, since the soul belongs to man sooner than it does to woman. The soul, that is, the essence of humanity, is something masculine rather than something feminine.

A similar idea about the inferiority of women probably underlies the Old Testament: According to Leviticus 12:1–5 a woman is un-clean forty days after the birth of a son, eighty days after the birth of a daughter. The ninety days before the emergence of the female soul in Aristotle and the eighty days of uncleanness in the Old Testament are fused together in Christian tradition, so that a soul was attributed to the female fetus eighty days after conception.

In keeping with this idea about successive animation, the term "murder" was incorrect not only for contraception but also for early abortion. Augustine follows Aristotelian biology in writing that no soul can live in an unformed body, and so there can be no talk of murder here (*On Exodus* 21, 80). Jerome too writes in a letter to Algasia: "The seed gradually takes shape in the uterus, and it does not count as killing until the individual elements have acquired their external appearance and their limbs" (*Epistle* 121, 4).

Nevertheless, Jerome too is inconsistent and speaks exaggeratedly of "murder" with reference to contraception. In a letter to Eustochium he writes to warn about some consecrated virgins: "Some even ensure barrenness by the help of potions, murdering human beings before they are fully conceived. Others, when they find that they are with child as a result of their sin, practice abortion with drugs, and so frequently bring about their own death, taking with them to the lower world the guilt of three crimes: suicide, adultery against Christ, and child murder" (*Epistle* 22, 13, translated by F. A. Wright, Loeb Library of Classics). . . .

We may note in passing that as bad as this degrading of women by the Church was, it must be made clear that the worst accusation—that the Church doubted women had souls or were human at all—is untrue. One often hears and reads that at the second Synod of Macon (585) the participants disputed whether women had souls, but that never happened. Souls were not the issue. Gregory of Tours, who was there, reports that a bishop raised the question, "whether woman could be called 'homo.'" Thus it was a philological question (though raised because of the higher value that men placed on themselves): *homo* in Latin means "person" as well as "man," as do cognate words in all the Romance languages, and as "man" does in English. The other bishops, Gregory reports, referred the questioner to the story of Creation, which says that God created man (*homo*), "male and female he created them," and to Jesus' title "Son of Man" (*filius hominis*), although he was the son of a virgin, and hence the son of a woman. These clarifications settled the issue: The term *homo* was to be applied to women as well as to men (Gregory of Tours, *Historia Francorum* 8, 20). . . .

[The] tightening of the rules on abortion took place in connection with a transformation of the thinking about the exact time when the embryo acquired a soul. From the end of the nineteenth century onward belief that animation occurred at the very moment of conception (simultaneous animation) won the day, and this brought with it an even stronger rejection of abortion in the earliest stages of pregnancy, not to mention the later stages. Up till the end of the nineteenth century the doctrine of successive animation had prevailed in theology. This, we recall, maintained that the male embryo received a soul on or about the fortieth day, the female embryo on or about the eighteenth. Hence canon law distinguished between the *fetus animatus,* and the *fetus inanimatus (anima* = soul). Only the abortion of an animate fetus was punished with excommunication. And since there was no way of determining the sex of the fetus, the penalty was not incurred until the eighteenth day. Only the fanatical Sixtus V had threatened abortion from the moment of conception, indeed had threatened contraception, with excommunication or even the death penalty. But in 1591, a year after his death, this decision was revoked by Gregory XIV.

Since the end of the nineteenth century canon law has gotten closer to the idea of Sixtus V: Excommunication now applies to abortion from the first moment of pregnancy. The distinction between the *fetus inanimatus* and the *fetus animatus* was dropped by Pius IX in 1869. The code of canon law, as revised in 1917 and 1983, speaks only of "the fetus."

The question of when the embryo became "ensouled" was always a controversial one. In the fourth century the Church Fathers Basil the Great and Gregory of Nyssa declared—drawing upon Stoic sources—that the animation of the human embryo occurred at the moment of conception, because the soul was infused into the uterus along with the semen. Albert the Great (d. 1280) also was an opponent of successive animation, while his disciple Thomas Aquinas also argued for it. Beginning in the seventeenth century there was a stronger trend toward simultaneous animation, after a physician from Louvain, Thomas Fienus, claimed that the human soul was infused not on the fortieth day, but on the third. In 1658 the Franciscan Hieronymus Florentinius demanded that every embryo, no matter how little time had passed since conception, had to be baptized when there was danger of death since it had a soul. In 1661 Innocent X's personal physician, Paul Zacchias, defended the view that the soul was infused at the moment of conception. (His main reason: Otherwise the subject of the feast of Mary's conception (December 8) would be a soulless cell.) By the beginning of the eighteenth century this was the prevailing opinion among doctors. In 1736 a theologian named Roncaglia spoke out for simultaneous animation. On the other hand, Alphonsus Liguouri echoed St. Thomas, while noting that such views were "very certain" (Moral Theology III, n. 394).

from *Eunuchs for the Kingdom of Heaven,*
translated by Peter Heinegg, pp. 74–75, 191, 305.

Soul, Conception, Abortion

Etienne-Emile Baulieu with Mort Rosenblum, French physician and
American correspondent

*"Most certainly," he said, "no experimental data can be in itself sufficient to
force recognition of a spiritual soul."*

Much of the serious opposition to RU-486 in America bases itself
on religion. It is hardly clear-cut, however. As time has gone on,
support has begun to crystallize among some church leaders who
had reserved judgment during the early controversy.

Too often, in the United States and elsewhere, the abortion
issue is seen as between "the church" on the one side and unde-
fined liberals on the other. The Roman Catholic church declares
that abortion is murder, based on the tenet that a person begins at
fertilization. In fact, the position dates only from 1869. Funda-
mentalist sects that take a similar position have no text to cite.

Neither Protestants, nor Jews, nor Moslems, nor the principal
Asian religions—not even Orthodox Catholics—insist that an embryo of a few days is sacred. Some faiths fix a time later in the continuum when a soul enters the fetus to form a new human being.
Others leave it up to an individual's conscience. Although most religions generally oppose abortion, several allow such contragestive
methods as menstrual regulation . . .

In the *New York Review of Books*, late 1990, Garry Wills . . .
noted the deep divisions among Catholics. Neither contraception
nor the origin of the soul is mentioned in the scriptures; they have
been discussed in various ways in successive papal decrees over
the centuries. The Church's second track of influence—moral per-
suasion based on the natural-law tradition—is all the weaker for
lack of clear definition of "natural law."

On the issue of abortion and birth control, even many devout
believers questioned the Church's authority. "Most Catholics,"
Wills observed, "have concluded that their clerical leaders are un-
hinged on the subject of sex . . . "

Organized religions have no clearer answer than science on
when a human life begins. The Bible condemns murder but is
silent on abortion. Protestants, for the most part, regard it as an
unfortunate necessity. Opinions vary among Protestant denomina-
tions, but few churchmen regard the early termination of pregnancy as murder. No major Asian faith attempts to name a precise
moment when a new person joins the world.

Jewish teachings fix a time, near quickening, when the soul enters the fetus. Until then, the fetus is considered a life form but not a human being, or *nefesh* in Hebrew. Orthodox Jews frown on abortion except to protect the mother's health. Conservative Jews accept "severe anguish" as a sufficient reason. Reform Judaism takes a liberal stand, including the grounds of "freedom of choice."

In a policy paper, Rabbi Aryeh Spero, of the Orthodox Civic Center Synagogue in Manhattan, noted that Jewish tradition dictates that abortions should be done as early as possible, preferably before the fortieth day.

Moslems accept the need for abortion under a number of circumstances. According to the Koran, it becomes the taking of a life only after a process described as "the blowing of the spirit." This is generally believed to occur at the end of the fourth month of pregnancy. I understand that menstrual regulation is not condemned by the Islamic religion.

The Roman Catholic church, in contrast, holds that fertilization implies the onset of human personhood.

At the height of the controversy over RU-486, Jean-Marie Cardinal Lustiger, the archbishop of Paris, wrote me, challenging my knowledge of Catholic doctrine. "You do not understand that the voluntary interruption of pregnancy is directly contrary to the commandment of God: Thou shalt not kill." No civilized person could disagree with God's commandment. The question is over what is murder.

But I had another view from the Reverend Norman Ford, an Australian priest whose book *When Did I Begin?*, published in 1988, is a classic work in the religious debate. He said he strongly disagreed with the philosophical reading of biology, common but not universal within the Church, that life begins at conception. Father Ford's own view is that an individual is defined after the primitive streak at fourteen days after fertilization. Among contemporary Catholic theologians, he is hardly alone.

Times change. Today's Catholic doctrine has its roots among the Romans, when every conception was the making of another member of an imperiled church. The verb itself, "to conceive," comes from the Latin, *concipere*, "to retain." That was how Aristotle saw it, in the wisdom of his age: A child is the result of the man's semen retained in the woman's menstrual blood.

St. Thomas Aquinas based his beliefs on the Aristotelian concept that, at some intermediate point, a soul entered the developing fetus—the defining moment when it became a human being. Church doctrine changed over the centuries. Pope Sixtus V ordered

severe punishment for abortion in 1588. Three years later, Pope
Gregory XIV repealed the ban. Pope Pius IX decreed the Church's
present stand, that life begins at conception, in 1869.

In the contemporary Vatican, abortion is roundly condemned,
but once again the moment of personhood is at issue. Joseph
Cardinal Ratzinger, prefect of the Congregation for the Doctrine
of Faith, declared in 1987 that the Church could not say with any
certainty that life, in fact, began at conception. "Most certainly,"
he said, "no experimental data can be in itself sufficient to force
recognition of a spiritual soul." Abortion was a sin, he said, because life *might* begin at conception.

"This declaration expressly leaves aside the question of the moment the spiritual soul is infused," he wrote. "There is not a unani-
mous tradition. . . . From a moral point of view, this is certain:
Even if a doubt existed [that] the fruit of conception is already a
human being, it is objectively a grave sin to dare to risk murder."
In public, the Church simplifies the issue. In its official "declaration" it makes the following prudent statement: "The Magisterium
has not expressly committed himself to an affirmation of a philo-
sophic nature." Ultimately, then, Vatican policy is not based on any
scientific or metaphysical considerations but on a moral stand-
point.

from *The Abortion Pill,* pp. 147–49, 183–85.

The Over-Soul

Ralph Waldo Emerson, American transcendentalist, 1803–1882

Before the revelations of the soul, Time and Space and Nature shrink away.

The philosophy of six thousand years has not searched the chambers and magazines of the soul. In its experiments there has always
remained, in the last analysis, a residuum it could not resolve.
Man is a stream whose source is hidden. Our being is descending
into us from we know not whence. The most exact calculator has
no prescience that somewhat incalculable may not balk the very
next moment. I am constrained every moment to acknowledge a
higher origin for events than the will I call mine. . . .

The Supreme Critic on the errors of the past and the present
and the only prophet of that which must be is that great nature in
which we rest as the earth lies in the soft arms of the atmosphere;
that Unity, that Over-Soul, within which every man's particular

being is contained and made one with all other; that common heart of which all sincere conversation is the worship to which all right action is submission; that overpowering reality which confutes our tricks and talents and constrains everyone to pass for what he is and to speak from his character and not from his tongue, and which evermore tends to pass into our thought and hand and become wisdom and virtue and power and beauty. We live in succession, in division, in parts, in particles. Meantime within man is the soul of the whole; the wise silence; the universal beauty, to which every part and particle is equally related; the eternal ONE. And this deep power in which we exist and whose beatitude is all accessible to us is not only self-sufficing and perfect in every hour, but the act of seeing and the thing seen, the seer and the spectacle, the subject and the object, are one. We see the world piece by piece, as the sun, the moon, the animal, the tree; but the whole, of which these are the shining parts, is the soul. Only by the vision of that Wisdom can the horoscope of the ages be read, and by falling back on our better thoughts, by yielding to the spirit of prophecy which is innate in every man, we can know what it saith. Every man's words who speaks from that life must sound vain to those who do not dwell in the same thought on their own part. I dare not speak for it. My words do not carry its august sense; they fall short and cold. Only itself can inspire whom it will, and behold! Their speech shall be lyrical and sweet and universal as the rising of the wind. Yet I desire, even by profane words if I may not use sacred, to indicate the heaven of this deity and to report what hints I have collected of the transcendent simplicity and energy of the Highest Law. . . .

The sovereignty of this nature whereof we speak is made known by its independency of those limitations which circumscribe all things. As I have said, it contradicts all experiences. In like manner, it abolishes time and space. The influence of the senses has in most men overpowered the mind to that degree that the walls of time and space have come to look real and insurmountable; and to speak with levity of these limits is, in the world, the sign of insanity. Yet time and space are but inverse measures of the force of the soul. The spirit sports with time,

> Can crowd eternity into an hour, Or stretch an hour to eternity.

. . . And so always the soul's scale is one, the scale of the senses and the understanding is another. Before the revelations of the soul, Time and Space and Nature shrink away. In common speech we refer all things to time, as we habitually refer the immensely sundered stars as one concave sphere. And so we say that the Judgment is distant or near, that the Millennium approaches, that a day of certain political, moral, social reforms is at hand, and the like when we mean that in the nature of things one of the facts we contemplate is external and fugitive and the other is permanent and connate with the soul. The things we now esteem fixed shall, one by one, detach themselves like ripe fruit from our experience and fall. The wind shall blow them none knows whither. The landscape, the figures, Boston, London, are facts as fugitive as any institution past, or any whiff of mist or smoke, and so is society, and so is the world. The soul looketh steadily forwards, creating a world before here, leaving worlds behind her. She has no dates, nor rites, nor persons, nor specialties, nor men. The soul knows only the soul; the web of events is the flowing robe in which she is clothed. . . .

from *The Best of Ralph Waldo Emerson,* pp. 206–10.

The Fall of Soul into Time
William Irwin Thompson, American philosopher

The nursery rhyme is a memory of the soul . . .

The edge of history is myth. If we study myth in a scientific way, we miss the experience of moving into a mythopoeic mode of consciousness. A line of events has a beginning and an end, but the matrix out of which events arise does not appear to be an event at all.

> *Humpty Dumpty sat on a wall,*
> *Humpty Dumpty had a great fall,*
> *And all the King's horses,*
> *And all the King's men*
> *Couldn't put Humpty together again.*

Humpty Dumpty is the cosmic egg, the wall, the edge between transcendence and existence. As nothing breaks up into the world of things, the movement toward entropy becomes irreversible. Humpty Dumpty is the immortal soul before its fall into time, and neither God's animals nor His angels can put him back into the world beyond time. The human condition is the fallen condition of time and fragmentation.

The nursery rhyme is a memory of soul, a piece of an old cosmology from a lost culture lingering on in the rational world of sci-

ence as a trivial piece of children's verse. When clairvoyants see
the aura of light and energy around the human body, they describe
it as egg-shaped. The human egg of Humpty Dumpty is an image
of ourselves and our complete history, a history that takes us beyond what this society will accept into the world of the immortal
soul.

In Vedic cosmology, as well as in the cosmology of the Dogon of
West Africa, the universe is an egg that shatters as it expands to
begin its career of unfoldment in time. As an archetypal image of
primordial unity, the cosmic egg suggests that there is unity and
fragmentation, eternity and time. The Fall into time is not so
much an event itself as the conditioning of time-space out of
which all events arise. The Fall exists prior to the world of events,
both logically and temporally, and so it seems as if it must be The
Event, the single action which echoes down throughout all ancient
mythologies, children's nursery rhymes, and modern stories: the
Fall of the One into the many, the emergence of the physical universe out of a transcendent God, the Fall of the soul into time, the
entrapment of an angelic soul into the body of Australopithecus
afrarensis, or the Fall of an unconditioned consciousness beyond
subject and object into the syntax of thought pounded into form by
each heartbeat. The Fall is not only once and long ago; it is reca-
pitulated in each instant of consciousness. The unfallen world beyond time remains as a background to the figured beats of the
heart in our world of serial progression. Like the white page that
surrounds the darkness of each letter you are reading here, eternity surrounds each heartbeat, and as the contemplative watches
his breath, he can move out of time through the doorway which
opens in the interval between each heartbeat. Each open space is
a spiritualization, each beat a materialization; and both are sacred,
for in one is the spiritualization of matter; in the other, the materialization of spirit.

As the ground out of which all events arise, the Fall is the archetype that stands over our understanding of time. The Fall of Adam
and Eve in the Old Testament, the Fall of Satan in Milton's *Paradise Lost,* the Fall of Tim Finnegan in the Irish folk song in Joyce's
Finnegans Wake, or the more recent expressions of the Fall in the
films *Kaspar Hauser* and *The Man Who Fell to Earth* are once, like
the voices in a fugue. The soul is, like Humpty Dumpty on the
wall, above time, seeing past, present, and future at once. From
the point of view of the ego, down in time, everything is linear: the
past is behind and the future is up ahead.

from The Time Falling Bodies Take to Light, pp. 8–10.

The Birth of Soul
Ray Charles, musician and soul singer

*Some people told me that I'd invented the sounds they call soul—but I
can't take any credit. Soul is just the way black folk sing when they leave
themselves alone.*

When I was writing songs, I concentrated on problems or feelings
everyone could understand. I wouldn't call the tunes biographical;
I just made 'em up. But I always tried to stick to common
themes—love, heartaches, money heartaches, pleasures of the
flesh, and pleasures of the soul.

"Hallelujah" clicked. It sold big among blacks, and I guess it was
my first record to enjoy some popularity among whites.

If these early hits sold two hundred thousand copies, I was
pleased. That was almost all in one market—the black market—
and two hundred thousand were a lot of records in those days. Oh,
sure, there'd be whites who bought my sides—even *sneak* and buy
'em if they had to—but up until "Hallelujah," the overwhelming
majority of those listening to me were black.

When I stopped imitating Nat King Cole and slid into my own
voice, I saw that my successes were exclusively at black clubs and
black dances. My music had roots which I'd dug up from my own
childhood, musical roots buried in the darkest soil. Naturally it
was music blacks could immediately take to heart.

Little by little, though, beginning around 1956, I saw that my
music had appeal beyond my own people. I saw it breaking
through to other markets, and now and then there'd be a date in a
city auditorium where whites would come along with blacks. It
probably took me longer to digest this gradual change than it
would have taken someone else. I couldn't see the increasing number of white faces.

It meant more work and more money. But it wasn't going to
change my music, and it wasn't going to change me. The more
people there were who like my stuff, the happier I was. But at this
point in my life that only convinced me to stick to my guns and follow my program.

The cats in the band could play the blues. That came first. Show
me a guy who can't play the blues and I'm through with him before
he can get started. If you can't get nasty and grovel down in the
gutter, something's missing. There are hundreds of versions of the
same blues—the same changes, the same patterns—just as there

are hundreds of versions of the same spirituals. The music is simple. But the feeling—the low-down gut-bucket feeling—has to be there or it's all for nothing. . . .

I noticed some interesting developments in popular music. White singers were picking up on black songs on a much more widespread basis. They had always done it, but now it was happening more frequently. George Gibbs and Pat Boone and Carl Perkins and Elvis were doing tunes which originally had been rhythm-and-blues hits.

It didn't bother me. It was just one of those American things. I've said before that I believe in mixed musical marriages, and there's no way to copyright a feeling or a rhythm or a style of singing. Besides, it meant that White America was getting hipper.

Something else happened in this time slot: rock 'n' roll. I have a hard time defining schools of music, and I've never been one to even try. I've been arguing against labels my whole life—I hate it when they're slapped on me—but finally they became so popular that even I have to use them.

I never considered myself part of rock 'n' roll. I didn't believe that I was among the forerunners of the music, and I've never given myself a lick of credit for either inventing it or having anything to do with its birth.

When I think of the true rock 'n' roll, cats like Chuck Berry and Little Richard and Bo Diddley come to mind. I think they're the main men. And there's a towering difference between their music and mine. My stuff was more adult. It was more difficult for teenagers to relate to; so much of my music was sad or down.

A tune like Little Richard's "Tutti Frutti" was fun. Less serious. And the kids could identify with it a lot easier than my "A Fool for You" or "Drown in My Own Tears."

I don't want to put down the others, and I don't want to butter myself up. Richard and Chuck and Bo sold millions of records, and they helped the whole industry. They did some spirited music and it broke through some thick barriers. Those guys sold a hell of a lot more records than I did back then. They sold to whites by the truckloads. Fats Domino had huge hits in the white market— "Blueberry Hill" and "Ain't That a Shame"—and I wasn't even in the same league.

Rock 'n' roll was also music that the teenagers were able to play themselves. Little Richard's or Jerry Lee Lewis's piano style—taking your thumb and scraping all they way up the keyboard—had a flare and a sound that the kids loved. And which they could duplicate.

I sang some happy songs, and I played tunes with tempos that moved. But if you compare, let's say, my "Don't You Know, Baby?"

to Little Richard's "Long Tall Sally," you'll know the difference; my
music is more serious, filled with more despair than anything
you'd associate with rock 'n' roll.

Since I couldn't see people dancing, the dance crazes passed me
by. I didn't try to write any jitterbugs or twists. I wrote rhythms
which moved me and figured they'd also make other folk move.

I've heard the Beatles say that they listened to me when they
were coming up. I believe them, but I also think that my influence
on them wasn't nearly as great as these other artists. I was really in
a different world, and if any description of me comes close, it's the
tag "rhythm-and-blues." I've fooled around in the same way that
blacks have been doing for years—playing the blues to different
rhythms.

That style requires pure heart singing. Later on they'd call it soul
music. But the names don't matter. It's the same mixture of gospel
and blues with maybe a sweet melody thrown in for good measure.
It's the sort of music where you can't fake the feeling.

Earlier I was telling you how I never test songs on the public before I record them. I've always been my own private testing service.
But there was one exception to this rule, even though I didn't
mean for it to happen the way it did. I'm talking about the accidental birth of "What I'd Say."

We happened to be playing one of my last dances—somewhere
in the Midwest—and I had another twelve minutes to kill before
the set closed. A typical gig of that kind lasted four hours, including a thirty-minute intermission. We played from 9:00 till 11:30,
took a half hour break, and then did the final hour.

It was nearly 1:00 A.M., I remember, and we had played our
whole book. There was nothing left that I could think of, so I finally said to the band and the Raeletts, "Listen, I'm going to fool
around and y'all just follow me."

So I began noodling. Just a little riff which floated up into my
head. It felt good and I kept on going. One thing led to another,
and suddenly I found myself singing and wanting the girls to re-
peat after me. So I told 'em, "Now!"

Then I could feel the whole room bouncing and shaking and
carrying on something fierce. So I kept the thing going, tightening
it up a little here, adding a dash of Latin rhythm there. When I got
through, folks came up and asked where they could buy the
record. "Ain't no record," I said, "just something I made up to kill a
little time."

The next night I started fooling with it again, adding a few more
lyrics and refining the riffs for the band. I did that for several

straight evenings until the song froze into place. And each time I sang it, the reaction was wild.

I called Jerry Wexler from the road and told him that I was coming to New York with something new to record. "I've been playing it," I said, "and it's pretty nice." That was further than I usually went with Jerry. I don't believe in giving myself advance notices, but I figured this song merited it.

We made the record in 1959, and it became my biggest hit to date. Like "Hallelujah," it sold to whites and blacks alike, although not everyone dug it. It was banned by several radio stations. They said it was suggestive. Well, I agreed. I'm not one to interpret my own songs, but if you can't figure out "What I'd Say," then something's wrong. Either that, or you're not accustomed to the sweet sounds of love.

from *Brother Ray: Ray Charles' Own Story,*
by Ray Charles and David Ritz, pp. 173–78, 190–91.

PART TWO

THE
SEAT
OF
THE
SOUL

Thou art a second world in miniature, the sun and moon are within thee, and also the stars.

—Origen

The seat of the soul is there where the inner world and the outer world meet. Where they overlap, it is in every point of the overlap.

—Novalis

The soul has a ghostly spot in her where she has all things matter-free, just as the first cause harbors in itself all things with which it creates all things. The soul also has a light in her with which she creates all things. When this light and this spot coincide so that each is the seat of the other, then, only, one is in full possession of one's mind. What more is there to tell?

—Dame Julian of Norwich

Introduction

Nobody really knows what the soul is, only that there are in-scrutable depths that require a tenacity of probing. What more *is* there to tell, as Julian of Norwich asks, other than soul is the source of light and movement, of profound beginnings? Once soul falls into time, what then? What do we see when we "turn the Tele-scope on our Soul," as Coleridge wondered? What is *resolved* by the focusing of our imaginations? How do we respond to the charges that soul is a mere social construction, a mystification of the work-ings of the body, an antiquated image for the hardwiring of the brain? How do we reply to those convinced that "silicon souls" will soon debut in the hallowed halls of science?

In Part 2 we explore a range of images of soul to help unravel the perennial confusion, from the heights of the Upanishads, those majestic "Himalayas of the Soul," to the depths of modern Swiss psychiatrist Carl Jung. What we discover in these passages, to para-phrase the architect Mies Van der Rohe, is that "the soul lives in the details." Here are richly imagined expressions of the soul's di-mensions, location, its metaphorical power, its hidden dream doors, its inhuman scale, and the confusion between mind, body, and soul. Here we roam history's long gallery and discover elabo-rate metaphors for soul: a multifaceted diamond, a many-roomed mansion, a circling river, a flaming tongue, a glowing sphere. William Law saw it this way:

> But there is a root or depth of thee from whence all these faculties come forth, as lines from a center or as branches from the body of the tree. This depth is called the center, fund, bot-tom of the soul. This depth is called the unity, the eternity. . . .

In order for us to comprehend this unity, William Blake wrote in "The Marriage of Heaven and Hell," "First, the notion that a man has a body distinct from his soul must be expunged." The Benedic-tine monk Brother David Steindl-Rast has made the critical dis-tinction elsewhere that what's important is how we *sense* ourselves as opposed to how we *think* about ourselves. From the outside we experience ourselves as body, but from the inside as soul. In every-day life we experience ourselves as soul-body beings, but it's in our articulation of the differences between our inner and outer experi-ences that confusion sets in, although "soul and body are existen-tially one in the same person."

This lyrical view of the ultimate unity of body and soul is beautifully rendered in a visionary scene in Cicero's *Republic,* called "Scipio's Dream," that charmed Boethius, Chaucer, and Shakespeare. From the dream appearance of Scipio Africanus to his grandson we have a panoramic view of the Roman universe based on the Pythagorean belief in the transmigration of souls, immortality, and the music of spheres. To the Roman philosopher the soul is living proof, so to speak, of the divinity in the body, and, echoing the Greek and Egyptian influences on him, the sacred source of motion.

To represent the vantage point of belief in a material soul I've chosen George Santayana's essay on Lucretius. There he illuminates the Roman Epicurean philosopher's often impenetrable arguments for the substantial reality of "the dancing atoms of the soul," which he saw as the prime mover and ground of consciousness.

For mystics like Dame Julian of Norwich and Saint Teresa of Avila there is no theory to be contrived about the soul, only a *unitive experience* of it, what Julian calls being "oned" to God, a kind of flute echo of the goal of mysticism everywhere: unity with ultimate reality, the universe. In one of the great masterpieces of mystical theology, *The Interior Castle,* Saint Teresa—writing obediently at the command of her religious superiors—describes the soul "as if it were a castle made of a single diamond," that can be explored in the mansions of the body. From the magnificent edifice of the *Introduction to St. Thomas Aquinas,* Thomas Aquinas seeks to explain the true nature of soul, challenging the "philosophy of old," that the soul is some sort of literal body. Rather, he writes, soul is not *a* body, but *in* the body, evidence of the "first principle" of life, echoing his master, Aristotle.

The deadend of the centuries-old debate about the substantial soul came in the work of sixteenth-century philosopher Descartes. His "discovery" of the soul in the pineal gland of the brain, the infamous "ghost in the machine," proceeded to become a poltergeist in the gears of Western philosophy for the next three centuries.

Why did the idea of a material soul, literally located in the body, arise at all? wonders philosopher William Barrett in his book *Death of the Soul.* When the immortality question was central, he surmises, the notion of the substantial soul was emphasized to console people about the uncertainty of its survival after death. Marsilio Ficino, however, the resident genius of the Florentine Academy, whose translations of Greek and Arab philosophers helped ignite the Renaissance, saw all things in the light of the soul. For Ficino the "eye of the soul" is the entryway for the life of the imagination, grounded in, requiring a deep awareness of body and a poetics to deepen the life of soul qualities that, as the Renaissance thinkers believed, give us our humanity. Speaking of being hip to the body, from Walt Whitman I've chosen two sections from his poem "I Sing the Body Electric," a positively galvanizing celebration of the fusion of mind, body, and soul.

As Thomas Moore sees in Ficino's "astropsychology" a way of knowing the "varieties of soul movement," philosopher Jacob Needleman finds in the Christian idea of a fixed soul a historical disaster because of the "lost" ability to detect just such mysterious movement. From his mentor, a certain Father Sylvan, we learn of a "lost tradition of soul," an unpredictable energy "activated and aborted a thousand times a day" (not unlike those fickle come-and-go subatomic particles). Seen in this open-ended manner, the "power of gathered attention" consciously creates soul.

Carl Jung, who did as much as anyone in our century to vindicate the "modern search for the soul," in my excerpt from his book of the same name, tackles the Doubting Thomases of scientific materialism as he attempts to demolish the modern argument against the substantial "otherness" of the soul. For Jung, like Carl Carus before him, the unconscious life of the soul forms the true basis of conscious life. Out of this inexhaustible source our sense of "I" emerges. But because we have virtually no control over our moods, emotions, dreams—the different manifestations of the soul—he seriously questions whether we are "masters in our own house." This suggestion of the "otherness" of soul has been believed in by aboriginal people for millennia but scoffed at by scientific rationalists, a ghostly reminder of Aiken's phantom.

For the sake of those still naturally confused by all the metaphysical hair-splitting about soul and spirit, I've chosen an illuminating passage from James Hillman's milestone work, *Re-Visioning Psychology*. In an excerpt I've dubbed "The Diverging Ways of Soul and Spirit" he traces the lost distinction to the Cartesian split and the subsequent "fuzzy blend" of mind, body, and soul. For Hillman, the difference between the soaring, transcendent qualities of spirit and the plunging, fantasy realm of soul (like the gap between mountain climbing and cave exploration?) is access to the "lost kingdom of imagination."

The seat of the soul is there where the inner and outer worlds overlap, where they converge in the hourglass point of energy, linking mind and body and soul. These passages represent different resolutions of one of the central dilemmas in human existence— the need to resolve what French surrealist Georges Bataille called the "anxiety of discontinuity" of the body after death—with images and ideas asserting a profound continuity. The poetry of this essential struggle is, as Al Young writes in his syncopated short story about the great Coleman Hawkin's record "Body and Soul," about "silent music, invisible art, and the clothing of time for the ages."

The Second Khanda Upanishad

Sixth century B.C.E.

The Great Soul to Be Found in the Heart

Where the channels are brought together
Like the spokes in the hub of a wheel—
Therein he moves about,
Becoming manifold.
Om!—Thus meditate upon the Soul [Atman].
Success to you in crossing to the farther shore beyond darkness!

He who is all-knowing, all wise,
Whose is this greatness on the earth—
He is in the divine Brahma city
And in the heaven established! The Soul [Atman]!
Consisting of mind, leader of the life-breaths and of the body,
He is established on food, controlling the heart.
By this knowledge the wise perceive
The blissful Immortal that gleams forth.

cited in *The Perennial Philosophy,* Aldous Huxley, p. 206.

Scipio's Dream

Marcus Tullius Cicero, Roman statesman and author, 106–43 B.C.E.

. . . so the frail body is quickened by an immortal soul.

[Scipio Africanus the Younger (185–129 B.C.E.) dreams of his
adopted grandfather, Scipio Africanus the Elder]

Strive earnestly and be assured that only this body of yours, and not your real self, is mortal. For you are not the mere physical form that you appear to be; but the real man is the soul and not that physical body which men can point to. Know, then, that your true nature is divine, if indeed it is a divine principle which lives, feels, remembers, and foresees, and which rules, guides, and activates the body beneath its sway, even as the supreme god directs the universe. And as the world, which is in part mortal, is stirred to motion by God Himself, who lives forever, so the frail body is quickened by an immortal soul.

For whatever possesses the power of ceaseless movement is eternal. On the other hand, whatever imparts movement to other things and is itself set in motion by external objects must end its life when its movement ends. Accordingly, only that which moves with self-originating motion never ceases to be moved, because it is never abandoned by itself; and it is, moreover, the source and beginning of motion for all other things that move. Beginning has no source, since all things arise from beginning, while beginning from something else could not be a beginning. If, then, beginning is never born, neither does it ever die. For beginning, if destroyed, will never itself receive new life from another source, nor will it create anything else from itself, since all things must arise from a beginning. Thus, it follows that the beginning of movement is derived from that which moves with self-originating motion and which can neither be born nor die. Otherwise, the whole heaven and the universe would collapse and stand still and would never receive any impulse by which they might again be stirred to motion.

Since, therefore, it is clear that whatever is self-moving is eternal, who will deny that this power has been given to soul? For everything that is stirred to movement by external forces is lifeless, but whatever possesses life is moved by an inner and inherent impulse. And this impulse is the very essence and power of soul. If, then, soul be the only thing which is self-moving, assuredly it is not created but is eternal. Train it in the noblest way! . . . The soul which is employed and disciplined in such pursuits will fly more speedily to this abode, its natural home. This journey it will make the swifter, if it looks abroad, while still imprisoned in the flesh, and if, by meditating upon that which lies beyond it, it divorces itself as far as may be from the body. For the souls of men who have surrendered themselves to carnal delights, who have made themselves as it were slaves of the passions, and who have been prompted by lust to violate the laws of gods and men, wander about near the earth itself, after their escape from the body, and do not return hither until they have been driven about for many ages.

He departed; I awoke from sleep.

from De re publica (On the Commonwealth), by Cicero and
translated by George H. Sabine and Stanley B. Smith.

Lucretius and the Material Soul
George Santayana, American philosopher, 1863–1952

For how are we to conceive that preexisting consciousness should govern the formation of the body, move, warm, or guide it?

To say that the soul is material has a strange and barbarous sound to modern ears. We live after Descartes, who taught the world that the essence of the soul was consciousness; and to call consciousness material would be to talk of the blackness of white. But ancient usage gave the word soul a rather different meaning. The essence of the soul was not so much to be conscious as to govern the formation of the body, to warm, move, and guide it. And if we think of the soul exclusively in this light, it will not seem a paradox, it may even seem a truism, to say that the soul must be material. For how are we to conceive that preexisting consciousness should govern the formation of the body, move, warm, or guide it? A spirit capable of such a miracle would in any case not be human, but altogether divine. The soul that Lucretius calls material should not, then, be identified with consciousness, but with the ground of consciousness, which is at the same time the cause of life in the body. This he conceives to be a swarm of very small and volatile atoms, a sort of ether, resident in all living seeds, breathed in abundantly during life and breathed out at death.

Even if this theory were accepted, however, it would not prove the point which Lucretius has chiefly at heart, namely, that an afterlife is impossible. The atoms of the soul are indestructible, like all atoms; and if consciousness were attached to the fortunes of a small group of them, or of one only (as Leibniz afterwards taught), consciousness would continue to exist after these atoms had escaped from the body and were shooting through new fields of space. Indeed, they might be the more aroused by that adventure, as a bee might find the sky or the garden more exciting than the hive. All that Lucretius urges about the divisibility of the soul, its diffused bodily seat, and the perils it would meet outside fails to remove the ominous possibility that troubles him.

To convince us that we perish at death he has to rely on vulgar experience and inherent probability: What changes is not indestructible; what begins, ends; mental growth, health, sanity accompany the fortunes of the body as a whole (not demonstrably those of the soul-atoms); the passions are relevant to bodily life and to an earthly situation; we should not be ourselves under a

different mask or in a new setting; we remember no previous existence if we had one, and so, in a future existence, we should not
remember this. These reflections are impressive, and they are enforced by Lucretius with his usual vividness and smack of reality.
Nothing is proved scientifically by such a deliverance, yet it is
good philosophy and good poetry; it brings much experience together and passes a loftly judgment upon it. The artist has his
eyes on the model; he is painting death to the life.

from *Three Philosophical Poets*, pp. 49–51.

When in the Fullness of Time
Hildegard of Bingen, German prophet and mystic, 1098–1179

When in the fullness of its time
this creation wilts,
its vigor returns to its own source.

This is the underlying natural law.
When the elements of the world fulfill
their function,
they come to ripeness
and their fruit is gathered back to God.

Now these things
are in reference to the soul's life:
spiritual vitality is alive in the soul
in the same way as the marrow of the hips in the flesh.

Out of the soul in good standing,
the vigor of the virtues flows out
as do the elements of creation,
it flows back in the same capacity
in attentive prayer.

The soul is a breath of living spirit,
that with excellent sensitivity,
permeates the entire body to give it life.

Just so,
the breath of the air makes the earth
fruitful.

Thus the air is the soul of the earth,
moistening it,
greening it.

from *Meditations with Hildegard of Bingen,*
version by Gabriele Uhlein, p. 60.

The Soul Is Oned to God
Dame Julian of Norwich, English mystic, 1343–ca. 1419

The soul,
that noble and joyful life
that is all peace and love,
draws the flesh to give its consent
by grace.

And both shall be oned
in eternal happiness.
Our soul is oned to God,
unchangeable goodness,
and therefore
between God and our soul
there is neither wrath nor forgiveness
because

there is no between.

Because of the beautiful oneing
that was made by God
between the body and the soul

it must be
that we will be restored
from double death.

from *Meditations with Julian of Norwich,*
version by Brendan Doyle, p. 31.

The Signature of All Things
Paracelsus, physician, alchemist, 1493–1541

Since nothing is so secret or hidden that it cannot be revealed, everything depends on the discovery of those things that manifest the hidden.

Explanation of *signatum* and its species: (*signatum* is divided into four species). There is nothing that Nature has not signed in such a way that man may discover its essence . . . the stars have their motions by which they are known. The same is true of man, save that they give him fixed lines by which one can establish the motion. And just as the motion of the stars has a complexion, so does the line of man. As you can see, each herb is given the form that befits its nature; similarly man is endowed with a form corresponding to his inneɪ nature. And just as the form shows what a given herb is, so the human sign indicates what a given man is. This does not refer to the name, sex, or similar characteristics, but to the properties inherent in the man. The art of signatures teaches us to give each being its true name in accordance with its innate nature. A wolf must not be called a sheep, a dove must not be called a fox; each being should receive a name that accords with its nature. Through these four species Nature makes apparent all the natural secrets which lie in man. Since nothing is so secret or hidden that it cannot be revealed, everything depends on the discovery of those things which manifest the hidden. It follows that chiromancy understands the signatures of such secrets, and the nature of each man's soul accords with these lines and veins. The same is true of the face, which is shaped and formed according to the content of the mind and soul, and the same is again true of the proportions of the human body. Thus can this member of astronomy describe each kind of soul. For the sculptor of Nature is so artful that he does not fashion the soul to fit the form, but the form to fit the soul; that is to say, the shape of a man is formed in accordance with the manner of his heart. Nature does not work like a painter who finishes a picture and gives it no signature, because the picture has none within it; it is like a shadow with no power. And yet, lacking power, the art proceeds from the Maker of living beings. And the more accomplished an artist would be, the more necessary it is that he master the art of signatures. The basis of these arts lies in these three species. The fourth species concerns the habits and behaviour of man, and whoever has knowledge of this is a consummate artist in signatures.

from *Paracelsus: Essential Readings,* selected and
translated by Nicholas Goodrick-Clarke, pp. 129–30.

The Interior Castle
Saint Teresa of Avila, Spanish Carmelite nun, 1515–1582

*I began to think of the soul as if it were a castle made of a single diamond
or of very clear crystal, in which there are many rooms, just as in Heaven
there are many mansions.*

While I was beseeching Our Lord today that He would speak
through me, since I could find nothing to say and had no idea how
to begin to carry out the obligation laid upon me by obedience a
thought occurred to me which I will now set down, in order to
have some foundation on which to build. I began to think of the
soul as if it were a castle made of a single diamond or of very clear
crystal, in which there are many rooms, just as in heaven there are
many mansions. Now if we think carefully over this, sisters, the
soul of the righteous man is nothing but a paradise, in which, as
God tells, He takes His delight. For what do you think a room will
be like which is the delight of a King so mighty, so wise, so pure
and so full of all that is good? I can find nothing with which to
compare the great beauty of a soul and its great capacity. In fact,
however acute our intellects may be, they will no more be able to
attain to a comprehension of this than to an understanding of
God; for, as He Himself says, He created us in His image and likeness. Now if this is so—and it is—there is no point in our fatiguing
ourselves by attempting to comprehend the beauty of this castle;
for, though it is His creature, and there is therefore as much difference between it and God as between creature and Creator, the
very fact that His Majesty says it is made in His image means that
we can hardly form any conception of the soul's great dignity and
beauty.

It is no small pity, and should cause us no little shame, that,
through our own fault, we do not understand ourselves, or know
who we are. Would it not be a sign of great ignorance, my daugh-
ters, if a person were asked who he was, and could not say, and had
no idea who his father or his mother was, or from what country he
came? Though that is great stupidity, our own is incomparably

greater if we make no attempt to discover what we are, and only know that we are living in these bodies, and have a vague idea, because we have heard it and because our Faith tells us so, that we possess souls. As to what good qualities there may be in our souls, or Who dwells within them, or how precious they are—those are things which we seldom consider and so we trouble little about carefully preserving the soul's beauty. All our interest is centered in the rough setting of the diamond and in the outer wall of the castle—that is to say, in these bodies of ours.

from *The Interior Castle,* translated and
edited by E. Allison Peers, pp. 28–29.

Whether the Soul Is a Body?

Thomas Aquinas, Italian philosopher, Dominican priest, 1225–1274

To seek the nature of the soul, we must premise that the soul is defined as the first principle of life . . .

We must proceed thus to the First Article:

Objection 1. It would seem that the soul is a body. For the soul is the mover of the body. Nor does it move unless moved. First, because apparently nothing can move unless it is itself moved, since nothing gives what it has not. For instance, what is not hot does not give heat. Secondly, because if there be anything that moves and is itself not moved, it must be the cause of eternal and uniform movement, as we find proved *Physics* viii. Now this does not appear to be the case in the movement of an animal, which is caused by the soul. Therefore the soul is a moved mover. But every moved mover is a body. Therefore the soul is a body.

Obj. 2. Further, all knowledge is caused by means of a likeness. But there can be no likeness of a body to an incorporeal thing. If, therefore, the soul were not a body, it could not have knowledge of corporeal things.

Obj. 3. Further, between the mover and the moved there must be contact. But contact is only between bodies. Since, therefore, the soul moves the body, it seems that the soul must be a body.

On the contrary, Augustine says the soul *is simple in comparison with the body, inasmuch as it does not occupy space by any bulk.*

I answer that, to seek the nature of the soul, we must premise that the soul is defined as the first principle of life in those things in our world which live; for we call living things *animate,* and those things which have no life, *inanimate.* Now life is shown principally by two activities, knowledge and movement. The philosophers of old, not being able to rise above their imagination, supposed that the principle of these actions was something corporeal; for they asserted that only bodies were real things, and that what is not corporeal is nothing. Hence they maintained that the soul is some sort of body. This opinion can be proved in many ways to be false; but we shall make use of only one proof, which shows quite universally and certainly that the soul is not a body.

It is manifest that not every principle of vital action is a soul, for then the eye would be a soul, as it is a principle of vision; and the same might be applied to the other instruments of the soul. But it is the *first* principle of life which we call the soul. Now, though a body may be a principle of life, as the heart is a principle of life in an animal, yet no body can be the first principle of life. For it is clear that to be a principle of life, or to be a living thing, does not belong to a body as a body, since, if that were the case, every body would be a living thing, or a principle of life. Therefore a body is competent to be a living thing, or even a principle of life, as *such* a body. Now that it is actually such a body it owes to some principle which is called its act. Therefore the soul, which is the first principle of life, is not a body, but the act of a body; just as heat, which is the principle of calefaction, is not a body, but an act of a body.

Reply Obj. 1. Since everything which is moved must be moved by something else, a process which cannot be prolonged indefinitely, we must allow that not every mover is moved. For, since to be moved is to pass from potentiality to actuality, the mover gives what it has to be the thing moved, inasmuch as it causes it to be in act. But, as is shown in *Physics* viii, there is a mover which is altogether immovable, and which is not moved either essentially or accidentally; and such a mover can cause an eternally uniform movement. There is, however, another kind of mover, which, though not moved essentially, is moved accidentally; and for this reason it does not cause a uniform movement. Such a mover is the soul. There is, again, another mover, which is moved essentially—namely, the body. And because the philosophers of old believed that nothing existed but bodies, they maintained that every mover is moved, and that the soul is moved essentially, and is a body.

Reply Obj. 2. It is not necessary that the likeness of the thing known be actually in the nature of the knower. But given a being which knows potentially, and afterwards knows actually, the likeness of the thing known must be in the nature of the knower, not actually, but only potentially; and thus color is not actually in the pupil of the eye, but only potentially. Hence it is necessary, not that the likeness of corporeal things be actually in the nature of the soul, but that there be a potentiality in the soul for such a likeness. But the ancient naturalists did not know how to distinguish between actuality and potentiality; and so they held that the soul must be a body in order to have knowledge of a body, and that it must composed of the principles of which all bodies are formed.

Reply Obj. 3. There are two kinds of contact, that of *quantity,* and that of *power.* By the former a body can be touched only by a body; by the latter a body can be touched by an incorporeal reality, which moves that body.

from *The Summa Theologica,*
edited by Anton C. Pegis, pp. 281–83.

The Seat of the Soul
René Descartes, French philosopher, 1596–1650
Article 31

That there is a small gland in the brain in which the soul exercises its functions more specifically than in the other parts of the body.

We must also know that, although the soul is joined to the entire body, there is nevertheless one part of the body in which it exercises its functions more specifically than in any of the others. It is generally believed that this part is the brain, or perhaps the heart: the brain because it is related to the organs of the senses, the heart because we feel our passions as though they were within it. But in carefully examining the matter, it seems to me that I have clearly ascertained that the part of the body in which the soul directly exercises its functions is neither the heart nor the brain as a whole but is only the innermost part of the brain, which is a certain very small gland, situated in the middle of its substance, and so suspended over the passage through which the animal spirits of the anterior cavities communicate with those of the posterior that the slightest movement on its part can do a great deal to alter the course of these spirits, and, reciprocally, that the slightest change in the course of the spirits can do a great deal to alter the movements of this gland.

from *Essential Works of Descartes,*
translated by Lowell Bair, pp. 123–24.

The Soul of the Voice
Henry David Longfellow, American poet, 1807–1882

How wonderful is the human voice! It is indeed the organ of the soul! The intellect of man sits enthroned visibly upon the forehead and in his eye; and the heart of man is written upon his countenance. But the soul reveals itself in the voice only, as God revealed himself to the prophet of old, in "the still, small voice," and in a voice from the burning bush. The soul of man is audible, not visible. A sound alone betrays the flowing of the eternal fountain, invisible to man!

cited in *Elbert Hubbard's Scrapbook,*
Elbert Hubbard, p. 228.

The Circling River of Psyche
Carl Gustav Carus, German court physician, 1789–1869

The key to an understanding of the nature of the conscious life of the soul lies in the sphere of the unconscious. All the difficulties, even the apparent impossibility, of a real understanding of the secrets of the psyche become obvious in this light. If it were absolutely impossible to be aware of the unconscious in consciousness, man would have to despair of ever understanding his psyche. If, however, this impossibility is only apparent, then the first task of a science of the psyche is to explain how man's mind can descend into these depths.

Before this attempt let us consider to what extent the unconscious life of the soul actually forms the true basis of conscious life.

At first glance into our inner life we see that the greatest part of our psychic life rests in the realm of the unconscious. While we are consciously aware of only a few ideas at a given moment, we create continually thousands of ideas which are completely unconscious,

unknown at the moment, and yet definitely existent. This is an indication that the greatest part of psychic life lies in the night of the
unconscious. Later, when we trace the remarkable evolution of an
idea, we shall see that the life of the psyche may be compared to a
great continuously circling river which is illuminated only in one
small area by the light of the sun. . . .

The close connection of the partial unconscious to pure consciousness, to the mature mind, can perhaps be clarified by the
following analogy. The fully conscious aspect of the soul is the
shining spire of a gothic cathedral, attracting the eye by its wealth
of ornament, a spire reaching to the skies, but it could not shine in
its beauty or attain such heights if the foundations resting deep in
the earth, and a firm structure of walls and iron did not support it.
All the finest qualities of the conscious life of the soul depend in
countless ways on the unconscious soul. The cathedral spire will
collapse if a single iron clamp breaks or the cornerstone gives way.
The most splendid products of the mind will also vanish if the
smallest obstacle obstructs the unconscious activity of the soul
governing the blood flow to the heart or regulating the phases of
breathing.

These considerations are usually neglected. If they are enter-
tained at all, regret is expressed that the mind depends on the
body. However, to the eye that can see these things in their totality,
it appears as a beautiful and necessary indication of the common
basis shared by consciousness and the unconscious spheres of the
soul in one and the same divine idea.

If those wonderful and mysterious processes of the unconscious
world of the soul are understood by the conscious mind; if it sees
itself supported by the unconscious like a rainbow floating lightly
over a dark wall of rain clouds; then the basis of essential understanding is at hand. . . .

If one attempts to penetrate carefully and deeply into the origin
of the life of our souls, one is inevitably brought back to the fundamental point that in the embryonic state the soul reigns unconsciously. All higher mental dispositions are potentially present, and
the structure of the nerves and the brain are unfolded in this unconscious state. Eventually, one will also understand where this
unconscious thinking process, which is responsible for the structure and transformation of the organism, becomes translated into
consciousness.

from *Psyche: On the Development of the Soul*, translation
prepared by Renata Welch and edited by Carlos Drake,
A. K. Donoghue, Thomas Logan, and Murray Stein,
pp. 1, 54–55.

The Physicians
Paul Jordan Smith, American storyteller and editor

It happened once that a group of physicians were in their cups and had fallen to quarreling about which part of the body was most important for life. As they could not agree among themselves, they decided to consult the rabbi.

"Of course it is the heart and blood vessels that are most important," said the first physician, "for on them the whole life of a man depends."

"Not at all," said the second physician. "It is the brain and nerves which are most vital, for without them, even the heart would not beat."

The third physician said, "You are both wrong. It is the stomach and the digestive passages which are important, for without the proper digestion of food, the body will die."

"The lungs are most important," declared the fourth, "for a man without air will surely die."

"You are all wrong," said the rabbi. "There are two vessels of the body only that are important, but you have no knowledge of them."

"What are they, then?" asked the physician.

The rabbi replied, "The channel that runs from the ear to the soul, and the one that runs from the soul to the tongue."

adaptation from *Parabola*, vol. III, no. 1, p. 57.

The Marriage of Heaven and Hell
William Blake, English visionary, 1757–1827

For the cherub with his flaming sword is hereby commanded to leave his guard at the tree of life, and when he does, the whole creation will be consumed, and appear infinite and holy whereas it now appears finite and corrupt.

This will come to pass by an improvement of sensual enjoyment.

But first the notion that man has a body distinct from his soul, is to be expunged; this I shall do, by printing in the infernal method, by corrosives, which in Hell are salutary and medicinal, melting apparent surfaces away, and displaying the infinite which was hid.

If the doors of perception were cleansed every thing would appear to man as it is, infinite.

For man has closed himself up, till he sees all things thro' narrow chinks of his caverns.

from *William Blake: A Selection of Poems and Letters,*
edited by J. Bronowski, pp. 100–101.

I Sing the Body Electric
Walt Whitman, American poet, 1819–1889

O I say these are not the parts and poems of the body only, but of the soul,
O I say now these are the soul!

1
I sing the body electric,
The armies of those I love engirth me and I engirth them,
They will not let me off till I go with them, respond to them,
And discorrupt them, and charge them full with the charm
of the soul.

Was it doubted that those who corrupt their own bodies conceal
themselves?
And if those who defile the living are as bad as they who defile
the dead?
And if the body does not do fully as much as the soul?
And if the body were not the soul, what is the soul?

9
O my body! I dare not desert the likes of you in other men and women,
nor the likes of the parts of you,
I believe the likes of you are to stand or fall with the likes of the soul
(and that they are the soul,)
I believe the likes of you shall stand or fall with my poems, and that
they are my poems,
Man's, woman's, child's, youth's, wife's, husband's, mother's, father's,
young man's, young woman's poems,
Head, neck, hair, ears, drop and tympan of the ears,
Eyes, eye-fringes, iris of the eye, eyebrows, and the waking or sleeping
of the lids,
Mouth, tongue, lips, teeth, roof of the mouth, jaws, and the
jaw-hinges,

Nose, nostrils of the nose, and the partition,
Cheeks, temples, forehead, chin, throat, back of the neck, neck-slue,
Strong shoulders, manly beard, scapula, hind-shoulders, and the
    ample side-round of the chest,
Upper-arm, armpit, elbow-socket, lower-arm, arm-sinews, armbones,
Wrist and wrist-joints, hand, palm, knuckles, thumb, forefingers,
    finger-joints, finger-nails,
Broad breast-front, curling hair of the breast, breast-bone, breast-side,
Hips, hip-sockets, hip-strength, inward and outward round,
    man-balls, man-root,
Strong set of thighs, well carrying the trunk above,
Leg-fibres, knee, knee-pan, upper-leg, under-leg,
Ankles, instep, foot-ball, toes, toe-joints, the heel;
All attitudes, all the shapeliness, all the belongings of my or your body
    or of any one's body, male or female,
The lung-sponges, the stomach-sac, the bowels sweet and clean,
The brain in its folds inside the skull-frame,
Sympathies, heart-valves, palate-valves, sexuality, maternity,
Womanhood, and all that is a woman, and the man that comes
    from woman,
The womb, the teats, nipples, breast-milk, tears, laughter, weeping,
    love-looks, love-perturbations and risings,
The voice, articulation, language, whispering, shouting aloud,
Food, drink, pulse, digestion, sweat, sleep, walking, swimming,
Poise on the hips, leaping, reclining, embracing, arm-curving and
    tightening,
The continual changes of the flex of the mouth, and around the eyes,
The skin, the sunburnt shade, freckles, hair,
The curious sympathy one feels when feeling with the hand the naked
    meat of the body,
The circling rivers the breath, the breathing it in and out,
The beauty of the waist, and thence of the hips, and thence downward
    toward the knees,
The thin red jellies within you or within me, the bones and the
    marrow in the bones,
The exquisite realization of health;
O I say these are not the parts and poems of the body only, but of
    the soul,
O I say now these are the soul!

from *Walt Whitman: The Complete Poems*, edited by
Francis Murphy, pp. 127–28, 134–36.

The Perennial Female Soul
Aldous Huxley, English writer, 1894–1963

In every exposition of the Perennial Philosophy the human soul
is regarded as feminine in relation to the Godhead, the personal
God, and even the Order of Nature. *Hubris,* which is the original
sin, consists in regarding the personal ego as self-sufficiently masculine in relation to the Spirit within and to Nature without, and
in behaving accordingly.

St. Paul drew a very useful and illuminating distinction between
the *psyche* and the *pneuma.* But the latter word never achieved any
degree of popularity, and the hopelessly ambiguous term, *psyche,*
came to be used indifferently for either the personal consciousness
or the spirit. And why, in the Western church, did devotional writers choose to speak of man's *anima* (which for the Romans signified
the lower, animal soul) instead of using the word traditionally reserved for the rational soul, namely *animus?* The answer, I suspect,
is that they were anxious to stress by every means in their power the
essential femininity of the human spirit in its relations with God.
Pneuma, being grammatically neuter, and *animus,* being masculine,
were felt to be less suitable than *anima* and *psyche.* Consider this
concrete example; given the structure of Greek and Latin, it would
have been very difficult for the speakers of these languages to identify anything but a grammatically feminine soul with the heroine of
the Song of Songs—an allegorical figure who, for long centuries,
played the same part in Christian thought and sentiment as the
Gopi Maidens played in the theology and devotion of the Hindus.

from *The Perennial Philosophy,* pp. 165–66.

The Flaming Tongue
Nikos Kazantzakis, Greek novelist, 1883–1957

The soul of man is a flame, a bird of fire that leaps from bough
to bough, from head to head, and that shouts: "I cannot stand
still, I cannot be consumed, no one can quench me!"

All at once the Universe becomes a tree of fire. Amidst the
smoke and the flames, reposing on the peak of conflagration,
immaculate, cool, and serene, I hold that final fruit of fire, the
Light.

From this lofty summit I look on the crimson line which ascends—a tremulous, blood-stained phosphorescence that drags itself like a lovesick insect through the raincool coils of my brain.

The ego, race, mankind, earth, theory, and action, God—all these phantasms made of loam and brain, good only for those simple hearts that live in fear, good only for those flatulent souls that imagine they are pregnant.

Where do we come from? Where are we going? What is the meaning of life? That is what every heart is shouting, what every head is asking as it beats on chaos.

And a fire within me leaps up to answer: "Fire will surely come one day to purify the earth. Fire will surely come one day to obliterate the earth. This is the Second Coming.

"The soul is a flaming tongue that licks and struggles to set the black bulk of the world on fire. One day the entire Universe will become a single conflagration.

"Fire is the first and final mask of my God. We dance and weep between two enormous pyres."

from The Saviors of God, translated by Kimon Friar, pp. 127–28.

The Appearance and Disappearance of the Soul
Jacob Needleman, American philosopher

A hundred, a thousand times a day, perhaps, "the soul is aborted."

In short, the soul is not a fixed entity. According to Father Sylvan, it is a movement that begins whenever man experiences the psychological pain of contradiction.

It is an actual energy, but one that is only at some beginning stage of its development and action. Every day, every more or less average human individual experiences the appearance of this energy in its most embryonic stage. Whenever there is pain or contradiction, this energy of the soul is released or "activated."

But almost always, almost without any exceptions whatsoever, this new energy is immediately dispersed and comes to nothing. A hundred, a thousand times a day, perhaps, "the soul is aborted."

An individual is completely unaware of this loss and remains so throughout his whole life. Without the necessary help and guidance, he never reaches the orientation necessary for enabling these everyday experiences to accumulate . . .

"Lost Christianity" is the lost or forgotten power of man to extract the pure energy of the soul from the experiences that make up his life. This possibility is distinct only in the most vivid or painful moments of our ordinary lives, but it can be discovered in all experiences if one knows how to seek it. Certain powerful experiences—such as the encounter with death or deep disappointment—are accompanied by the sensation of *presence;* an attention appears that is simultaneously open to a higher, freer mind ("Spirit") and to all the perceptions, sensations, and emotions that constitute our ordinary self. One feels both separate and engaged in a new and entirely extraordinary way. One experiences "I Am." This is the soul (in inception).

It was a disaster for Christianity, according to Father Sylvan, when it adopted the notion that the soul of man already exists in finished form within human nature. This assumption about the given existence of the soul led to our identification of ordinary kinds of thoughts, emotions and sensations with the soul, the higher part of ourselves, and hence to the futile and mistaken effort to perfect our being by perfecting our thoughts, emotions, or sensations, that is, the futile effort of thought to alter emotion or vice versa. The Christian teaching, as Father Sylvan presents it, says on the contrary that these psychological functions are incapable of altering each other. Change, transformation, can come only through the action of an objectively higher force: the Spirit. And this Spirit cannot find channels of action unless there exists something in man that can receive it and pass it on to all the parts of himself.

The immensity and revolutionary nature of this idea can be seen when it is applied to the efforts of mankind, everywhere, to find "happiness." The quest for happiness, which in one form or another is the main impetus of the whole mass of human life and moral idealism, is from this point of view little more than the vain effort by the mind to alter the emotions, or vice versa.

But the power to alter the structure of human life, inwardly as well as outwardly, does not reside in a partial function of the psyche. Only that function which can be in actual relationship, actual contact, with all the parts of the self has the possibility of altering the self, or of serving as the channel for the force that can alter the whole of the self. That function Father Sylvan identifies as the power of gathered attention, the power of the soul.

from *Lost Christianity,* 1985, pp. 175–76.

Marsilio Ficino's Astropsychology

Thomas Moore, American psychologist

The planets correspond, then, to deeply felt movements of the soul. . . .

A good portion of *The Planets* consists of advice for accommodating oneself to the various planetary centers. Each planet is described roughly, then the material things associated with each are listed, as we are advised to use the proper material objects. Some of the objects mentioned have obvious physical properties related to a particular planet, such as the golden things connected with the sun. Others have stories behind them linking them to the deity of a planet.

Interpreting this procedure of accommodation, we may understand the details metaphorically. There are seven planets in the classical system, but there are many more archetypal possibilities one can imagine for the soul. We may begin to understand the process of accommodation by studying the planets, along with Ficino, as archetypal images, but we do not have to stop there. An imaginative symbol system helps, and there are many to be found in the religions of the world and even in art and psychology, but sometimes we need only an idiosyncratic metaphor against which to view an actual situation and glimpse the fantasies congealed in it. A dream will do, or a novel, or science, or a walk in the woods. Everything is metaphor and food for the soul. All of the material world contains sparks of the kindred sky, flashes of the psychological lumen.

If accommodation is a posturing of oneself toward the world so that the psychological dimension is revealed and put in action, then what happens to the psyche itself is an "arrangement." Recall the title of Ficino's book: *De Vita Coelitus Comparanda.* I am translating *comparanda* as "arrange," though it could also mean "dispose" or "prepare." The title of the book refers, then, to arranging life according to planetary spirit, but we could also think of the arrangement to planetary spirit, but we could also think of the arrangement as a constellation of psyche itself, all parts awakened and in place. When one's psychological life reflects the sky, *its* planets are in motion. It is not stuck under the domination of a single planetary focus. . . . The ultimate purpose is to know the varieties of soul-movement so that this variety can become part of psychological life. Movement itself is essential to the soul, for without movement there is no feeling, no valuing, and no vitality.

It is apparent that Ficino's astropsychology suggests a picture of the psyche which embraces many extremes of experience without sacrificing any of them or, worse, rubbing them out through harmonizing or reconciliation of opposites. Ficino affirms both sides of paradoxes consistently, always keeping a Janus face. He affirms the role of cyclic, transpersonal factors (planets) in human life while at the same time emphasizing the important task of discovering one's uniqueness and individuality. Among the planets he recognizes those which are particularly painful to the soul, like Mars and Saturn, but he doesn't suggest flight from these influences—they are part of life. True to his pervasive Platonism he strongly advocates a dying to materialistic attitudes, yet his theory remarkably places great value on the ordinary, the mundane, and the worldly.

One final point should be made about the interpretation of the planets and their characters. I am suggesting that we read all of this astrology in terms of a sky within. The planets correspond, then, to deeply felt movements of the soul and not to either ego attitudes, that is, conscious values and positions, or to persona qualities. I mean the latter in the Jungian sense: social, gender, and ego roles we play. Mars is not simply a surface tendency toward anger, nor is Venus the trappings of body awareness. These planetary centers are deep in the psyche, generating many complexes, fantasies, and behaviors. The sky within truly seems as vast as the sky without, and the planets are just as massive, mysterious, and unearthly.

from *The Planets Within*, pp. 125–26.

The Architecture of the Soul
Keith Critchlow, English architect

Plotinus weaves a beautiful analogy when he compares the Soul to "a huge light, which shining to its uttermost limits becomes darkness. The soul seeing this darkness, which it has made subsist, forms this darkness (as a hollow of light)." The most apt formal analogy to clothe this image is a sphere—the uninterrupted radiant form of a light to its limits. The sphere also aptly answers to Plato's description in the Laws: "Soul is among the primal things, elder-born than all bodies and prime source of all their changes and transformations."

The sphere as light is a beautiful symbol of the total transparency of space to light and the "original" nonseparation of center, interspace, and periphery of the undifferentiated unified form. Philoponus, a seventh-century commentator of the Platonic succession, was probably making an accurate representation of the esoteric tradition when he describes the more subtle bodies of ourselves: "There is moreover, beyond this (spiritual body) another kind of body, that is forever attached to (the Soul), of a celestial nature, and for this reason everlasting, which they call radiant (*augoeides*) or star-like (*astroeides*)." Furthermore he goes on to establish the radiant sphere analogy by saying: "Matter of celestial bodies is not of the four elements, but there is another body—the fifth element or quintessence, and its form (*eidos*) is spherical." We will explore the image of the sphere as analogy to Soul. It is simplicity, compoundness, completeness (in terms of rotational symmetry). It is all-embracing, "just" in its equality, unbiased (on any radii from center to periphery). The shortest distance between any two points on a sphere's surface will always be a segment of the circle that exactly divides it into two equal halves. The sphere "at rest in the perfection of itself," then, is an apt symbol for the Androgyne—as both the origin and the resolving of duality. In its relation to Soul it also represents the centering of the individual soul with the Soul of the All.

from *Parabola*, vol. III, no. 4, pp. 35–36.

The Empirically Justified Psyche
Carl Jung, Swiss psychologist, 1875–1961

> . . . we can perhaps summon up the courage to consider the possibility of a "psychology with the psyche"—that is, of a field of study based on the assumption of an autonomous psyche.

It is quite evident that, since breath is the sign of life, breath is taken for life, as are also movement and moving force. According to another primitive view the soul is regarded as fire or flame, because warmth is also a sign of life. A very curious, but by no means rare, primitive conception identifies the soul with the name. The name of an individual is his soul, and hence arises the custom of using the ancestor's name to reincarnate the ancestral soul in the newborn child. We can infer from this that the ego-consciousness was recognized as an expression of the soul. Not infrequently the soul is identified with the shadow, for which reason it is a deadly insult to tread upon a person's shadow. For the same reason, noonday, the ghost hour of southern latitudes, is considered threatening; the shadow then grows small, and this means that life is endangered. This conception of the shadow contains an idea which was indicated by the Greeks in the word *synopados*, "he who follows behind." They expressed in this way the feeling of an intangible, living presence—the same feeling which led to the belief that the souls of the departed were shadows.

These indications may serve to show how primitive man experienced the psyche. To him the psyche appears as the source of life, the prime mover, a ghostlike presence which has objective reality. Therefore the primitive knows how to converse with his soul; it becomes vocal within him because it is not he himself and his consciousness. To primitive man the psyche is not, as it is to us, the epitome of all that is subjective and subject to the will; on the contrary, it is something objective, contained in itself, and living its own life.

This way of looking at the matter is empirically justified, for not only on the primitive level, but with civilized man as well, psychic happenings have an objective side. In large measure they are withdrawn from our conscious control. We are unable, for example, to suppress many of our emotions; we cannot change a bad mood into a good one, and we cannot command our dreams to come or go. The most intelligent man may at times be obsessed with thoughts which he cannot drive away with the greatest effort of will. The mad tricks that memory plays sometimes leave us in helpless amazement, and at any time unexpected fantasies may run through our minds. We only believe that we are masters in our own house because we like to flatter ourselves. Actually, however, we are dependent to a startling degree upon the proper functioning of the unconscious psyche and must trust that it does not fail us. If we study the psychic processes of neurotic persons, it seems perfectly ludicrous that any psychologist could take the psyche as the equivalent of consciousness. And it is well known that the psychic processes of neurotics differ hardly at all from those of so-called normal persons—for what man today is quite sure that he is not neurotic?

This being so, we shall do well to admit that there is justification for the old view of the soul as an objective reality—as something independent, and therefore capricious and dangerous. The further assumption that this being, so mysterious and terrifying, is at the same time the source of life, is also understandable in the light of psychology. Experience shows us that the sense of the "I"—the ego-consciousness—grows out of unconscious life. The small child has psychic life without any demonstrable ego-consciousness, for which the earliest years leave hardly any traces in memory. Where do all our good and helpful flashes of intelligence come from? What is the source of our enthusiasms, inspirations, and of our heightened feeling for life? The primitive senses in the depths of his soul the springs of life; he is deeply impressed with the life-dispensing activity of his soul, and he therefore believes in everything that affects it—in magical practices of every kind. That is why, for him, the soul is life itself. He does not imagine that he directs it, but feels himself dependent upon it in every respect.

However preposterous the idea of immortality of the soul may seem to us, it is nothing extraordinary to the primitive. After all, the soul is something out of the common. While everything else that exists takes up a certain amount of room, the soul cannot be located in space. We suppose, of course, that our thoughts are in our heads, but when it comes to our feelings we begin to be uncertain; they appear to dwell in the region of the heart. Our sensations are distributed over the whole body. Our theory is that the seat of consciousness is in the head, but the Pueblo Indians told me that Americans were mad because they believed their thoughts were in their heads, whereas any sensible man knows that he thinks with his heart. Certain Negro tribes locate their psychic functioning neither in the head nor in the heart, but in the belly.

To this uncertainty about the localization of psychic functions another difficulty is added. Psychic contents in general are nonspatial except in the particular realm of sensation. What bulk can be ascribed to thoughts? Are they small, large, long, thin, heavy, fluid, straight, circular, or what? If we wished to form a vivid picture of a nonspatial being of the fourth dimension, we should do well to take thought, as a being, for our model.

It would all be so much simpler if we could only deny the existence of the psyche. But here we are with our immediate experiences of something that *is*—something that has taken root in the midst of our measurable, ponderable, three-dimensional reality, that differs bafflingly from this in every respect and in all its parts, and yet reflects it. The psyche may be regarded as a mathematical point and at the same time as a universe of fixed stars. It is small wonder, then, if to the unsophisticated mind, such a paradoxical being borders on the divine. If it occupies space, it has no body. Bodies die, but can something invisible and incorporeal disappear? What is more, life and psyche existed for me before I could say "I," and when this "I" disappears, as in sleep or unconsciousness, life and psyche still go on, as our observation of other people and our own dreams inform us. Why should the simple mind deny, in the face of such experiences, that the "soul" lives in a realm beyond the body? I must admit that I can see as little nonsense in this so-called superstition as in the findings of research regarding heredity or the basic instincts.

from *Modern Man in Search of a Soul*,
translated by W. S. Dell and Cary F. Baynes,
pp. 181–85.

Our Unknown Soul
William Barrett, American philosopher

Thus at the center of the self there is a hole and a mystery. Our own soul is unknown to us.

Consider the chairs and tables in this room. I go out of the room for a half hour, and when I come back everything looks as it did. But did these chairs and this table persist during that interval of absence? Common sense and instinct say that they did. In the Kantian view, it is sufficient, to say that we *can* think of them as persisting throughout that interval. Common sense is here more dogmatic than Kant, and on this matter, I prefer to side with common sense.

What I wish to present, in short, is a far more concrete and substantial view of the human self, or soul, than can be found in Kant. The soul as substance! Horrors! What a dreadful lapse back to Descartes and all his attendant errors! But perhaps we have to look farther back than that; in our time the idea of substance itself has become shaky and suspect, and we may as well go back for a moment to Aristotle for a look at it.

For Aristotle, a "primary substance" is a concrete individual object: this table, this chair, or the individual man Socrates. The characteristic of such a substance is that it is capable of separate existence: the color of an object must inhere in the object, but the object itself is capable of separate existence. The object is more substantial than its colors. When the question of the immortality of soul was central, this characteristic of substance naturally became emphasized. What was required was a substantial soul capable of surviving the dissolution of the body.

But there is another characteristic of substance that Aristotle takes note of: A substance is that which persists through change. It may have altered in the process, but it is still recognizably the same: a persisting identity through time. It is in this latter sense that I wish to stress the substantiality of the human self. We are persisting identities, both physically and mentally. However we may grow, develop, and change, we recognize the self as the same person throughout.

This fact of persisting personal identity is so large and overwhelming a part of our common experience that it is hard to understand why modern philosophy has passed it by. Philosophers have written about the self as if the greater part of our experience were spent in a lonely chamber, in solitary introspection, hunting for a fugitive and ghostly identity. In fact, however, most of us live amid friends and family, where the reality of personal identity is so bedrock a fixture of our world that we hardly even single it out for special comment. We know and are known by our intimates, and in the course of our everyday life we do not take this phenomenon of persisting identity as puzzling. Why, then, should it have been turned into so puzzling a matter by the philosophers?

In Kant's case, the puzzle comes from his epistemological doctrine. According to this Kantian doctrine, we know the appearances of things, but the thing-in-itself remains hidden from us. Of this table before me, for example, so familiar, so commonplace, I know many aspects, but of the thing-in-itself, the table in and of itself, I remain ignorant. And the same state of affairs would hold for the mind as a persisting identity. We are familiar with aspects of that self—indeed there is nothing in our experience that is closer to us than our self—but of the self as a Ding-an-sich, a thing-in-itself, we have no intellectual grasp. I have no clear-cut intellectual concept of this I who I am twenty-four hours a day. Thus at the center of the self there is a hole and a mystery. Our own soul is unknown to us.

from *Death of the Soul: From Descartes to the Computer*, pp. 113–15.

The Diverging Ways of Soul and Spirit
James Hillman, American psychologist

I have drawn apart soul and spirit in order to make us feel the differences, and especially to feel what happens to soul when its phenomena are viewed from the perspective of spirit.

Here we need to remember that the ways of the soul and those of the spirit only sometimes coincide and that they diverge most in regard to psychopathology. A main reason for my stress upon pathologizing is just to bring out the differences between soul and spirit, so that we end the widespread confusions between psychotherapy and spiritual disciplines. There is a difference between Yoga, transcendental meditation, religious contemplation and retreat, and even Zen, on the one hand, and the psychologizing of psychotherapy on the other. This difference is based upon a distinction between spirit and soul.

Today we have rather lost this difference that most cultures, even tribal ones, know and live in terms of. Our distinctions are

Cartesian: between outer tangible reality and inner states of mind, or between body and a fuzzy conglomerate of mind, psyche, and spirit. We have lost the third, middle position which earlier in our tradition, and in others too, was the place of soul: a world of imagination, passion, fantasy, reflection that is neither physical and material on the one hand, nor spiritual and abstract on the other, yet bound to them both. By having its own realm psyche has its own logic—psychology—which is neither a science of physical things nor a metaphysics of spiritual things. Psychological pathologies also belong to this realm. Approaching them from either side, in terms of medical sickness or religion's suffering, sin, and salvation, misses the target of soul.

But the threefold division has collapsed into two, because soul has become identified with spirit. This happens because we are materialists, so that everything that is not physical and bodily is one undifferentiated cloud; or it happens because we are Christians. Already in the early vocabulary used by Paul, *pneuma* or spirit had begun to replace *psyche* or soul. The New Testament scarcely mentions soul phenomena such as dreams but stresses spirit phenomena such as miracles, speaking in tongues, prophecy, and visions.

Philosophers have tried to keep the line between spirit and soul by keeping soul altogether out of their works or assigning it a lower place. Descartes confined soul to the pineal gland, a little enclave between the opposing powers of internal mind and external space. More recently, Santayana has put soul down in the realm of matter and considered it an antimetaphysical principle. Collingwood equated soul with feeling and considered that psychology had no business invading the realm of thought and ideas. The spiritual point of view always posits itself as superior and operates particularly well in a fantasy of transcendence among ultimates and absolutes.

Philosophy is therefore less helpful in showing the differences than is the language of the imagination. Images of the soul show first of all more feminine connotations. *Psyche,* in the Greek language, besides being soul, denoted a night moth or butterfly and a particularly beautiful girl in the legend of Eros and Psyche. Our discussion in the previous chapter of the anima as a personified feminine idea continues this line of thinking. There we saw many of her attributes and effects, particularly the relationship of psyche with dream, fantasy, and image. This relationship has also been put mythologically as the soul's connection with the night world, the realm of the dead, and the moon. We still catch our soul's most essential nature in death experiences, in dreams of the night, and in the images of *lunacy*.

The world of spirit is difference indeed. Its images blaze with light, there is fire, wind, sperm. Spirit is fast, and it quickens what it touches. Its direction is vertical and ascending; it is arrow straight, knife sharp, powder dry, and phallic. It is masculine, the active principle, making forms, order, and clear distinctions. Although there are many spirits, and many kinds of spirit, more and more the notion of *spirit* has come to be carried by the Apollonian archetype, the sublimations of higher and abstract disciplines, the intellectual mind, refinements, and purifications.

We can experience soul and spirit interacting. At moments of intellectual concentration or transcendental meditation, soul invades with natural urges, memories, fantasies, and fears. At times of new psychological insights or experiences, spirit would quickly extract a meaning, put them into action, conceptualize them into rules. Soul sticks to the realm of experience and to reflections within experience. It moves indirectly in circular reasonings, where retreats are as important as advances, preferring labyrinths and corners, giving a metaphorical sense to life through such words as *close, near, slow,* and *deep*. Soul involves us in the pack and welter of phenomena and the flow of impressions. It is the "patient" part of us. Soul is vulnerable and suffers; it is passive and remembers. It is water to the spirit's fire, like a mermaid who beckons the heroic spirit into the depths of passions to extinguish its certainty. *Soul is imagination,* a cavernous treasury—to use an image from St. Augustine—a confusion and richness, both. Whereas spirit chooses the better part and seeks to make all one. Look up, says spirit, gain distance; there is something beyond and above, and what is above is always, and always superior.

They differ in another way: Spirit is after ultimates and it travels by means of a *via negativa*. "*Neti, neti,*" it says, "not this, not that." Strait is the gate and only first or last things will do. Soul replies by saying, "Yes, this too has place, may find its archetypal significance, belongs in a myth." The cooking vessel of the soul takes in everything, everything can become soul; and by taking into its imagination any and all events, psychic space grows.

I have drawn apart soul and spirit in order to make us feel the differences, and especially to feel what happens to soul when its phenomena are viewed from the perspective of spirit. Then, it seems, the soul must be disciplined, its desires harnessed, imagination emptied, dreams forgotten, involvements dried. For soul, says spirit, cannot *know*, neither truth, nor law, nor cause. The soul is fantasy, all fantasy. The thousand pathologizings that soul is heir to by its natural attachments to the ten thousand things of life in the world shall be cured by making soul into an imitation of spirit. The *imitatio Christi* was the classical way; now there are other models, gurus from the Far East or Far West, who, if followed to the letter, put one's soul on a spiritual path which supposedly leads to freedom from pathologies. Pathologizing, so says spirit, is by its very nature confined only to soul; only the psyche can be pathological, as the word *psychopathology* attests. There is no *pneumopathology* and as one German tradition has insisted, there can be no such thing as *mental* illness (*Geisteskrankheit*), for the spirit cannot pathologize. So there must be spiritual disciplines for the soul, ways in which soul shall conform with models enunciated for it by spirit.

But from the viewpoint of the psyche the humanistic and Oriental movement upward looks like repression. There may well be more psychopathology actually going on while transcending than while being immersed in pathologizing. For any attempt at self-realization without full recognition of the psychopathology that resides, as Hegel said, inherently in the soul is in itself pathological, an exercise in self-deception. Such self-realization turns out to be a paranoid delusional system, or even of charlatanism, the psychopathic behavior of an emptied soul.

from *Re-Visioning Psychology,* pp. 67–70.

"Body and Soul: Coleman Hawkins, 1939"
Al Young, African-American music critic

When the record came out, saxophonists all over the world, hearing it and sensing that things would never be the same started woodshedding Hawkins' impassioned licks in their closets and on the stand.

My father, who used to bicycle thirty miles one way to court my mother, had this record among his dust-needled 78s. He'd already worn out several copies before I learned to love it from memory, never knowing until much later what a cause it had stirred.

Imagine it's 1939. You talk about a hellraising year, that one had to take the cake with Hitler taking Czechoslovakia, Bohemia, Moravia, and Poland; with Stalin taking Finland and Poland (poor Poland); Franco taking Spain; Great Britain and France declaring war on Germany; Mussolini taking Albania; Stalin and Hitler signing their infamous non-aggression pact that would splinter and split all the left-leaning parents of kids I would later meet at college and beyond. My own folks, peasants and proles, knew next to nothing about the left-wing or right-wing of anything but chickens, but they did know right from wrong. Politics to them had something to do with money and power, which in white Mississippi were one and the same.

History and truth are so easily misconstrued. Even dates, names, facts and figures can lie—"Aught's an aught/Figger's a figger/All for the white man/None for the nigger"—depending on who's doing the dating, doing the naming, doing the figuring. The telling of the truth is the poet's proper domain and in the head-whipping nations of this darkening, fact-ridden world, people still look to poets and the music they make for light, sweet light illumining everything.

If it's true that in this alleged 1939 the New York World's Fair "World of Tomorrow" ran for five straight months and that TVA got the Supreme Court go-ahead and that TV in the U.S. was first broadcast publicly from the Empire State Building (covering the opening of that same World's Fair), then it's equally fair to imagine Coleman Hawkins in that crowded year. In October, the Golden Gate Bridge closed down for repairs while on the eleventh day of that same month, Hawkins, just back from a rewarding stay in war-hungry Europe, repaired to the RCA Victor New York studios with some musical friends and cut "Body and Soul"—just like that, in the shadow of the Empire State Building

You can even picture him slouched in front of one of those weighty old condenser boom mikes, surrounded by smoke, suspendered and hatted, thinking something like: Well, let's see how what I'm feeling's gonna come out sounding this time, so we can get this session wrapped up and get back to the gig and really do some blowing. After the take he probably remembered how he'd performed this wee hours ballad better a hundred times before. "I'll get it down yet," he told himself, "but this'll have to do for now." And, children, that was that.

When the record came out, saxophonists all over the world, hearing it and sensing that things would never be the same, started woodshedding Hawkins' impassioned licks in their closets and on the stand. Why'd he have to go and do that? Of course, everybody fell in love with it. My father would play it, take it off, play something else, then put it back on. This went on for years. What was he listening for? What were we listening to? What did it mean? What were all those funny, throaty squawks and sighs and cries all about? I knew what a body was, but what was a soul? You kept hearing people say, "Well, bless his soul!" You thought you knew what they meant, but really, you could only imagine as you must now. You knew what they meant when they said, "Bless her heart!" because you could put your hand to your heart and feel the beat, and your Aunt Ethel sometimes fried up chicken hearts along with gizzards, livers, and feet. But a soul was unseeable. Did animals have souls too? Did birds, dogs, cows, mules, pigs, snakes, bees? And what about other stuff, like corn, okra, creeks, rivers, moonlight, sunshine, trees, the ground, the rain, the sky? Did white folks have souls?

Was a soul something like a breeze: something you couldn't picture or grab but could only feel like you could the wind off the Gulf when the day cooled down, or the way the ground would tremble when the train roared past across the street from where we lived?

Thirty-nine, forty, fifty, a hundred, thousands—who's to say how many rosy-chilled Octobers have befallen us, each one engraved in micro-moments of this innocent utterance, electrically notated, but, like light in a photography, never quite captured in detail, only in essence. Essence in this instance is private song, is you hearing your secret sorrow and joy blown back through Coleman Hawkins, invisibly connected to you and played back through countless bodies, each one an embodiment of the same soul force.

All poetry is about silent music, invisible art and the clothing of time for the ages.

                                                  from *Bodies & Soul*, pp. 1–4.

PART THREE

HEART
AND
SOUL

Lady butterfly
perfumes her wings
by floating
over the orchid
            —Basho

O remember
In your narrow dark hours
That more things move
Than blood in the heart.
            —Louise Bogan

From every human being there rises a light that reaches straight to heaven,
and when two souls that are destined to be together find each other, the
streams of light flow together and a single brighter light goes forth from that
united being.

                                            —Baal Shem Tov

Introduction

From the philosophers gathered around Socrates at his sympo-
siums in ancient Athens to the torchsingers gathered around
honkytonk pianos in the blues bars of Kansas City, we hear again
and again that while soul may be the breath surge, love, sweet love,
is the heartbeat of the universe. The bittersweet attraction between
the two is one of the supreme mysteries of the human adventure. If
it's any consolation to us mere mortals, while love and soul each
hold out the promise of magical metamorphosis of the other, getting the two into sync is a problem that plagued even the gods, as
we learn from the tale of Eros and Psyche by the Roman writer
Apuleius.

Is this how the world is ensouled, by such torturous enchant-
ments? How do we reconcile the needs of the heart with the desires
of the soul? What does Apuleius's classic tale of love's long-winged
journey in pursuit of soul really tell us? That our main task involves
love? That the soul realizes itself not only in contemplative solitude
and racking isolation but also in erotic embraces and deep pleasure
and joy? Or simply that a mysterious transformation happens with
each trembling encounter of heart and soul?

All we know for certain is that where Eros stirs, Psyche is sure to
be found; where Psyche performs her tasks, Eros draws near; when
love nourishes soul, the soul is deepened through love. And that no
one touches the depths of the soul without love, the awakening
god. Poet David Whyte captures the tremulous movement, how
"the soul lives encontented by listening" when he writes:

> . . . The voice hesitant,
> and her hand trembling
> in the dark for yours. . . .

The allusive imagery of poets, lovers, and madmen alike attempt
to describe the supreme moment, when, as Plato writes in the passage of the chariot, rider, and horses I've selected from "The Phaedrus," "desire enters the soul." From June Singer's *A Gnostic Book
of Hours*, I've found an adaptation of the esoteric fourth-century
The Exegesis on the Soul that illuminates the "hidden river of wisdom" that sages have drunk from to "liberate the sparks of divinity."
The unknown Jewish—Christian authors of ancient Alexandria
who composed this romantic allegory pictured a feminine soul only
able to rejoice after rejoining her beloved.

More than eight centuries later, in the excruciatingly exquisite letters of the beloved French abbess Heloise to her notorious teacher, Abelard, one of the world's most celebrated tragic love affairs, we find evidence of the mad swirl left behind by blind passion. Exiled by their scandal, Heloise writes her former teacher (who once confessed that they spoke of love more than philosophy on their strolls in the gardens near Notre Dame!) how their sweet pleasures "can scarcely be banished from my thoughts"—even during the holy celebration of Mass.

For Meister Eckhart, "the nearly indefatigably imaginative theologian and mystic," as Matthew Fox describes him, the relationship between love and soul is divine, as cosmic as the pouring forth of God's energies, as natural as a horse running free in a meadow.

For an inspiring example of an epiphany of love, I've gone to James Joyce. In my selection from *A Portrait of the Artist as a Young Man* Joyce gloriously described the "uplifting" of a vision of love on Sandymount Beach outside Dublin, an image of love that awakens the slumbering soul of the young hero, Stephen Daedalus.

From *Psyche's Sisters,* an intensely moving account of Christine Downing's clarification of "the role of sisterhood" in her life, we find confirmation of the significance of engagement with the "otherness" of actual women, an affirmation of the nurturing power of lesbian love. In "Your Breast Is Enough," by the incomparable Chilean poet Pablo Neruda, is a recapitulation of the entire round of love and soul imagery all in one splendid poem: breath, heart, wings, freedom, sleep, heaven.

From Apuleius's tale of Eros and Psyche, perhaps the most seminal tale of love in the Western world, I've chosen the revelation scene. As rendered by storyteller Diane Wolkstein in her ravishing book *The First Love Stories,* Psyche is cajoled by her sisters to murder her unwitting midnight mystery lover, Eros, but "to her utter amazement and bewilderment, and guilt," as psychiatrist Robert Johnson describes the moment elsewhere, she "sees that he is the god of love." She accidentally pricks herself on one of his arrows, instantly falling in love with him, or more precisely, "in love with Love." The completion of her famous tasks through the rest of the story help her "cut through that fog of projection," in Johnson's mythopoetic reading, before she can make the critical move from romance to true love, which is seeing through the fog. Psyche, or soul, the myth is also telling us, must reconnect with the god of love, before encountering the other gods. If she does, she can give birth, and the child's name, according to tradition, is called Pleasure or Joy. Coincidentally, Czech novelist Milan Kundera's *The Unbearable*

Lightness of Being also uses the bow-inspired image of the "drawing power" of love upon the soul when Tomas first meets Tereza, even if the novelist represents the position of the "irreconcilable duality of body and soul" as the fundamental human experience.

If there is a secret love potion, it is in the embrace of Eros and Psyche, of love and soul intertwined, "the wine of lust deriving its strength from the soul's sap," as Marguerite Yourcenar described the inner movement. By drinking from the flagon of ambrosia, Eros and Psyche are promised immortality, as Zeus vows, which is to say, the suspension of time and space, eternity measured not in longevity but intensity, the intensity of the fusion between heart and soul. Love drawn out of dark turbulence by fierce desire, drawn out like fine wine from the old oak cask of the soul.

When Desire Enters Heart and Soul
Plato, Greek philosopher, ca. 427–348 B.C.E.

Now when the charioteer beholds the vision of love, and has his whole soul warmed through sense. . . .

As I said at the beginning of this tale, I divided each soul into three—two horses and a charioteer; and one of the horses was good and the other bad: The division may remain, but I have not yet explained in what the goodness or badness of either consists, and to that I will proceed. The right-hand horse is upright and cleanly made; he has a lofty neck and an aquiline nose; his color is white, and his eyes dark; he is a lover of honor and modesty and temperance, and the follower of true glory; he needs no touch of the whip but is guided by word and admonition only. The other is a crooked, lumbering animal, put together anyhow; he has a short, thick neck; he is flat-faced and of a dark color, with grey eyes and blood-red complexion; the mate of insolence and pride, shag-eared and deaf, hardly fielding to whip and spur. Now when the charioteer beholds the vision of love, and has his whole soul warmed through sense, and is full of the prickings and ticklings of desire, the obedient steed, then as always under the government of shame, refrains from leaping on the beloved; but the other, heedless of the pricks and of the blows of the whip, plunges and runs away, giving all manner of trouble to his companion and the charioteer, whom he forces to approach the beloved and to remember the joys of love.

They at first indignantly oppose him and will not be urged on to do terrible and unlawful deeds; but at last, when he persists in plaguing them, they yield and agree to do as he bids them. And now they are on the spot and behold the flashing beauty of the beloved; which, when the charioteer sees, his memory is carried to the true beauty, whom he beholds in company with Modesty like an image placed upon a holy pedestal. He sees her, but he is afraid and falls backwards in adoration, and by his fall is compelled to pull back the reins with such violence as to bring both the steeds on their haunches, the one willing and unresisting, the unruly one very unwilling; and when they have gone back a little, the one is overcome with shame and wonder, and his whole soul is bathed in perspiration; the other, when the pain is over which the bridle and the fall had given him, having with difficulty taken breath, is full of wrath and reproaches, which he heaps upon the charioteer and his fellow-steed, for want of courage and manhood, declaring that they have been false to their agreement and guilty of desertion. Again they refuse, and again he urges them on and will scarce yield to their prayer that he would wait until another time. When the appointed hour comes, they make as if they had forgotten, and he reminds them, fighting and neighing and dragging them on, until at length he, on the same thoughts intent, forces them to draw near again. And when they are near he stoops his head and puts up his tail and takes the bit in his teeth and pulls shamelessly. Then the charioteer is worse off than ever; he falls back like a racer at the barrier, and with a still more violent wrench drags the bit out of the teeth of the wild steed and covers his abusive tongue and jaws with blood, and forces his legs and haunches to the ground and punishes him sorely. And when this has happened several times and the villain has ceased from his wanton way, he is tamed and humbled, and follows the will of the charioteer, and when he sees the beautiful one he is ready to die of fear. And from that time forward the soul of the lover follows the beloved in modesty and holy fear.

And so the beloved who, like a god, has received every true and loyal service from his lover, not in pretense but in reality, being also himself of a nature friend to his admirer, if in former days he has blushed to own his passion and turned away his lover because his youthful companions or others slanderously told him that he would be disgraced, now, as years advance, at the appointed age and time, is led to receive him into communion. For fate, which has ordained that there shall be no friendship among the evil, has also ordained that there shall ever be friendship among the good. And the beloved, when he has received him into communion and intimacy, is quite amazed at the goodwill of the lover; he recognizes that the inspired friend is worth all other friends or kinsmen; they have nothing of friendship in them worthy to be compared with his. And when his feeling continues and he is nearer to him and embraces him in gymnastic exercises and at other times of meeting, then the fountain of that stream, which Zeus when he was in love with Ganymede named Desire, overflows upon the lover, and some enters into his soul, and some when he is filled flows out again; and as a breeze or an echo rebounds from the smooth rocks and returns whence it came, so does the stream of beauty, passing through the eyes, which are the windows of the soul, come back to the beautiful one; there arriving and quickening the passages of the wings, watering them and inclining them to grow, and filling the soul of the beloved also with love. And thus he loves, but he knows not what; he does not understand and cannot explain his own state; he appears to have caught the infection of blindness from another; the lover is his mirror in which he is beholding himself, but he is not aware of this. When he is with the lover, both cease from their pain, but when he is away then he longs as he is longed for, and has love's image, lover for love [Anteros], lodging in his breast, which he calls and believes to be not love but friendship only, and his desire is as the desire of the other, but weaker; he wants to see him, touch him, kiss, embrace him, and probably not long afterwards his desire is accomplished. When they meet, the wanton steed of the lover has a word to say to the charioteer; he would like to have a little pleasure in return for many pains, but the wanton steed of the beloved says not a word, for he is bursting with passion which he understands not; he throws his arms round the lover and embraces him as his dearest friend; and, when they are side by side, he is not in a state in which he can refuse the lover anything, if he ask him; although his fellow-steed and the charioteer oppose him with the arguments of shame and reason. After this their happiness depends upon their self-control; if the better elements of the mind which lead to order and philosophy prevail, then they pass their life here in happiness and harmony—masters of themselves and orderly—enslaving the vicious and emancipating the virtuous elements of the soul; and when the end comes, they are light and winged for flight, having conquered in one of the three heavenly or truly Olympian victories; nor can human discipline or divine inspiration confer any greater blessing on man than this. If, on the other hand, they leave philosophy and lead the lower life of ambition, then probably, after wine or in some other careless hour, the two wanton animals take the two souls when off their guard and bring them together, and they accomplish that desire of their hearts which to the many is bliss; and this having once enjoyed they continue to enjoy, yet rarely, because they have not been so dear to one another as the others, either at the time of their love or afterwards. They consider that they have given and taken from each other the most sacred pledges, and they may not break them and fall into enmity. At last they pass out of the body, unwinged, but eager to soar, and thus obtain no mean reward of love and madness. For those who have once begun the heavenward pilgrimage may not go down again to darkness and the journey beneath the earth, but they live light always; happy companions in their pilgrimage, and when the time comes at which they receive their wings they have the same plumage because of their love.

from "The Phaedrus," *The Dialogues of Plato,* translated by
Benjamin Jowett, pp. 25–28.

When the Soul Is Joined to Her Beloved
Anonymous fourth-century Gnostic

Gradually the soul recognizes her beloved
and she rejoices once more,
yet weeping before him
as she remembers the disgrace of her former widowhood.
She adorns herself still more,
so that he might be pleased to stay with her.
He requires her to turn to face from her people
and the multitude of her adulterers
in whose midst she once was,
To devote herself only to her kind, her real lord,
and to forget the house of the earthly father
where things went so badly with her
But to remember her Father who is in heaven.
And the prophet said in the Psalms:
"Hear, my daughter, and see, then incline your ear,
Forget your people and your father's house
for the king has desired your beauty; he is your lord."

from *The Exegesis on the Soul,* Nag Hammadi Gospels, p. 196.
Cited in *A Gnostic Book of Hours: Keys to Inner Wisdom,*
transcribed by June Singer, p. 108.

Tearing Heart from Soul
A Letter from Heloise to Abelard
(Twelfth century)

Everything we did and also the times and places are stamped on my heart along with your image.

For if I truthfully admit to the weakness of my unhappy soul, I can find no repentance whereby to appease God, whom I always accuse of the greatest cruelty in regard to this outrage. By rebelling against his ordinance, I offend him more by my indignation than I placate him by making amends through penitence. How can it be called repentance for sins, however great the mortification of the flesh, if the mind still retains the will to sin and is on fire with its old desires? It is easy enough for anyone to confess sins, to accuse himself, or even to mortify his body in outward show of penance, but it is very difficult to tear the heart away from hankering after its dearest pleasures. Quite rightly then, when the saintly Job said "I will speak out against myself," that is, "I will loose my tongue and open my mouth in confession to accuse myself of my sins". . .

In my case, the pleasures of lovers which we shared have been too sweet—they can never displease me and can scarcely be banished from my thoughts. Wherever I turn they are always there before my eyes, bringing with them awakened longings and fantasies which will not even let me sleep. Even during the celebration of the Mass, when our prayers should be purer, the lewd visions of those pleasures take such a hold upon my unhappy soul that my thoughts are on their wantonness instead of on prayers. I should be groaning over the sins I have committed, but I can only sigh for what I have lost. Everything we did and also the times and places are stamped on my heart along with your image, so that I live through it all again with you. Even in sleep I know no respite. Sometimes my thoughts are betrayed in a movement of my body, or they break out in an unguarded word. In my utter wretchedness, that cry from a suffering soul could well be mine: "Miserable creature that I am, who is there to rescue me out of the body doomed to this death?" Would that in truth I could go on: "The grace of God through Jesus Christ our Lord." This grace, my dearest, came upon you unsought—a single wound of the body by freeing you from these torments has healed many wounds in your soul. Where God may seem to you an adversary he has in fact proved himself kind: like an honest doctor who does not shrink from giving pain if it will bring about a cure. But for me, youth and passion and experience of pleasures which were so delightful intensify the torments of the flesh and longings of desire, and the assault is the more overwhelming as the nature they attack is the weaker.

Men call me chaste; they do not know the hypocrite I am. They consider purity of the flesh a virtue, though virtue belongs not to the body but to the soul. I can win praise in the eyes of men but deserve none before God, who searches our hearts and loins and sees in our darkness. I am judged religious at a time when there is little in religion which is not hypocrisy, when whoever does not offend the opinions receives the highest praise. And yet perhaps there is some merit and it is somehow acceptable to God, if a person whatever his intention gives no offense to the Church in his outward behavior, does not blaspheme the name of the Lord in the hearing of unbelievers nor disgrace the Order of his profession amongst the worldly. And this too is a gift of God's grace and comes through his bounty—not only to do good but to abstain from evil—though the latter is vain if the former does not follow from it, as it is written: "Turn from evil and do good." Both are vain if not done for love of God.

from *The Letters of Abelard and Heloise*,
translated by Betty Radice, pp. 132–34.

The Divine Love of the Soul

Meister Eckhart, German theologian and mystic, 1260–ca.1329

God
> loves the soul so deeply
> that were anyone to take away from God
> the divine love of the soul,
that person would kill God.

If you were to let a horse
> run about in a green meadow,
the horse would want to pour forth its whole strength
> in leaping about the meadow.

So too
it is a joy to God
>> to have poured out
> the divine nature and being
>> completely into us

> who are divine images.

from *Meditations with Meister Eckhart*,
version by Matthew Fox, p. 29.

Let Us Love This Enduring Beauty
Marsilio Ficino, Italian philosopher, 1433–1499

Therefore let us concede without argument that Love is a great
and wonderful god, and also noble, and very useful, and let us in-
dulge to love in such a way as to be content with his own end,
which is beauty. We enjoy this with the same faculty by which we
know it. We know it with the intellect, the sight, and the hearing.
Hence with these faculties we enjoy it. With the other senses we
enjoy not beauty, which Love desires, but something else, which
the body desires. Therefore we shall hunt beauty with these three
faculties, and by means of the beauty which appears in sounds and
bodies, as if by means of certain footprints, we shall track down
the beauty of the soul. We shall praise the former, but be satisfied
only with the latter; and we shall always strive to remember that
the greater the beauty was, the greater the love is. And where the
body is certainly beautiful but the soul is not, let us love the body
very little if at all, as a shadowy and fleeting image of beauty.
Where the soul alone is beautiful, let us love this enduring beauty
of the soul ardently. But where both beauties occur together, let us
admire them vehemently. . .

from *Commentary on Plato's Symposium on Love,*
translated by Sears Jayne, pp. 42–43.

Sonnets from the Portuguese
Elizabeth Barrett Browning, English poet, 1806–1851

XLIII

How do I love thee? Let me count the ways.
I love thee to the depth and breadth and height
My soul can reach, when feeling out of sight
For the ends of Being and Ideal Grace.
I love thee to the level of every day's
Most quiet need, by sun and candle-light.
I love thee freely, as men strive for Right.
I love thee purely, as men turn from Praise.
I love thee with the passion put to use
In my old griefs, and with my childhood's faith.
I love thee with a love I seemed to lose

With my lost saints—I love thee with the breath,
Smiles, tears of all my life!—and, if God choose,
I shall but love thee better after death.

from *Selected Poems*, p. 237.

Salvation in a Concentration Camp
Viktor E. Frankl, German psychiatrist and author

But soon my soul found its way back from the prisoner's existence to
another world, and I resumed talk with my loved one. . . .

In spite of all the enforced physical and mental primitiveness of
the life in a concentration camp, it was possible for spiritual life to
deepen. Sensitive people who were used to a rich intellectual life
may have suffered much pain (they were often of a delicate consti-
tution), but the damage to their inner selves was less. They were
able to retreat from their terrible surroundings to a life of inner
riches and spiritual freedom. Only in this way can one explain the
apparent paradox that some prisoners of a less hardy make-up
often seemed to survive camp life better than did those of a robust
nature. In order to make myself clear, I am forced to fall back on
personal experience. Let me tell what happened on those early
mornings when we had to march to our work site.

There were shouted commands: "Detachment, forward march!
Left 2-3-4! Left 2-3-4! Left 2-3-4! Left 2-3-4! First man about, left
and left and left and left! Caps off!" These words sound in my ears
even now. At the order "Caps off!" we passed the gate of the camp,
and searchlights were trained upon us. Whoever did not march
smartly got a kick. And worse off was the man who, because of the
cold, had pulled his cap back over his ears before permission was
given.

We stumbled on in the darkness, over big stones and through
large puddles, along the one road leading from the camp. The accompanying guards kept shouting at us and driving us with the
butts of their rifles. Anyone with very sore feet supported himself
on his neighbor's arm. Hardly a word was spoken; the icy wind did
not encourage talk. Hiding his mouth behind his upturned collar,
the man marching next to me whispered suddenly: "If our wives
could see us now! I do hope they are better off in their camps and
don't know what is happening to us."

That brought thoughts of my own wife to mind. And as we stumbled on for miles, slipping on icy spots, supporting each other time

and again, dragging one another up and onward, nothing was said, but we both knew: Each of us was thinking of his wife. Occasionally I looked at the sky, where the stars were fading and the pink light of the morning was beginning to spread behind a dark bank of clouds. But my mind clung to my wife's image, imagining it with an uncanny acuteness. I heard her answering me, saw her smile, her frank and encouraging look. Real or not, her look was then more luminous than the sun which was beginning to rise.

A thought transfixed me: For the first time in my life I saw the truth as it is set into song by so many poets, proclaimed as the final wisdom by so many thinkers. The truth—that love is the ultimate and the highest goal to which man can aspire. Then I grasped the meaning of the greatest secret that human poetry and human thought and belief have to impart: *The salvation of man is through love and in love.* I understood how a man who has nothing left in this world still may know bliss, be it only for a brief moment, in the contemplation of his beloved. In a position of utter desolation, when man cannot express himself in positive action, when his only achievement may consist in enduring his sufferings in the right way—an honorable way—in such a position man can, through loving contemplation of the image he carries of his beloved, achieve fulfillment. For the first time in my life I was able to understand the meaning of the words, "The angels are lost in perpetual contemplation of an infinite glory."

In front of me a man stumbled and those following him fell on top of him. The guard rushed over and used his whip on them all. Thus my thoughts were interrupted for a few minutes. But soon my soul found its way back from the prisoner's existence to another world, and I resumed talk with my loved one: I asked her questions, and she answered; she questioned me in return, and I answered.

"Stop!" We had arrived at our work site. Everybody rushed into the dark hut in the hope of getting a fairly decent tool. Each prisoner got a spade or a pickax.

"Can't you hurry up, you pigs?" Soon we had resumed the previous day's positions in the ditch. The frozen ground cracked under the point of the pickaxes, and sparks flew. The men were silent, their brains numb.

My mind still clung to the image of my wife. A thought crossed my mind: I didn't even know if she were still alive. I knew only one thing—which I have learned well by now: Love goes very far beyond the physical person of the beloved. It finds its deepest meaning in his spiritual being, his inner self. Whether or not he is actually present, whether or not he is still alive at all, ceases somehow to be of importance.

I did not know whether my wife was alive, and I had no means of finding out (during all my prison life there was no outgoing or incoming mail); but at the moment it ceased to matter. There was no need for me to know; nothing could touch the strength of my love, my thoughts, and the image of my beloved. Had I known then that my wife was dead, I think that I would still have given myself, undisturbed by that knowledge, to the contemplation of her image, and that my mental conversation with her would have been just as vivid and just as satisfying. "Set me like a seal upon thy heart, love is as strong as death."

from *Man's Search for Meaning,*
translated by Ilse Lasch, pp. 56–61.

The Rapture of Divine Love
Evelyn Underhill, English poet, novelist, and mystic, 1875–1941

The anonymous author of the "Mirror" writes, in one of his most daring passages, " 'I am God,' says Love, 'for Love is God, and God is Love. And this soul is God by condition of love: but I am God by Nature Divine. And this [state] is hers by righteousness of love, so that this precious beloved of me, is learned, and led of Me without her [working]. . . . This [soul] is the eagle that flies high, so right high and yet more high than doth any other bird; for she is feathered with fine love' ". . . .

I think no one can deny that the comparison of the bond between soul and the Absolute to "ghostly glue," though crude, is wholly innocent. Its appearance in ["The Epistle of Prayer"] as an alternative to the symbol of wedlock may well check the uncritical enthusiasm of those who hurry to condemn at sight all "sexual" imagery. That it has seemed to the mystics appropriate and exact is proved by its reappearance in the next century in the work of a greater contemplative. "Thou givest me," says Petersen, "Thy whole Self to be mine whole and undivided, if at least I shall be Thine whole and undivided. And when I shall be thus all Thine, even as from everlasting Thou hast loved Thyself, so from everlasting Thou has loved me: for this means nothing more than that Thou enjoy Thee in myself and myself in Thee. And when in Thee I shall love myself, nothing else but Thee do I love, because *Thou art in me and I in Thee, glued together as one and the selfsame thing,* which henceforth and forever cannot be divided."

From this kind of language to that of the Spiritual Marriage, as understood by the pure minds of the mystics, is but a step. They mean by it no rapturous satisfactions, no dubious spiritualizing of earthly ecstasies, but a lifelong bond "that shall never be lost or broken," a close personal union of will and of heart between the free self and that "Fairest in Beauty" Whom it has known in the act of contemplation.

The Mystic Way has been a progress, a growth, in love: a deliberate fostering of the inward tendency of the soul towards its source, an eradication of its disorderly tendencies to "temporal goods." But the only proper end of love is union: "a perfect uniting and coupling together of the lover and the loved into one." It is "a unifying principle," the philosophers say: life's mightiest agent upon every plane. Moreover, just as earthly marriage is understood by the moral sense less as a satisfaction of personal desire, than as a part of the great process of life—the fusion of two selves for new purposes—so such spiritual marriage brings with it duties and obligations. With the attainment of a new order, the new infusion of vitality, comes a new responsibility, the call to effort and endurance on a new and mighty scale. It is not an act but a state. Fresh life is imparted, by which our lives are made complete: New creative powers are conferred. The self, lifted to the divine order, is to be an agent of the divine fecundity: an energizing center, a parent of transcendental life.

from *Mysticism,* pp. 427–28.

The Soul's Silence, Exile and Cunning
James Joyce, Irish novelist, 1882–1941

Her image had passed into his soul for ever and no word had broken the holy silence of his ecstasy.

There was a long rivulet in the strand: and, as he waded slowly up its course, he wondered at the endless drift of seaweed. Emerald and black and russet and olive, it moved beneath the current, swaying and turning. The water of the rivulet was dark with endless drift and mirrored the high-drifting clouds. The clouds were drifting above him silently and silently the seatangle was drifting below him; and the grey warm air was still: And a new wild life was singing in his veins.

Where was his boyhood now? Where was the soul that had hung back from her destiny, to brood alone upon the shame of her wounds and in her house of squalor and subterfuge to queen it in faded cerements and in wreaths that withered at the touch? Or, where was he.

He was alone. He was unheeded, happy, and near to the wild heart of life. He was alone and young and willful and wildhearted, alone amid a waste of wild air and brackish waters and the seaharvest of shells and tangle and veiled grey sunlight and gayclad lightclad figures of children and girls and voices childish and girlish in the air.

A girl stood before him in midstream: alone and still, gazing out to sea. She stood like one whom magic had changed into the likeness of a strange and beautiful seabird. Her long slender bare legs were delicate as a crane's and pure save where an emerald trail of seaweed had fashioned itself as a sign upon the flesh. Her thighs, fuller and softhued as ivory, were bared almost to the hips where the white fringes of her drawers were like feathering of soft white down. Her slate-blue skirts were kilted boldly about her waist and dovetailed behind her. Her bosom was as a bird's, soft and slight, slight and soft as the breast of some dark-plumaged dove. But her long fair hair was girlish: and girlish, and touched with the wonder of mortal beauty, her face.

He was alone and still, gazing out to sea; and when she felt his presence and the worship of his eyes her eyes turned to him in quiet sufferance of his gaze, without shame or wantonness. Long, long she suffered his gaze, and then quietly withdrew her eyes from his and bent them towards the stream, gently moving water broke the silence, low and faint and whispering, faint as the bells of sleep; hither and thither, hither and thither: and a faint flame trembled in his cheek.

—Heavenly God! cried Stephen's soul, in an outburst of profane joy.—

He turned away from her suddenly and set off across the strand. His cheeks were aflame; his body was aglow; his limbs were trembling. On and on and on and on he strode, far out over the sands, singing wildly to the sea, crying to greet the advent of the life that had called out to him.

Her image had passed into his soul for ever and no word had broken the holy silence of his ecstasy. Her eyes had called him and his soul had leaped at the call. To live, to err, to fail, to triumph, to recreate life out of life! A wild angel had appeared to him, the angel of mortal youth and beauty, an envoy from the fair courts of life, to throw open before him in an instant of ecstasy the gates of all the ways of error and glory. On and on and on and on!

from A *Portrait of the Artist as a Young Man*,
pp. 132–33.

The Significance of Soul for Women
Christine Downing, American author

The exploration of sisterhood seems to lead toward a deeper understanding of human mortality and of the significance for the soul of the sometimes painful engagement with the real otherness of actual women. . . .

It seems not at all accidental that the need to come to a more conscious understanding of my relation to both my outer and my inner sister, to the personal sister and the archetypal one, appears just as I find myself in that phase of my life whose major task is preparation for death. That preparation, as I see it, is the soul work laid upon us when we have completed the passage through menopause. The themes of sisterhood and mortality are complexly interfused.

I believe this may be why the sorting through with the sister comes last—after all the other tasks. The objective is not patching-up, correction, or resolution; the task is reimaging, questioning, going deeper. It is an initiation into Hades, the realm where psyches live. The purpose is not primarily a better understanding of my past or our shared past, though that may be part of the way. The point, I came to recognize, would not be literal reconciliation with an estranged sister or, as I had at first imagined, the re-creation of a long-lost intense intimacy. It is not even primarily to help make me more capable in the present of giving and receiving love uncontaminated with unworked-through sister feeling— though that is very important to me. The pull to clarify the role of sisterhood in my life is certainly strengthened by my longing to love women (and especially the woman who is my mate) well. But the rediscovery of the sister is also a new and necessary discovery of self, and beyond that, it may be, as I have already intimated, an initiation into a new relationship to the earth herself, now perceived not as mother (as she so often is in mythology) but as sister, not simply as my source but as a being toward whom I have responsibility. . . .

That the two themes of mortality and sisterhood should in Greek mythology be so closely interwoven feels, in retrospect, so right as to be almost inevitable. In my life, too, as I have noted, these themes appeared together. Being fully human, being fully ourselves as *human* women, seems to require the refraction provided by a sisterly other. The exploration of sisterhood seems to lead to-

ward a deeper understanding of human mortality and of the significance for the soul of the sometimes painful engagement with the
real *otherness* of actual women. . . .

For well-educated Europeans of Freud's and Jung's time the
word *psyche* immediately conjured up this story, the only classical
tale in which Psyche appears. They found deeply moving its implication that *the* true story about Psyche is one that involves Eros,
that the soul realizes itself in relationship, that human love is directed toward soul-making. . . .

The discovery of the importance of sisterhood has led me to a
new appreciation of Apuleius's tale. How we understand it may depend on what we focus on: Psyche's relation to Aphrodite, to Eros,
or to her sisters. . . .

The tales about sister-brother relationships suggest the deep
meaning this bond has in the inner lives of men: "Sister" seems to
signify that which connects them to the realm of feeling, to their
own inner depths, their soul, and what enables them to turn trust-
ingly toward death. The sister represents a relation to what men
seem truly to experience as their own inner but often inaccessible
and mysterious "femininity"—a relation to that femininity that is
life-bringing rather than death-dealing, less frightening than the
otherness represented by the mother. For men this contrasexual
relationship carries tremendous power. For women, the brother,
the contrasexual other, seems to mean less than the same-sex
other, the sister.

For us, too, the sister carries the soul-meaning that the sister
carries for men. For us, too, she embodies that same connection to
the source of our lives, the source of meaning, that the mother
originally embodies—but less fearfully. . . .

from *Psyche's Sisters*, pp. 9–10, 17, 43–45.

Eros and Psyche
Diane Wolkstein, American storyteller

*So it was that by her own will, yet unknowingly, Psyche fell in love with
Eros, God of Love.*

Psyche was left alone, except for her rages which tormented her.
All day her mind tossed back and forth like the waves of the sea.
At first she was clear and determined, but soon she began to
waver, distracted by the implications of what she was about to do.

She delayed. She hurried. She dared. She feared. She despaired. She raged. And what was most curious was that in the same moment, in the same body, she hated the beast and she loved the husband.

As night approached, she made her decision and prepared the necessary equipment. In the darkness, her husband slipped into her bed, and they wrapped themselves in the combats of love. Then he fell into a deep sleep. By nature, Psyche did not possess a particularly bold spirit or body, yet the cruelty of her fate hardened her. She took the lamp and seized the knife. But the moment the light shone on the bed, the mystery was revealed. Lying on the bed, in all his beauty, was the sweetest and gentlest of all creatures, Eros, the God of Love. At the sight of him, the light of the lamp burned more brightly and the knife dulled in edge in shame.

Psyche was terrified. Pale and shaking, she fell to her knees. She tried to hide the knife by plunging it into her own heart, but the knife, fearful of such a crime, fell from her hands onto the floor. Then despite her weakness and fear, her spirit revived when she gazed at Eros's divine beauty. His golden hair was still wet with nectar. His playful curls drifted across his rosy cheeks and milky white neck. They glowed with such splendor that the light of the lamp flickered in awe. On his shoulders the flying god's dewy white wings sparkled with beauty, and although they were not in flight, the outermost feathers reverberated in continuous quivering. The rest of his body was so smooth and splendid that Venus herself would not have been ashamed to have brought such a child into the world. At the foot of the bed lay the weapons of the great god: his bow, quiver, and arrows.

Psyche's insatiable curiosity impelled her to examine and touch each of her husband's weapons. She took an arrow from his quiver and, wishing to test its sharpness, pressed her skin, and several drops of blood ran from her finger. So it was that by her own will, yet unknowingly, Psyche fell in love with the God of Love. Burning with desire, she leaned over and kissed him impulsively, impetuously, with kiss after kiss, fearful he would waken before she had finished.

While the anguished and delighted Psyche hovered over him, the lamp she was holding, whether from treachery or jealousy or simply from desire to touch and kiss such a body, spurted a drop of boiling oil onto the right shoulder of the god. Oh rash, bold lamp! Oh paltry minister of love, how could you burn the God of Fire, you who were surely invented by some lover who wished to behold the sight of his beloved past the moment of darkness?

Eros awoke and leapt out of bed in dreadful pain. When he saw his wife holding the lamp in her hand and the knife lying on the floor, he understood. Without a word, he spread his wings and flew into the air. Psyche caught hold of his right leg and held fast. With her weight dragging him, they flew into the cloudy regions. She held on until her strength gave out. Then she let go and fell to the ground, exhausted.

Eros did not desert her as she lay on the ground. He flew to the nearest cypress tree and, swaying from its top branches, reproached her. "Oh most simple Psyche, why didn't you trust me? Rather than obey the commands of my mother, Venus, who ordered me to cause you to love and be bound in marriage to myself. Yes, I acted rashly. I, the famous archer, wounded myself with my own weapon so that my wife might take me for a monster and try to cut off my head with a knife—my head and eyes which once bore you so much love. Oh Psyche, did I not try to warn you? Did I not plead with you to listen to me? Well, your other advisors will soon pay their penalty. As for you, you will be punished by my flight." With these words, he flew away.

Psyche lay on the ground and let out dreadful cries as she watched her husband fly farther and farther away. When she could no longer see him, she sprang up and threw herself into the river to end her life, but the waters of the river, fearful of the God of Love, who can even burn waters, would not let her die. They lifted her up and carried her to the other shore.

from *The First Love Stories*, pp. 128–30.

The Soul Rush
Milan Kundera, Czechoslovakian novelist

He called to her in a kind voice, and Tereza felt her soul rushing up to the surface. . .

Tereza was therefore born of a situation which brutally reveals the irreconcilable duality of body and soul, that fundamental human experience.

A long time ago, man would listen in amazement to the sound of regular beats in his chest, never suspecting what they were. He was unable to identify himself with so alien and unfamiliar an object as the body. The body was a cage, and inside that cage was something which looked, listened, feared, thought, and marveled; that something, that remainder left over after the body had been accounted for, was the soul.

Today, of course, the body is no longer unfamiliar: We know that the beating in our chest is the heart and that the nose is the nozzle of a hose sticking out of the body to take oxygen to the lungs. The face is nothing but an instrument panel registering all the body mechanisms: digestion, sight, hearing, respiration, thought.

Ever since man has learned to give each part of the body a name, the body has given him less trouble. He has also learned that the soul is nothing more than the gray matter of the brain in action. The old duality of body and soul has become shrouded in scientific terminology, and we can laugh at it as merely an obsolete prejudice.

But just make someone who has fallen in love listen to his stomach rumble, and the unity of body and soul, that lyrical illusion of the age of science, instantly fades away. . . .

Tereza's mother demanded justice. She wanted to see the culprit penalized. That is why she insisted her daughter remain with her in the world of immodesty, where youth and beauty mean nothing, where the world is nothing but a vast concentration camp of bodies, one like the next, with souls invisible.

Now we can better understand the meaning of Tereza's secret vice, her long looks and frequent glances in the mirror. It was a battle with her mother. It was a longing to be a body unlike other bodies, to find that the surface of her face reflected the crew of the soul charging up from below. It was not an easy task: her soul— her sad, timid, self-effacing soul—lay concealed in the depths of her bowels and was ashamed to show itself.

So it was the day she first met Tomas. Weaving its way through the drunks in the hotel restaurant, her body sagged under the weight of the beers on the tray, and her soul lay somewhere at the level of the stomach or pancreas. Then Tomas called to her. That call meant a great deal, because it came from someone who knew neither her mother nor the drunks with their daily stereotypically scabrous remarks. His outsider status raised him above the rest.

Something else raised him above the others as well: He had an open book on his table. No one had ever opened a book in that restaurant before. In Tereza's eyes, books were the emblems of a secret brotherhood. For she had but a single weapon against the world of crudity surrounding her: the books she took out of the municipal library, and above all, the novels. She had read any number of them, from Fielding to Thomas Mann. They not only offered the possibility of an imaginary escape from a life she found unsatisfying; they also had a meaning for her as physical objects: She loved to walk down the street with a book under her arm. It had the same significance for her as an elegant cane for the dandy a century ago. It differentiated her from others.

(Comparing the book to the elegant cane of the dandy is not absolutely precise. A dandy's cane did more than make him different; it made him modern and up to date. The book made Tereza different, but old-fashioned. Of course, she was too young to see how old-fashioned she looked to others. The young men walking by with transistor radios pressed to their ears seemed silly to her. It never occurred to her that they were modern.)

And so the man who called to her was simultaneously a stranger and a member of the secret brotherhood. He called to her in a kind voice, and Tereza felt her soul rushing up to the surface through her blood vessels and pores to show itself to him.

from *The Unbearable Lightness of Being,*
pp. 40, 47–48.

Your Breast Is Enough
Pablo Neruda, Chilean poet, 1904–1973

Your breast is enough for my heart,
and my wings for your freedom.
What was sleeping above your soul will rise
out of your mouth to heaven.

In you is the illusion of each day.
You arrive like the dew to the cupped flowers.
You undermine the horizon with your absence.
Eternally in flight like the wave.

I have said that you sang in the wind
like the pines and like the masts.
Like them you are tall and taciturn,
and you are sad, all at once, like a voyage.

You gather things to you like an old road.
You are peopled with echoes and nostalgic voices.
I awoke and at times birds fled and migrated
that had been sleeping in your soul.

from *Twenty Love Poems and a Song of Despair,*
translated by W. S. Merwin, p. 37.

The Vase

Gabriela Mistral, Chilean poet, 1889–1957

I dream of a vase of humble and simple clay,
to keep your ashes near my watchful eyes;
and for you my cheek will be the wall of the vase
and my soul and your soul will be satisfied.

I will not sift them into a vase of burning gold,
not into a pagan urn that mimics carnal lines;
I want only a vase of simple clay to hold
you humbly like a fold in this skirt of mine.

One of these afternoons I'll gather clay
by the river, and I'll shape it with trembling hand.
Women, bearing sheaves, will pass my way,
not guessing I fashion a bed for a husband.

The fistful of dust, I hold in my hands,
will noiselessly pour, like a thread of tears.
I will seal this vase with an infinite kiss,
and I'll cover you only with my endless gaze!

from *Love Poems: From Spain and Spanish America*,
translated by Perry Higgins, p. 147.

PART FOUR

SOUL CRISIS

For whosoever will save his life shall lose it; but whosoever shall lose his life for my sake and the gospel's, the same shall save it.
For what shall it profit a man, if he shall gain the whole world, and lose his own soul?
Or what shall a man give in exchange for his soul?

—Mark: 8:36

Truly one learns only by sorrow; it is a terrible education the soul gets, and it requires a terrible grief that shakes the very foundation of one's being to bring the soul into its own.

—British Major Lanoe Hawker VC,
CO of No. 24 Squadron, 1916

Soul loss can be observed today as a psychological phenomenon in the everyday lives of the human beings around us. Loss of soul appears in the form of a sudden onset of apathy and listlessness; the joy has gone out of life, initiative is crippled, one feels empty, everything seems pointless.

—Marie-Louise von Franz

Introduction

Then something strange our soul touches. The black edge of fury, the blue rim of sorrow, the bruised shadow of the world. Through the glass darkly we suddenly see the heartrending truth of our lives. We learn that beyond the splendors of the soul there is also a darkness dangerous to deny, where often blows a wind of crushing madness.

Sometimes precipitously, more often imperceptibly, something essential in us steals—or is stolen—away, leaving us in icy detachment, incomprehensible blue moods, unimaginable emptiness, tranquilized, resistant to the tenderizing advances of eros, lost in a raging garden wet with rain. Alone at the crossroads.

What shamans traditionally called soul loss we now think of as emptiness, alienation, or pain in the core of our being where we know there was once something full and vital. There is a hole where once was soul. The crisis seizes us when we're in the steely grip of grief, betrayal, physical terror, numbing routine, or an inauthentic life. Philosopher Jacob Needleman has described one of the most prevalent fears clawing at his readers and students as a loss of meaning in their lives. Many of them have felt compelled to ask him, "How do I make money and keep my soul? How do I hold on to my self and not have my soul sucked dry? . . ."

But soul crisis can also occur because of what James Hillman brands the psyche's "autonomous ability to create illness, morbidity, abnormality, suffering," creating, he writes further, the "troubled, old, disembodied, immortal, lost, innocent, inspired, moody, depressed facets of the soul." Could this be the contrary nature of the soul meeting the sorrows of the world halfway, an instinctual knowledge that we cannot bear the pain of things until we somehow *resemble* them? How is it that for the soul to be truly moved some, a "tortured psychology" may be necessary? That there is an "unfathomable longing in the soul to vex itself," as Edgar Allan Poe darkly described it? That the first step may be to lose the way? To lose our soul so that we may regain it? In this section of the anthology we follow the tortuous path of the soul in crisis, a path of many crossroads, moving gingerly through several accounts of harrowing episodes of human experience: the terrors of war, rape, abortion, seizure, imprisonment, heartbreak, depression, breakdown. Though the ferocious reality of soul crisis may often be sanitized today with clinical nomenclature, the ancients said it best: *People can and do lose their souls.*

And yet, within the following passages are examples of what Thomas Moore describes as the hidden truth within the contortions of the soul in crisis. "Often when imagination twists the commonplace into a slightly new form," he writes, "suddenly we see soul where formerly it was hidden."

Our earliest example of crisis in the soul is the sixteenth-century Mesoamerican poem, "A Song of Lamentation," in which a chillingly anonymous voice ritually responds to the imminent destruction of her people and their sacred rain forests. From the prisons of the Spanish Inquisition comes the tortured rapture of "Dark Night of the Soul," the immortal poem that tells of Saint John of the Cross's mystical visions of his soul uniting with God. Another excerpt from a milestone work I've set along the roadside of our journey is Goethe's *Faust*, the eponymous Western story for the battle for the soul between the forces of light and darkness. The harrowing soul-bargaining scene between Mephistopheles and Faust is included here not only for the splendid poetry, but also for the metaphorical power of Goethe's eerie premonition of the coming spiritual crisis in the West.

For an example of soul loss on a cultural level, I've included an excerpt from psychologist Bruno Bettelheim's long essay on the consequences of the century-long mistranslation of the very word for soul in the work of Sigmund Freud. Instead of encouraging a deep feeling for the mysteries of the soul, "that which is most spiritual and worthy in man . . . [and] what makes us human," Bettelheim writes, "the unfortunate translations lured the reader into developing a . . . 'scientific' understanding of the unconscious." The repercussion for psychology in America was that analysis itself suffered—with tragic irony—"to the complete neglect of the psyche or soul."

Willa Cather, in her short story, "Eric Hermannson's Soul," comes a jolting scene of the struggle between a piously vengeful preacher and a young musician whose violin is his "only bridge to the kingdom of soul."

From the blistered prose of a classic of Gothic literature, Robert Louis Stevenson's *Strange Case of Dr. Jekyll and Mr. Hyde,* we find a kind of infrared view of the dark pit of the human soul. When Stevenson gazes into the abyss, he sees how "causeless" hatred can "destroy the balance of the soul."

No less harrowing is Sue Nathanson-Elkin's courageous description of her anguish over her abortion, a physical pain, she writes with adagio sadness, less unbearable than her soul-agony. For her the crisis was more than an emotional reaction to the trauma; instead it "involves the shattering of one's beliefs about oneself." Another devastating crisis is explored in an excerpt I've called "The Annihilation of the Soul" from Susan Griffin's searing book on rape. There she counters her discovery of "rage and fear at the existence of rape" with a vision of a world without it.

"Every man acutely alive is acutely wrestling with his own soul," admitted D. H. Lawrence. Any life lived to the hilt defies despair, honors the blue moods that sweep down us like the mistrals of southern France. And like the blustery winter winds soul crisis may be an inevitable season in our lives. For as T. S. Eliot reminds us in "East Coker":

> To arrive where you are, to get from where you are not,
>   You must go by a way wherein there is no ecstasy.

Closing out this section is a modern version of Goethe's legend of losing the soul in a Faustian pact with the devil, rock journalist Greil Marcus's version of the legend of guitar genius Robert Johnson. According to Southern blues tradition, Johnson sold his soul to the devil at the crossroads outside New Orleans to be able to play soul-seizing blues. The legend tells us that some transformations in the human soul can only be explained with tales from the "Crossroads," as Johnson himself immortalized the desperate life of being chased, guitar in hand, by the hellhounds.

If no excellent soul is exempt from madness, as Plato consoled us, is it possible no madness is exempt from excellence?

A Song of Lamentation
Anonymous Mexican, ca. 1500

(Tico, toco, tocoto, and then it ends, ticoto, ticoto.)

The sweet-voiced quetzal there, ruling the earth, has intoxicated my soul.

I am like the quetzal bird, I am created in the house of the one only God;

I sing sweet songs among the flowers; I chant songs and rejoice in my heart.

The fuming dew-drops from the flowers in the field intoxicated my soul.

I grieve to myself that ever this dwelling on earth should end.

I foresaw, being a Mexican, that our rule began to be destroyed,
I went forth weeping that it was to bow down and be destroyed.

Let me not be angry that the grandeur of Mexico is to be destroyed.

The smoking stars gather against it; the one who cares for flowers is
about to be destroyed.

He who cared for books wept, he wept for the beginning of the
destruction.

translated from the Nahuatl by Daniel G. Brinton, cited in
Poems of War Resistance, edited by Scott Brinton, p. 27.

The Soul-Eater
A West African Folktale

. . . it was not an ordinary animal but one which had the power to eat a
man's soul.

Once there was an old man who had four sons. One was a soldier,
one a hunter, one a farmer, and the youngest one lived in a nearby
town and had no work. The father lived in a large forest with the
hunter and the farmer.

One day, the hunter set out with his gun to provide meat for the
family. He trapped an animal that looked like a giant rat and carried it back to the compound. As soon as the father saw the animal
he told his son that they must not eat it because it was not an ordinary animal but one which had the power to eat a man's soul.

The boy laughed at his father, saying, "Old men are as superstitious as old women. Meat is meat, Pa, and I intend to eat this animal."

The father said nothing more but went out to tap some palm-
wine. While he was out the hunter skinned his prey and put it on
the fire to cook.

When Papa returned his son told him, "Hey Pa, I threw out that
other meat and I am now cooking a goat. Come and eat."

Still Papa refused, and he advised his other son not to eat the
meat either. The meat smelt very good, but only the hunter ate it,
and he ate and ate until he had eaten it all.

Next morning the father called his farmer son and told him that they must go out hunting. The farmer went to waken his brother but the brother did not move. The farmer pulled and shook his brother but he did not move. He looked as if he were only sleeping but he was not breathing. The farmer felt very sad and went outside to dig a grave.

While he was digging his father came out and said, "Why are you digging a grave? Your brother is not dead. Leave him where he is."

The farmer was annoyed with his father. "Pa," he insisted, "my brother is dead. I cannot just leave his body in the house to corrupt. I must bury him. He's dead, Pa."

Papa just looked at his son. "You young men," he said, "you think you know everything. Your brother wouldn't listen to me yesterday and today you won't listen."

The brother stopped digging and followed his father into the forest. They saw a tiger but Papa said, "We are not hunting tigers."

They saw a leopard but Papa said, "We are not hunting leopards."

All day they searched and each time they saw an animal Papa refused to hunt it, until they saw one that looked like a giant rat. "This is the animal we must hunt," said the father.

He and his son struggled with the animal, which cried like a child each time they hit it. At last the father hit it a mighty blow on the skull and it died. The farmer bent to pick it up but his father insisted, "Don't touch it. Leave it where it is."

The son and his father went home. They found the hunter lying in blood with his skull cracked open. "Now you can bury him," said the father.

And the farmer buried his brother and wondered at the wisdom of old men.

from *Tortoise the Trickster and Other Folktales from Cameroon*,
by Loreto Todd, pp. 65–66.

Dark Night of the Soul
Saint John of the Cross, Spanish mystic and poet, 1542–1591

On a dark secret night,
starving for love and deep in flame,
O happy lucky flight!
unseen I slipped away,
my house at last was calm and safe.

Blackly free from light,
disguised and down a secret way,
O happy lucky flight!
in darkness I escaped,
my house at last was calm and safe.

On that happy night—in
secret; no one saw me through the dark—
and I saw nothing then,
no other light to mark
the way but fire pounding my heart.

That flaming guided me
more firmly than the noonday sun,
and waiting there was he
I knew so well—who shone
where nobody appeared to come.

O night, my guide!
O night more friendly than the dawn!
O tender night that tied
lover and the loved one,
loved one in the lover fused as one!

On my flowering breasts
which I had saved for him alone,
he slept and I caressed
and fondled him with love,
and cedars fanned the air above.

Wind from the castle wall
while my fingers played in his hair:
its hands serenely fell
wounding my neck, and there
my senses vanished in the air.

I lay. Forgot my being,
and on my love I leaned my face.
All ceased. I left my being,
leaving my cares to fade
among the lilies far away.

from *The Poems of St. John of the Cross*,
translated by Willis Barnstone, p. 38.

Faust's Pact with the Devil

Johann Wolfgang von Goethe, German poet, novelist, scientist, 1749–1832

But in return what must I do for you?

FAUST: When from that dreadful conflict drawn away
By sounds of sweet familiar harmony,
Fragments of childish feeling lingering in me
Betrayed me with echoes of a happier day.
Therefore I curse what seeks to cheat
The soul with luring phantasy,
Binding it with flattery and deceit
Into this pit of misery!
Cursed before all that lofty thought
In which the spirit itself doth shroud!
Cursed be the dazzling forms which sought
Upon our senses to press and crowd!
Cursed be all dissembling dreams
Of fame and everlasting life!
Cursed be all we flatter ourselves we own,
As vassal, plough, as child and wife!
Cursed be Mammon when with treasure
He spurs us on to daring deeds,
While merely for our idle pleasure
Spreading the cushions for our needs!
Cursed be the soothing juice of the grape!
Cursed be love's ecstatic call!
Cursed be hope! Cursed be faith!
Yet cursed be patience most of all!

CHORUS OF SPIRITS *invisible:*
Woe! Woe!
Thou has laid low
The beautiful world
By the force of thy blow!
It totters, it crashes!
A demigod smashes!
We carry the fragments
Into the void
To bemoan and deplore
The beauty destroyed.
Earth-born,
Thou hast both power and might!

Create it anew
More glowingly bright;
In your breast let it spring.
A new life commence
With clarified sense,
Then, if you do,
New songs will ring!

MEPHISTOPHELES: These are my tiny agents.
Hark! They aspire
To counsel you wisely
To deed and desire,
To lure you out of this lonely state
Where the senses and life-force
Seek to stagnate!

Cease to play with your affliction then,
Which like a vulture feeds upon your life!
The worst of company would make you feel
Only that you are a man amongst men.
Yet I don't mean to thrust you back
Into the common pack.
I am not of the very great,
But if you'll take me as a mate
And go your way through life with me,
I shall willingly agree
To be yours on the spot.
I'll be your comrade to the grave
And if I suit—
I'll be your servant, be your slave.

FAUST: But in return what must I do for you?

MEPHISTOPHELES: You have a long time ere that note is due.

FAUST: No, no! The devil is an egoist,
And does not casually assist
Another person—just for God's sake too!
State all conditions plain and clear:
A servant such as you brings danger near.

MEPHISTOPHELES: Here I'll pledge myself at your command
To serve implicitly and without rest,
If when in the beyond we stand
You'll do the same for me at my request.

FAUST: The beyond fills me with small concern;
If you dash this world to fragments first,

The other may arise in turn.
Out of this earthly source my joy must spring,
And this sun shines upon my sufferings.
From both conditions could I separate,
Then let what will and can, appear!
Further, I do not care to hear
If in a future one feels love or hate,
Or if in any other sphere
There is a higher or a lower state.

MEPHISTOPHELES: On these terms you may well say yes.
Commit yourself. In days to come I mean
To show you all the arts which I possess;
I'll give you what no mortal yet has seen.

FAUST: What, poor Devil, could you give at best?
When was the human spirit in its striving quest
Ever understood by such a beast?
Yet have you food which never satisfies,
Red gold that like quicksilver flies,
Melting in the outstretched palms?
A game at which one never wins,
A girl though clasped within my arms,
Upon a neighbor casts her eyes,
The honor of a godlike aim,
Vanishing like a meteor's flame?
Show me fruits which rot ere gathered from the tree,
Show me trees which daily bloom anew!

MEPHISTOPHELES: Such demands do not embarrass me!
Such treasure I can offer you.
But then a time will also come, my friend,
When you'll desire to feast in peace instead.

FAUST: If ever I stretch upon an idler's bed,
Then let my doom descend!
If ever through lying flattery
You lure me into self-complacency,
If ever through pleasure you succeed
And trick me into feeling satisfied,
Let that day be my last!
This is my wager.

MEPHISTOPHELES: Done!

FAUST: Agreed!
If I should ever to the moment say,
"O stay! Thou art so fair!"

Clap me into fetters then and there,
And to destruction I shall gladly go!
Then may the death-bells toll,
Then from your service you are freed at last.
The clock may stop, the hands may fall,
My time will be forever past.

MEPHISTOPHELES: Consider it well! I shall remember all.

FAUST: You have the fullest right thereto;
This compact was not entered wantonly.
I'm a vassal if I persist in what I do;
Yours or whose—what difference can there be?

from *Faust*, translated by Alice Raphael, pp. 55–58.

A Soul Boiling

Robert Louis Stevenson, Scottish novelist, 1850–1894

. . . a soul boiling with causeless hatreds, and a body that seemed not strong enough to contain the raging energies of life.

There comes an end to all things; the most capacious measure is filled at last; and this brief condescension to my evil finally destroyed the balance of my soul. And yet I was not alarmed; the fall seemed natural, like a return to the old days before I had made my discovery. It was a fine, clear, January day, wet under foot where the frost had melted, but cloudless overhead; and the Regent's Park was full of winter chirrupings, and sweet with spring odors. I sat in the sun on a bench; the animal within me licking the chops of memory; the spiritual side a little drowsed, promising subsequent penitence, but not yet moved to begin. After all, I reflected, I was like my neighbors; and then I smiled, comparing myself with other men, comparing my active goodwill with the lazy cruelty of their neglect. And at the very moment of that vainglorious thought, a qualm came over me, a horrid nausea and the most deadly shuddering. These passed away, and left me faint; and then, as in turn the faintness subsided, I began to be aware of a change in the temper of my thoughts, a greater boldness, a contempt of danger, a solution of the bonds of obligation. I looked down; my clothes hung formlessly on my shrunken limbs; the hand that lay on my knee was corded and hairy. I was once more Edward Hyde. A moment before I had been safe of all men's respect, wealthy, beloved—the cloth laying for me in the dining-room at home; and now I was the common quarry of mankind, hunted, houseless, a known murderer, thrall to the gallows . . .

When I came to myself at Lanyon's, the horror of my old friend perhaps affected me somewhat; I do not know; it was at least but a drop in the sea to the abhorrence with which I looked back upon these hours. A change had come over me. It was no longer the fear of the gallows, it was the horror of being Hyde that racked me. I received Lanyon's condemnation partly in a dream; it was partly in a dream that I came home to my own house and got into bed. I slept after the prostration of the day, with a stringent and profound slumber which not even the nightmares that wrung me could avail to break. I awoke in the morning shaken, weakened, but refreshed. I still hated and feared the thought of the brute that slept within me, and I had not of course forgotten the appalling dangers of the day before; but I was once more at home, in my own house, and close to my drugs; and gratitude for my escape shone so strong in my soul that it rivaled the brightness of hope.

I was stepping leisurely across the court after breakfast drinking the chill of the air with pleasure, when I was seized again with those indescribable sensations that heralded the change; and I had but the time to gain the shelter of my cabinet, before I was once again raging and freezing with the passions of Hyde. It took on this occasion a double dose to recall me to myself; and alas! six hours after, as I sat looking sadly in the fire, the pangs returned, and the drug had to be readministered. In short, from that day forth it seemed only by a great effort as of gymnastics, and only under the immediate stimulation of the drug, that I was able to wear the countenance of Jekyll. At all hours of the day and night, I would be taken with the premonitory shudder; above all, if I slept, or even dozed for a moment in my chair, it was always as Hyde that I awakened. Under the strain of this continually impending doom and by the sleeplessness to which I now condemned myself, ay, even beyond what I had thought possible to man, I became, in my own person, a creature eaten up and emptied by fever, languidly weak both in body and mind, and solely occupied by one thought: the horror of my other self. But when I slept, or when the virtue of the medicine wore off, I would leap almost without transition (for the pangs of transformation grew daily less marked) into the possession of a fancy brimming with images of terror, a soul boiling with causeless hatreds, and a body that seemed not strong enough to contain the raging energies of life.

The powers of Hyde seemed to have grown with the sickliness of Jekyll. And certainly the hate that now divided them was equal on each side. With Jekyll, it was a thing of vital instinct. He had now seen the full deformity of that creature that shared with him some of the phenomena of consciousness, and was co-heir with him to death; and beyond these links of community, which in themselves made the most poignant part of his distress, he thought of Hyde for all his energy of life, as of something not only hellish but inorganic. This was the shocking thing; that the slime pit seemed to utter cries and voices; that the amorphous dust gesticulated and sinned; that what was dead and had no shape should usurp the offices of life. And this again, that this insurgent horror was knit to him closer than a wife, closer than an eye lay caged in his flesh, where he heard it mutter and felt it struggle to be born; and at every hour of weakness, and in the confidence of slumber, prevailed against him, and deposed him out of life.

The hatred of Hyde for Jekyll was of a different order. His order of the gallows drove him continually to commit temporary suicide, and return to his subordinate station of a part instead of a person; but he loathed the necessity, he loathed the despondency into which Jekyll was now fallen, and he resented the dislike with which he was himself regarded. Hence the apelike tricks that he would play me, scrawling in my own hand blasphemies on the pages of my books, burning the letters and destroying the portrait of my father; and indeed, had it not been for his fear of death, he would long ago have ruined himself in order to involve me in the ruin. But his love of life is wonderful; I go further; I who sicken and freeze at the mere thought of him, when I recall the abjection and passion of this attachment, and when I know how he fears my power to cut him off by suicide, I find it in my heart to pity him.

It is useless, and the time awfully fails me, to prolong this description; no one has ever suffered such torments, let that suffice; and yet even to these, habit brought—no, not alleviation—but a certain callousness of soul, a certain acquiescence of despair; and my punishment might have gone on for years, but for the last calamity which has now fallen, and which has finally severed me from my own face and nature. My provision of the salt, which had never been renewed since the date of the first experiment, began to run low. I sent out for a fresh supply, and mixed the draught; the ebullition followed, and the first change of color, not the second; I drank it, and it was without efficacy. You will learn from Poole how I have had London ransacked; it was in vain; and I am now persuaded that my first supply was impure, and that it was that unknown impurity which lent efficacy to the draught.

About a week has passed, and I am now finishing this statement under the influence of the last of the old powders. This, then, is the last time, short of a miracle, that Henry Jekyll can think his own thoughts, or see his own face (now how sadly altered!) in the glass. Nor must I delay too long to bring my writing to an end; for if my narrative has hitherto escaped destruction, it has been by a combination of great prudence and great good luck. Should the throes of change take me in the act of writing it, Hyde will tear it in pieces; but if some time shall have elapsed after I have laid it by, his wonderful selfishness and circumspection for the moment will probably save it once again from the action of his apelike spite. And indeed the doom that is closing on us both, has already changed and crushed him. Half an hour from now, when I shall again and forever reindue that hated personality, I know how I shall sit shuddering and weeping in my chair, or continue, with the most strained and fear-struck ecstasy of listening, to pace up and down this room (my last earthly refuge), and give ear to every sound of menace. Will Hyde die upon the scaffold? or will he find courage to release himself at the last moment? God knows; I am careless; this is my true hour of death, and what is to follow concerns another than myself. Here then, as I lay down the pen and proceed to seal up my confession, I bring the life of that unhappy Henry Jekyll to an end.

from *Strange Case of Dr. Jekyll and Mr. Hyde*, pp. 114–23.

Ishmael's November Soul
Herman Melville, American novelist, 1819–1891

Call me Ishmael. Some years ago—never mind how long precisely—having little or no money in my purse, and nothing particular to interest me on shore, I thought I would sail about a little and see the watery part of the world. It is a way I have of driving off the spleen, and regulating the circulation. Whenever I find myself growing grim about the mouth; whenever it is a damp, drizzly November in my soul; whenever I find myself involuntarily pausing before coffin warehouses, and bringing up the thread of every funeral I meet; and especially whenever my hypos get such an upper hand of me, that it requires a strong moral principle to prevent me from deliberately stepping into the street, and methodically knocking people's hats off—then, I account it high time to get to sea as soon as I can. This is my substitute for pistol and ball. With a philosophical flourish Cato throws himself upon the sword;

I quietly take to the ship. There is nothing surprising in this. If they but knew it, almost all men in their degree, some time or other, cherish very nearly the same feelings towards the ocean with me.

from Moby Dick, p. 1.

The Anguish of the Infantry Officer
Herbert Read, English poet and art critic

My Company
But, God! I know that I'll stand
Someday in the loneliest wilderness,
Someday my heart will cry
For the soul that has been, but that now
Is scattered with the winds,
Deceased and devoid.

I know that I'll wander with a cry:
"O beautiful men, O men I loved,
O whither are you gone, my company?"

1917

from Collected Poems, cited in "The Great War" by Paul Fussell.

Waking the Sleeping Soul
Albert Schweitzer, Alsatian theologian, musician, medical missionary, 1875–1965

You know of the disease in Central Africa called sleeping sickness. . . . There also exists a sleeping sickness of the soul. Its most dangerous aspect is that one is unaware of its coming. That is why you have to be careful. As soon as you notice the slightest sign of indifference, the moment you become aware of the loss of a certain seriousness, of longing, of enthusiasm and zest, take it as a warning. You should realize that your soul suffers if you live superficially. People need times in which to concentrate, when they can search their inmost selves. It is tragic that most men have not achieved this feeling of self-awareness. And finally, when they hear the inner voice they do not want to listen anymore. They carry on

as before so as not to be constantly reminded of what they have
lost. But as for you, resolve to keep a quiet time both in your
homes and here within these peaceful walls when the bells ring on
Sundays. Then your souls can speak to you without being drowned
out by the hustle and bustle of everyday life.

cited in *The Search for Meaning,*
by Phillip L. Berman, epigraph.

The Pilgrim Soul
Anonymous nineteenth-century Russian Christian monk

*I said, "but I beg you to give me some spiritual teaching. How can I save
my soul?"*

For a long time I wandered through many places. I read my Bible
always, and everywhere I asked whether there was not in the
neighborhood a spiritual teacher, a devout and experienced guide,
to be found. One day I was told that in a certain village a gentle-
man had long been living and seeking the salvation of his soul. He
had a chapel in his house. He never left his estate, and he spent
his time in prayer and reading devotional books. Hearing this,
I ran rather than walked to the village named. I got there and
found him.

"What do you want of me?" he asked.

"I have heard that you are a devout and clever person," said I.
"In God's name please explain to me the meaning of the Apostle's
words, 'Pray without ceasing.' How is it possible to pray without
ceasing? I want to know so much, but I cannot understand it all."

He was silent for a while and looked at me closely. Then he said,
"Ceaseless interior prayer is a continual yearning of the human
spirit toward God. To succeed in this consoling exercise we must
pray more often to God to teach us to pray without ceasing. Pray
more, and pray more fervently. It is prayer itself which will reveal
to you how it can be achieved unceasingly; but it will take some
time."

So saying, he had food brought to me, gave me money for my
journey, and let me go.

He did not explain the matter.

from *The Way of a Pilgrim,*
translated by R. M. French, p. 4.

The Soul Agony of Abortion
Sue Nathanson-Elkin, American psychologist

I know that there is no bandage that human beings can apply, no medicine for this open boundary, for my wounded soul.

The psychological tasks I faced in working with my suffering at first seemed overwhelming. For me, mothering, like hunger, is a primordial instinct that begins to function automatically at conception; consequently I felt the abstract potentiality of the fetus as a tangible reality. Central to the mothering instinct within me is a predisposition to recognize and meet the needs of my children, voluntarily sacrificing my own at times when there is a conflict. The abrupt severing of the powerful mothering energy that surged forth in response to my fourth pregnancy resulted in nearly unendurable emotional pain. I had found my best self in the exquisite harmony of loving children, who need love above all else (infants whose physical needs are fully met fail to thrive without an attachment to a mothering person). Committed to life, not death, having always celebrated my fertility and joy in giving birth, I fell into an abyss of despair from which I could see no exit. How would I find a way to accept the loss of my unborn child, to bear the sudden excising of my fertility, and to live with myself after choosing to deny life to the fourth child I had already begun to protect and nurture?

These necessary yet inconceivable tasks precipitated a crisis at the deepest center of my being—a crisis of soul—unlike any other experience of suffering I have encountered. "Soul-crisis" is my name for an experience that consists of much more than an intense emotional reaction to loss and trauma. It involves the shattering of one's beliefs about oneself and one's life into fragments that cannot be put back together again in exactly the same way. It is an experience that forces an assessment of one's basic mode of being in the world, that compels the examination of familiar assumptions, that requires the loss of innocence and a simple worldview, that demands the rebuilding of one's basic foundation. . . .

I feel the medication from the I.V. and then the medication takes over. I remain conscious but, as if in a dream, see the bright lights, the white, focus of the doctor and the nurses. Through a haze I feel the cramping and pain, as if it is happening to another body, that my mind is only watching from an unfathomable distance.

Somehow I find myself in a bed in a recovery room, alone with my husband. For the first time, I feel the emptiness, and worse, the raw and bleeding edges of my empty womb, and I know that there is no bandage that human beings can apply, no medicine for this open boundary, for my wounded soul. I am lost in an anguish that I never imagined I could possibly feel. I know Michael is sitting close to me, trying to hold my hand, but I barely feel his presence. I am lost in a chaotic realm of multicolored pain washing over me in gulping waves, hot and burning. This realm is all there is; the observer-self is gone. I do not know how long I remain at the hospital, nor do I have any awareness of being removed and driven home.

Later I find myself at home in my own bed, alone in the room. I feel crazed as never before in my life. I scream aloud into my pillow to muffle the sound, afraid to frighten my children or anyone else who might hear, afraid to hear myself. I scream and scream, an inhuman sound rasping across my throat, carving grooves in it. I grip the headboard with all my might to prevent myself from acting upon my overwhelming impulse to claw my stomach. I want to tear my skin and rip out my insides. I will strew them across the bed, scratching and clawing, ripping away until there is no life left within. But I grip the headboard instead, because I know deep within me that I cannot create a physical pain that will be as unbearable as my soul-agony, that no amount of physical pain can divert me from such anguish. I am frightened by the intensity of my impulses and by the thin thread that enables me to control them. The strength with which I grip the headboard feels superhuman to me, as if it would lift a car.

I realize, as I ruminate about crises of soul, that abortion is only one trigger for crisis of soul. There are others. I think of the many issues that arise from being female—miscarriage, having a child with birth defects, infertility, menopause, hysterectomy, ovarian cancer, mastectomy. Any one of these might precipitate a profound crisis for a woman (and men who are involved with women grappling with such crises may also be vulnerable to crises of soul). Even normal life transitions, such as having one's children grow up and leave home, can trigger a crisis of soul, the crisis that occurs when a former sense of self is irretrievably lost and a new one has not yet evolved. As women become increasingly able to take their life experiences seriously, I know we will begin to create forms that will mark, honor, and hold the feelings that events such as these evoke.

from *Soul Crisis*, pp. 6, 45, 228–29.

Freud's Soul Lost in Translation
Bruno Bettelheim, German-American psychologist, 1903–1990

The poet H. D. (Hilda Doolittle), speaking of her experience with Freud during her analysis, said, "He is midwife to the soul."

In *The Interpretation of Dreams* (1900), which opened to our understanding not just the meaning of dreams but also the nature and power of the unconscious, Freud told about his arduous struggle to achieve ever greater self-awareness. In other books, he told why he felt it necessary for the rest of us to do the same. In a way, all his writings are gentle, persuasive, often brilliantly worded intimations that we, his readers, would benefit from a similar spiritual journey of self-discovery. Freud showed us how the soul could become aware of itself. To become acquainted with the lowest depth of soul—to explore whatever personal hell we may suffer from—is not an easy undertaking. Freud's findings and, even more, the way he presents them to us give us the confidence that this demanding and potentially dangerous voyage of self-discovery will result in our becoming more fully human, so that we may no longer be enslaved without knowing it to the dark forces that reside in us. By exploring and understanding the origins and the potency of these forces, we not only become much better able to cope with them but also gain a much deeper and more compassionate understanding of our fellow man. In his work and in his writings, Freud often spoke of the soul—of its nature and structure, its development, its attributes, how it reveals itself in all we do and dream. Unfortunately, nobody who reads him in English could guess this, because nearly all his many references to the soul, and to matters pertaining to the soul, have been excised in translation. . . .

There really was no reason—apart from a wish to interpret psychoanalysis as a medical specialty—for this corruption of Freud's references to the soul. There was no reason for the English translators to misunderstand these references. The first three definitions of the word "soul" given in *The Shorter Oxford English Dictionary* express very well what Freud had in mind. The first definition, "the principle of life in man," is declared to be obsolete, and is quoted only for the sake of completeness. The second and third definitions, "the spiritual part of man in contrast to the purely physical" and "the emotional part of man's nature," are most pertinent. It is true that in common American usage the word "soul" has been more or less restricted to the sphere of religion. This is not the case of Freud's Vienna, and it is not the case in German-speaking countries today. In German the word *Seele* has retained its full meaning as man's essence, as that which is most spiritual and worthy in man. *Seele* ought to have been translated in this sense.

What Freud considered as forming or pertaining to the essence of man, man's soul, the translators have relegated entirely to the I, the thinking and resigning part of man. They have disregarded the nonthinking it, the irrational world of the unconscious and of the emotions. Freud uses *Seele* and *seelisch* rather than *geistig* because *geistig* refers mainly to the rational aspects of the mind, to that of which we are conscious. The idea of the soul, by contrast, definitely includes much of which we are not consciously aware. Freud wanted to make clear that psychoanalysis was concerned not just with man's body and his intellect, as his medical colleagues were, but—and most of all—with the dark world of the unconscious which forms such a large part of the soul of living man—or, to put it in classical terms, with that unknown netherworld in which, according to ancient myths, the souls of men dwell.

from *Freud and Man's Soul*, pp. 4, 76–77.

The Kingdom of Soul
Willa Cather, American novelist, 1873–1947

The final barrier between Eric and his mother's faith was his violin, and to that he clung as a man sometimes will cling to his dearest sin, to the weakness more precious to him than all his strength.

The final barrier between Eric and his mother's faith was his violin, and to that he clung as a man sometimes will cling to his dearest sin, to the weakness more precious to him than all his strength. In the great world beauty comes to men in many guises, and art in a hundred forms, but for Eric there was only his violin. It stood, to him, for all the manifestations of art; it was his only bridge into the kingdom of the soul.

It was to Eric Hermannson that the evangelist directed his impassioned pleading that night.

"*Saul, Saul, why persecutest thou me?* Is there a Saul here tonight who has stopped his ears to that gentle pleading, who has thrust a spear into that bleeding side? Think of it, my brother; you are offered this wonderful love and you prefer the worm that dieth not and the fire which will not be quenched. What right have you to lose one of God's precious souls? *Saul, Saul, why persecutest thou me?"*

A great joy dawned in Asa Skinner's pale face, for he saw that Eric Hermannson was swaying to and fro in his seat. The minister fell upon his knees and threw his long arms over his head.

"O my brothers! I feel it coming, the blessing we have prayed for. I tell you the Spirit is coming! Just a little more prayer, brothers, a little more zeal, and he will be here. I can feel his cooling wing upon my brow. Glory be to God forever and ever, amen!"

The whole congregation groaned under the pressure of this spiritual panic. Shouts and hallelujahs went up from every lip. Another figure fell prostrate upon the floor. From the mourners' bench rose a chant of terror and rapture:

> *"Eating honey and drinking wine,*
> *Glory to the bleeding Lamb!*
> *I am my Lord's and he is mine,*
> *Glory to the bleeding Lamb!"*

The hymn was sung in a dozen dialects and voiced all the vague yearning of these hungry lives, of these people who had starved all the passions so long, only to fall victims to the basest of them all, fear.

A groan of ultimate anguish rose from Eric Hermannson's bowed head, and the sound like the groan of a great tree when it falls in the forest.

The minister rose suddenly to his feet and threw back his head, crying in a loud voice:

"*Lazarus, come forth!* Eric Hermannson, you are lost, going down at sea. In the name of God, and Jesus Christ his Son, I throw you the life line. Take hold! Almighty God, my soul for this!" The minister threw his arms out and lifted his quivering face.

Eric Hermannson rose to his feet; his lips were set and the lightning was in his eyes. He took his violin by the neck and crushed it to splinters across his knee, and to Asa Skinner the sound was like the shackles of sin broken audibly asunder.

from "Eric Hermannson's Soul," *Willa Cather: 24 Stories,*
selected and with an introduction by Sharon O'Brien, pp. 94–96.

Rage in the Dark, the Wind
Fernando Pessoa, Portuguese poet, 1888–1935

Rage in the dark, the wind—
Huge sound of on and on.

My thought has nothing in it
Except that it can't die down.

The soul contains, it seems,
A dark where there hardens and
Blows a madness that comes
From trying to understand.

Raving in dark, the wind—
It can't shake free out there.
My thought—I am caught in it
Like the wind caught in the air.

(23.5.32)

from *Selected Poems: Fernando Pessoa,*
selected and translated by Jonathan Griffin, p. 44.

The Annihilation of the Soul
Susan Griffin, American feminist and poet

I discovered my rage and fear at the existence of rape. And beyond this?
Solitude. Myself. What am I if I exist unprotected in the world?

I discovered my rage and fear at the existence of rape. And beyond this? Solitude. Myself. What am I if I exist unprotected in the world? These are beginning to be questions for the soul, and these are the questions, after seven years of political questioning, which like the kernel of wheat after it has been held up to the wind, remain. But is this not what we have meant all along when we have demanded to be human? . . .

One physical act is not equal to another physical act. Rape is not a matter of spiritless atoms penetrating other dead matter. Mind comes to play. Will comes to play. The act is informed by centuries of the hatred of women, by a tradition of violence and fear toward our bodies, by Saint Paul's words that we ought to keep silent, by the old rule that we must cover our heads in church. This is what makes rape a qualitatively different act than assault, or robbery. In both cases, one is forced, one is injured. But in the case of rape, the very odor of the body of the rapist, his gestures of brutality, the menace of his threats echo back into centuries of debasement and his penetration penetrates the very soul of his victim with, as the French women wrote, annihilation.

But isn't the thought that women have no soul one of the pre-
conditions of rape, and is not rape, after all, a ritualistic playing
out of that belief? Two monks in the fourteenth century wrote that
women are not to be trusted in the realm of the spiritual, that this
is why they are more open to possession by the devil. After the
death by suicide of a film actress, another publicly declares, "They
treat us like meat," by which she means that the men who hire
them treat them as less than human, as matter without spirit. A
young man who has committed a rape confesses that, as he forced
the young woman, a stranger to him, her cries of fear made him realize suddenly, as if this had never before occurred to him, that she
was a human being.

But this may be the reason, finally, that our very selfish motion,
to heal ourselves, to tend to our own wounds, may turn out to be
the most radical motion of all, one that heals not only ourselves
but eventually all, and thus transforms the social order absolutely.
For indeed, the rapist does not feel the agony of rape; the nature of
his particular mutilation is a numbing. To fail to see the soul of another is to truncate perception utterly. But the one who is raped
cannot rest still with her situation. She is turned on a rack, herself
and her own body put in direct opposition to the state of the world
as society has asked her to accept it. . . .

How could a woman be more quintessentially inessential except
when she is being raped? Her very life is under threat of extinc-
tion. The dictates of her soul are rendered without effect. And any
sense of being essential in this context must therefore be an ex-
tremity, an act which strikes at the core of patriarchy. Isn't this the
reason why under the law it has been so much more acceptable for
a man to strike out against the rape of his wife or his daughter
than it is for the woman herself to do so? Behind the letter of the
law is a reasoning based on property rights, so that even here the
crime of rape is not a crime against an inessential being but
against her owner, the essential being who is her husband or her
father. . . .

And essence, after all, is another word for soul, is another word
for spirit—the spirit which is lost to the rapist and the raped, in
this transgression. And so there is a shape here after all, moving
from the political to the spiritual. . . .

[Women have] received the suggestion that those women who
were burned by the Christian Fathers as witches were indeed the
priestesses of a different religion, one which was more female not
only in its offices, but in the more transcendent meanings of the
word female: closer to the earth, listening to natural spirits, emotional, sexual, dark. We recovered images from prehistory.

Rounded female goddesses, found buried in fields, left from older civilizations. A goddess with snakes as symbols of power wound about her arms. The sacred calf. The tree of life. The symbols which the patriarchal religion had called evil.

And indeed we found that in this mythological world the story of rape was told with great clarity. That the sites of matriarchal temples, such as Knossos on Crete, were chosen because the surrounding hills made the shape of a female body. That a female deity preceded Zeus. That Zeus raped Hera. And then we listened with new ears to the story of the rape of Persephone—how the daughter was stolen from her mother, how she was raped with her father's blessings, how her mother made the earth unyielding in revenge and received her daughter back only by compromise.

All this knowledge worked a kind of alchemy in us which cannot easily be described by rational means. Can I say simply that a woman who can perceive in herself the Goddess cannot so easily be shamed by rape? That she is more likely to shame her rapist? For we are not protesting anymore that we too are human. We are not bent and strained to argue that we do not want rape, eager to prove that rape is a crime. We take our essentialness as self-evident now, and our work begins with this. So we begin to see, and we see differently. We see what is not there. We see visions. We know there is a world without rape and this world is in our minds.

from Rape: The Politics of Consciousness, pp. 41–47.

Soul on Ice
Eldridge Cleaver, African-American author and activist

I was twenty-two when I came to prison and of course I changed tremendously over the years. But I had always had a strong sense of myself and in the last few years I felt I was losing my identity.

Getting to know someone, entering that new world, is an ultimate, irretrievable leap into the unknown. The prospect is terrifying. The stakes are high. The emotions are overwhelming. The two people are reluctant really to strip themselves naked in front of each other, because in doing so they make themselves one to the other. How often they inflict pain and torment upon each other! Better to maintain shallow, superficial affairs; that way the scars are not too deep. No blood is hacked from the soul.

But I do not believe a beautiful relationship has to end always in carnage, or that we have to be fraudulent and pretentious with one another. If we project fraudulent, pretentious images, or if we fantasize each other into distorted caricatures of what we really are, then, when we awake from the trance and see beyond the sham and front, all will dissolve, all will die or be transformed into bitterness and hate. I know that sometimes people fake on each other out of genuine motives to hold onto the object of their tenderest feelings. They see themselves as so inadequate that they feel forced to wear a mask in order continuously to impress the second party.

If a man is free—not in prison, the Army, a monastery, hospital, spaceship, submarine—and living a normal life with the usual multiplicity of social relations with individuals of both sexes, it may be that he is incapable of experiencing the total impact of another individual upon himself. The competing influences and conflicting forces of other personalities may dilute one's psychic and emotional perception, to the extent that one does not and cannot receive all that the other person is capable of sending.

Yet I believe that a man whose soul or emotional apparatus had lain dormant in a deadening limbo of desuetude is capable of responding from some great sunken well of his being, as though a potent catalyst had been tossed into a critical mass, when an exciting, lovely, and lovable woman enters the range of his feelings. What a deep, slow, torturous, reluctant, frightened stirring! He feels a certain part of himself in a state of flux, as if a bodiless stranger has stolen inside his body, startling him by doing calisthenics, and he feels himself coming slowly back to life. His body chemistry changes and he is flushed with new strength.

When she first comes to him his heart is empty, a desolate place, a dehydrated oasis, unsolaced, and he's craving womanfood, without which sustenance the tension of his manhood has unwound and relaxed. He has imperative need of the kindness, sympathy, understanding, and conversation of a woman, to hear a woman's laughter at his words, to answer her questions and be answered by her, to look into her eyes, to sniff her primeval fragrance, to hear—with slaughtered ears—the sensuous rustling of frivolous garments as legs are crossed and uncrossed beneath a table, to feel the delicate, shy weight of her hand in his—how painfully and totally aware is he of her presence, her every movement! It is as if one had been left to die beneath a bush on a lonely trail. The sun is hot and the shade of the bush, if not offering an extension of life, offers at least a slowing-down of death. And just when one feels the next breath will surely be the last, a rare and rainbow-colored bird settles on a delicate twig of the bush, and, with the magic of melodious trillings and beauty of plumage, charms the dying one back to life. The dying man feels the strength flowing into and through the conduits of his body from the charged atmosphere created by the presence of the bird, and he knows intuitively in his clinging to life that if the bird remains he will regain his strength and health—and live.

Seeing her image slipping away from the weak fingers of his mind as soon as she has gone, his mind fights for a token of her on which to peg memory. Jealously, he hoards the fading the memory of their encounter, like a miser gloating over a folio of blue-chip stock. The unfathomable machinery of the subconscious projects an image onto the conscious mind: her bare right arm, from curve of shoulder to fingertip. (Had his lips quivered with desire to brand that soft, cool-looking flesh with a kiss of fire, had his fingers itched to caress?) Such is the magic of a woman, the female principle of nature which she embodies, and her power to resurrect and revitalize a long-isolated and lonely man.

I was twenty-two when I came to prison and of course I changed tremendously over the years. But I had always had a strong sense of myself and in the last few years I felt I was losing my identity. There was a decision in my body that eluded me, as though I could not exactly locate its site. I would be aware of this numbness, this feeling of atrophy, and it haunted the back of my mind. Because of this numb spot, I felt peculiarly off balance, the awareness of something missing, of a blank spot, a certain intimation of emptiness. Now I know what it was. After eight years of prison, I was visited by a woman, a woman who was interested in my work and cared about what happened to me. And since encountering her, I feel life, strength flowing back into that spot. My step, the tread of my stride, which was becoming tentative and uncertain, has begun to recover a definiteness, a confidence, a boldness which makes me want to kick over a few tables. I may even swagger a little, and, as I read in a book somewhere, "push myself forward like a train."

from *Soul on Ice*, pp. 33–36.

They Want Your Soul
Alice Walker, African-American author

To such people, your color, your sex, yourself make you an object. But an object, strangely, perversely, with a soul. A soul.

[Sometime during the early seventies I was asked to write a letter to an imaginary young black woman, giving her some sense of my own experiences and telling her things she might need to know. I

wrote a long letter, which I sent off to the person who asked for it.
(I no longer recall who this was), but then discovered I wanted to
say even more.]

Dear Joanna:
Forgive me for writing again so soon. I realize you are busy
reading the words of all your other sisters who also love you,
but you have been constantly on my mind each day. I think
of new things to share with you. Today I wanted to tell you
about beauty.

In you, there is beauty like a rock.

So distilled, so unshatterable, so ageless, it will attract
great numbers of people who will attempt, almost as an exercise of will (and of no more importance to them than an exercise), to break it. They will try ignoring you, flattering you,
joining you, buying you, simply to afford themselves the opportunity of finding the one crack in your stone of beauty by
which they may enter with their tools of destruction. Often
you will be astonished that, while they pursue their single-
minded effort to do this, they do not seem to see your sorrowing face (sorrowing because some of them will have come
to you in the disguise of friends, even sisters) or note the
quavering of your voice, or the tears of vulnerability in your
eyes. To such people, your color, your sex your*self* make you
an object. But an object, strangely, perversely, with a soul. A
soul.

It is your soul they want.

They will want to crack it out of the rock and wear it somewhere—not inside them, where it might do them good, but
about them—like, for example, a feather through their hair,
or a scalp dangling from their belt.

As frightening as this is, it has always been so.

Your mother and father, your grandparents, *their* parents,
all have had your same beauty like a rock, and all have been
pursued, often hunted down like animals, because of it. Perhaps some grew tired of resisting, and in weariness relin-
quished the stone that was their life. But most resisted to the
end. The end, for them, being merely you. Your life. Which is
not an end.

That resistance is your legacy.

Inner beauty, an irrepressible music, certainly courage to
say No or Yes, dedication to one's own Gods, affection for
one's own spirit(s), a simplicity of approach to life, will survive all of us through your will.

You are, perhaps, the last unconquered resident on this earth. And must live, in any case, as if it *must* be so.

from *Living by the Word: Selected Writings 1973–1987*, pp. 75–78.

The Postmodern Soul
Sam Keen, American author

Once we abandon the age-old quest for consistency, for forging a single identity, for a unifying vision we are left with no guiding principle except to follow the dictates of the moment.

Today, the notion of postmodernism is all the rage. Around 1960, we entered the era characterized by a new style of life, art, and identity. While the modern world was shaped by the industrial revolution and mass production, the postmodern era is shaped by the information revolution, the ethic of consumption, fast-changing styles, and lack of commitment to any single perspective. According to Todd Gitlin, "Postmodernism is completely indifferent to the questions of consistency and continuity. It self-consciously splices genres, attitudes, styles. It relishes the blurring or juxtaposition of forms (fiction-nonfiction), stances (straight-ironic), moods (violent-comic), cultural levels (high-low) . . . It neither embraces nor criticizes, but beholds the world blankly, with a knowingness that dissolves feeling and commitment into irony . . . It takes pleasure in the play of surfaces, and derides the search for depth as mere nostalgia."

At best, postmodern man has gone for the gusto, done away with pleasure anxiety, and thrown off the old capitalist tyranny of scarcity-consciousness and postponed gratification. He is no longer trying to improve his soul, develop his willpower, or save himself for some future heaven. He has given up the quest for a single identity, a consistent point of view or triumph over tragedy. His stance is one of irony rather than romance.

At worst, postmodern man is the concupiscent consumer. He might be called a dilettante except that he is too cool to dive into delight. His tastes, life-style, and convictions are formed by fashion. Like the god Proteus, and unlike the substantial self-made men of the last century, he changes shape at will. His life is organized more around the idea of "taste" than of "right or wrong"; his world is aesthetic rather than moral. You could call him disillusioned except that he has never dared care about anything passionately enough to have developed hope or illusion.

In truth the postmodern man is not so new as he thinks.
Kierkegaard described him a century ago as Don Juan, the aesthetic man whose life is a series of one-night stands and fleeting
romances. He is a blank page, a tabula rasa, upon which the moment writes its tale. Weightless, he suffers, in the words of Milan
Kundera, "the unbearable lightness of being." Unlike the classical
"hero with a thousand faces," he avoids the depths and keeps himself satiated with a thousand amusing facades. The mall, the auto-
mobile showroom, and the electronic supermarket are his
catharsis. If he turns to more "serious" matters he becomes what
Trungpa Rinpoche called a "spiritual materialist." He samples religions and salvation schemes.

With the postmodern man we reach a point where moral reasoning gives out. Once we abandon the age-old quest for consistency,
for forging a single identity, for a unifying vision we are left with
no guiding principle except to follow the dictates of the moment.
"Taste" replaces "ought," and as the old proverb says, "About taste
there is no dispute."

Without an organizing center, postmodern man is lost, wandering in a wilderness of confusing plurality. But, paradoxically, being
bereft of set moral landmarks, he is in a unique position to under-
take a new journey.

from *Fire in the Belly,* pp. 110–11.

Once Dipped in Dark Oblivion
D. H. Lawrence, English novelist and poet, 1885–1930

The End, The Beginning

If there were not an utter and absolute dark
of silence and sheer oblivion
at the core of everything,
how terrible the sun would be,
how ghastly it would be to strike a match, and make a light.

But the very sun himself is pivoted
upon the core of pure oblivion
so is a candle, even as a match.

And if there were not an absolute, utter forgetting
and a ceasing to know, a perfect ceasing to know
and a silent, sheer cessation of all awareness
how terrible life would be!
how terrible it would be to think and know, to have consciousness!

But dipped, once dipped in dark oblivion
the soul has peace, inward and lovely peace.

from The Complete Poems of D. H. Lawrence, p. 144.

A Lien on His Soul: The Legend of Robert Johnson

Greil Marcus, American music critic

[Robert] Johnson's music is so strong that in certain moods it can make you feel that he is giving you more than you could have bargained for—that there is a place for you in these lines of his: "She's got a mortgage on my body, a lien on my soul." It is no exaggeration to say that Johnson changed the lives of people as distant from each other as Muddy Waters, who began his career as a devoted imitator; Dion, who made his way through the terrors of his heroin habit with Johnson's songs for company; and myself. After hearing Johnson's music for the first time—listening to that blasted and somehow friendly voice, the shivery guitar, hearing a score of lines that fit as easily and memorably into each day as Dylan's had—I could listen to nothing else for months. Johnson's music changed the way the world looked to me. Over the years, what had been a fascination with a bundle of ideas and dreams from old American novels and texts—a fascination with the foreboding and gentleness that is linked in the most interesting Americans—seemed to find a voice in Johnson's songs. It was the intensity of his music that changed fascination into commitment and a bundle of ideas into what must serve as a point of view.

But commitment is a tricky, Faustian word. When he first appeared, Robert couldn't play guitar to save his life, Son House told Pete Welding; Johnson hung out with the older bluesmen, pestering them for a chance to try his hand, and after a time he went away. It was months later, on a Saturday night, when they saw him again, still looking to be heard. They tried to put him off, but he persisted; finally, they let him play for a lull and left him alone with the tables and chairs.

Outside, taking the air, House and the others heard a loud, devastating music of a brilliance and purity beyond anything in the memory of the Mississippi Delta. Johnson had nothing more to learn from *them.*

"He sold his soul to the devil to get to play like that," House told Welding.

Well, they tell a lot of stories about Robert Johnson. You could call that one superstition, or you could call it sour grapes. Thinking of voodoo and gypsy women in the back country, or of the black man who used to walk the streets of Harlem with a briefcase full of contracts and a wallet full of cash, buying up souls at $100 a throw, you could even take it literally.

If there were nothing else, the magic of Johnson's guitar would be enough to make that last crazy interpretation credible. But in a way that cannot be denied, selling his soul and trying to win it back are what Johnson's bravest songs are all about, and anyone who wants to come to grips with his music probably ought to entertain Son House's possibility. I have the feeling, at times, that the reason Johnson has remained so elusive is that no one has been willing to take him at his word.

Let us say that Johnson sought out one of the Mississippi Delta devil-men, or one of the devil-women, and tried to sell his soul in exchange for the music he heard but could not make. Let us say he did this because he wanted to attract women; because he wanted to be treated with the kind of awe that is in Son House's voice when he speaks of Robert Johnson and the devil; because music brought him a fierce joy, made him feel alive like nothing else in the world. Or let us say that the idea of the devil gave Johnson a way of understanding the fears that overshadowed him; that even if no deal was made, the promises passing from one to another, Johnson believes that his desires and his crimes were simple proof of a consummation quite beyond his power to control; that the image of the devil appealed to Johnson when he recognized (singing, "I mistreated my baby, but I can't see no reason why") that his soul was not his own, and, looking at the disasters of his life and the evil of the world, drew the one conclusion as to whom it did belong.

Blues grew out of the need to live in the brutal world that stood ready in ambush the moment one walked out of the church. Unlike gospel, blues was not a music of transcendence; its equivalent to God's Grace was sex and love. Blues made the terrors of the world easier to endure, but blues also made those terrors more real. For a man like Johnson, the promises of the church faded; they could be remembered—as one sang church songs; perhaps even when one prayed, when one was too scared not to—but those promises could not be lived. Once past some unmarked border, one could not go back. The weight of Johnson's blues was strong enough to make salvation a joke; the best he could do was cry for its beautiful lie. "You run without moving from a terror in which you cannot believe," William Faulkner wrote in one of his books about the landscape he shared with Robert Johnson, just about the time Johnson was making his first records, "toward a safety in which you have no faith."

from *Mystery Train*, pp. 32–36.

PART FIVE

SOUL
WORK

Phantasy abandoned by reason produces impossible monsters; united with her, she is the mother of the arts and origin of their marvel.

— **Francisco Goya**

Art must recreate, in full consciousness, and by means of signs, the total life of the universe, that is to say, the soul where the varied dream we call the universe is played.

— **Teodar de Wyzema**

Who knows what form the forward momentum of life will take in the time ahead or what use it will make of our anguished searching. The most any one of us can seem to do is to fashion something—an object or ourselves—and drop it into the confusion, make an offering of it, so to speak, to the life force.

— **Ernest Becker**

Introduction

When Socrates addressed the senators of Athens at his trial he didn't ask for their mercy or forgiveness or even defend himself. Instead, he asked why they weren't ashamed of spending their lives hoarding money and fame and "caring so little about wisdom and truth and the greatest improvement of the soul, which you never regard or heed at all?"

Today it's common for people to dismiss the great hovering question about the soul by saying, "I don't know what it is" or that the whole foolhardy concept died with God in the asylum with Nietzsche or on the front cover of *Time* magazine. Or who cares?

Nevertheless, the legacy of Socrates lives on. Care of the soul, working the soul, the crafting of the good life are still ways of activating the depths of the imagination. By cultivating what Keats called "negative capability," the ability of living in uncertainty without despair or surrender, we can respond to the godless hours and spiritless days with soulful moves from the garret and pulpit back to the street to answer the ground level question, "How should I actually *live* my life?"

In Part 5 I pursue the theme of soul as something that develops and actually shapes consciousness, by citing passages of those through the centuries who have believed ardently in working the soul, in Thoreau's image, like a farmer works the soil. From the anonymous hand behind Psalm 23 who spoke of "recreating" the self, through the French adventurer Isabelle Eberhardt who traveled to "fashion a soul," to the forging of bluesy music and "the application of Poetics to everyday life," in the memorable phrase of Thomas Moore, there is a venerable tradition about the soul that refuses to believe it is endowed like a royal title, but instead is something, after all the cold shivers of doubt, that unfolds from within. For as Alan Jones writes, "We are not self-made. . . . Soul making . . . has something to do with paying attention to the Things Invisible, things which do not lend themselves to manipulation and control." As he describes it, soul work is less Herculean than humbling, more of an inner stretching exercise than an outer bulking up of spiritual muscles, in order to simply "become more and more who we are."

Ironically, the trouble with culture-vultures, adventure-junkies, and practitioners of "holier-than-thou" spiritual calisthenics, is, as James Hillman constantly reminds us, that, lo and behold, "Events are not essential to the soul's experience . . . nor dreams, journeys, loves . . . they do not differentiate or deepen one's psychic capacity to become an old wise soul." A much harder task than climbing Mt. Kilimanjaro with your Indian guru or Berkeley astrologer is the realization that "There must be a *vision* of what's happening, *deep ideas* to create the experience of soul."

This notion is not unlike the Avalik Eskimo artists who ask the ivory bone they are about to carve, "Who are you? Who hides in you?" The contributors of this chapter ask themselves, What must I pay attention to to become myself? What must I do to "struggle to know the world as man knows an apple in the mouth," as Rollo May describes the task elsewhere in *The Quest for Beauty.*

For the exultant Plotinus, soul was the immeasurable beginning of all things, the touchstone for beauty, and capable of being "trained" like a disciplined sculptor working marble with a chisel. His treasure trove of a book, *The Enneads,* is full of rapturous insights that recommend searching "the souls of those that have shaped beautiful forms." French architect Ferdnand Pouillon's languorously contemplative book about medieval cathedral building, *The Stones of the Abbey,* evokes the soul of work as ultimate attention to one's craft, which in turn becomes a source of courage.

Is there a shadow side to soul making? Consider Mary Wollstonecroft Shelley's *Frankenstein.* In my excerpt, a Swiss student experiments with literally animating—"infusing the spark of life"—into the inanimate form of a soulless monster cobbled together from churchyard corpses.

In her classic Maine diary, *Journal of a Solitude,* May Sarton describes a more benevolent form of soul-making: poetry, a tool she uses to help lead her to a resurgence of life. To painter Wassily Kandinsky soul is the "guiding principle" for the beauty that springs from the soul in the form of color, harmony, vibration.

Considering the absolute absence of any music from classical Greece, it is tantalizing to consider that Plato said, "Music and rhythm find their way into the secret places of the soul," a sentiment that could easily be liner notes for soul music album. With the ignition of soul music in the 1950s, what had been called rather self-consciously "going down into the depths," as with mystics or depth psychologists, became "getting down." "That is the gospel truth" became "Ain't that the truth, baby?" "Let's go back to your childhood" became "Let me take you back, let me take you *waaayyy back,*" a way to open up a blues concert. The difference was you didn't need to live alone for years in desert caves, you didn't need footnotes, and you could dance to it. Music historian Peter Guralnick sums up the history in his definitive book, *Sweet*

Soul Music, that soul derives from the Southern dream of freedom, and as such is a music that "keeps hinting at a conclusion, keeps straining at the boundaries—of melody and convention. . . ." Soul is a music where feeling dictated rhythm and pace, music sung from the heart with fiery emotional truth but with "quiet moments at the center . . . moments of stillness," that dramatically echo age-old gospel techniques of soaring and swooping between the sacred and the profane.

Reaching down into his soul, James Brown cries out to his audience to reach down with him, *"Can I get a witness?"*

Psalm 23
Eighth(?) through fifth(?) century B.C.E.

The Lord is my shepherd;
I shall not want.
He maketh me to lie down
in green pastures: he leadeth
me beside the still waters.
He restoreth my soul: he
leadeth me in the paths of
righteousness for his name's
sake.
Yea, though I walk through
the valley of the shadow of
death, I will fear no evil: for
thou art with me; thy rod and
thy staff they comfort me.
Thou preparest a table
before me in the presence of
mine enemies: thou anointest
my head with oil; my cup
runneth over.
Surely goodness and mercy
shall follow me all the days of
my life: and I will dwell in the
house of the LORD for ever.

King James Version

The Smith of My Soul

Bayazid of Bistun, ninth-century Islamic mystic

For twelve years I was the smith of my soul. I put it in the furnace of austerity and burned it in the fire of combat, I laid it on the anvil of reproach and smote it with the hammer of blame until I made of my soul a mirror. Five years I was the mirror of myself and was ever polishing that mirror with divers acts of worship and piety. Then for a year I gazed in contemplation. On my waist I saw a girdle of pride and vanity and self-conceit and reliance on devotion and approbation of my works. I labored for five years more until that girdle became worn out and I professed Islam anew. I looked and saw that all created things were dead. I pronounced four *akbirs* over them and returned from the funeral of them all, and without intrusion of creatures, through God's help alone, I attained unto God.

cited in *The Perennial Philosophy*,
Aldous Huxley, pp. 276–77.

Soul and Beauty

Plotinus, Neoplatonist, Greek philosopher, 205–270

Therefore the Soul must be trained—to the habit of remarking, first, all noble pursuits, then the works of beauty . . . you must search the souls of those that have shaped these beautiful forms.

8. But what must we do? How lies the path? How come to vision of the inaccessible Beauty, dwelling as if in consecrated precincts, apart from the common ways where all may see, even the profane?

He that has the strength, let him arise and withdraw into himself, foregoing all that is known by the eyes, turning away for ever from the material beauty that once made his joy. When he perceives those shapes of grace that show in body, let him not pursue: he must know them for copies, vestiges, shadows, and hasten away towards That they tell of. For if anyone follow what is like a beautiful shape playing over water—is there not a myth telling in symbol of such a dupe, how he sank into the depths of the current and was swept away to nothingness? So too, one that is held by material beauty and will not break free shall be precipitated, not in body but in Soul, down to the dark depths loathed of the Intellective-Being, where, blind even in the Lower-World, he shall have commerce only with shadows, there as here.

'Let us flee then to the beloved Fatherland': this is the soundest counsel. But what is this flight? How are we to gain the open sea? For Odysseus is surely a parable to us when he commands the flight from the sorceries of Circe of Calypso—not content to linger for all the pleasure offered to his eyes and all the delight of sense filling his days.

The Fatherland to us is There whence we have come, and There is the Father. What then is the course, what manner of our flight? This is not a journey for the feet; the feet bring us only from land to land; nor need you think of coach or ship to carry you away; all this order of things you must set aside and refuse to see: you must close the eyes and call instead upon another vision which is to be waked within you, a vision, the birth-right of all, which few turn to use. .

9. And this inner vision, what is its operation?

Newly awakened it is all too feeble to bear the ultimate splendour. Therefore the Soul must be trained—to the habit of remarking, first, all noble pursuits, then the works of beauty produced not by the labour of the arts but by the virtue of men known for their goodness: lastly, you must search the souls of those that have shaped these beautiful forms.

But how are you to see into a virtuous Soul and know its loveliness?

Withdraw into yourself and look. And if you do not find yourself beautiful yet, act as does the creator of a statue that is to be made beautiful: he cuts away here, he smoothes there, he makes this line lighter, this other purer, until a lovely face has grown upon his work. So do you also: cut away all that is excessive, straighten all that is crooked, bring light to all that is overcast, labour to make all one glow of beauty and never cease chiselling your statue, until there shall shine out on you from it the godlike splendour of virtue, until you shall see the perfect goodness surely established in the stainless shrine.

When you know that you have become this perfect work, when you are self-gathered in the purity of your being, nothing now remaining that can shatter that inner unity, nothing from without clinging to the authentic man, when you find yourself wholly true to your essential nature, wholly that only veritable Light which is not measured by space, not narrowed to any circumscribed form nor again diffused as a thing void of term, but ever unmeasurable as something greater than all measure and more than all quantity—when you perceive that you have grown to this, you are now become very vision: now call up all your confidence, strike forward yet a step—you need a guide no longer—strain, and see

This is the only eye that sees the mighty Beauty. If the eye that adventures the vision be dimmed by vice, impure, or weak, and unable in its cowardly blenching to see the uttermost brightness, then it sees nothing even though another point to what lies plain to sight before it. To any vision must be brought an eye adapted to what is to be seen, and having some likeness to it. Never did eye see the sun unless it had first become sunlike, and never can the Soul have vision of the First Beauty unless itself be beautiful.

Therefore, first let each become godlike and each beautiful who cares to see God and Beauty. So, mounting, the Soul will come first to the Intellectual-Principle and survey all the beautiful Ideas in the Supreme and will avow that this is Beauty, that the Ideas are Beauty. For by their efficacy comes all Beauty else, by the offspring of Being and of the Intellectual-Principle. What is beyond the Intellectual-Principle we affirm to be the nature of Good radiating Beauty before it. So that, treating the Intellectual-Cosmos as one, the first is the Beautiful: if we make distinction there, the Realm of Ideas constitutes the Beauty of the Intellectual Sphere; and the Good, which lies beyond, is the Fountain at once and Principle of Beauty: the Primal Good and the Primal Beauty have the one dwelling-place and, thus, always, Beauty's seat is There.

from *The Enneads,* I, 8–9,
translation by Stephen McKenna, pp. 71–72.

Frankenstein, or the Modern Prometheus
Mary Wollstonecraft Shelley, English novelist, 1797–1851

I had worked hard for nearly two years, for the sole purpose of infusing life into an inanimate body.

It was on a dreary night of November that I beheld the accomplishment of my toils. With an anxiety that almost amounted to agony, I collected the instruments of life around me, that I might infuse a spark of being into the lifeless thing that lay at my feet. It was already one in the morning; the rain pattered dismally against the panes, and my candle was nearly burnt out, when, by the glimmer of the half-extinguished light, I saw the dull yellow eye of the creature open; it breathed hard, and a convulsive motion agitated its limbs.

How can I describe my emotions at this catastrophe, or how delineate the wretch whom with such infinite pains and care I had endeavored to form? His limbs were in proportion, and I had selected his features as beautiful. Beautiful!—Great God! His yellow skin scarcely covered the work of muscles and arteries beneath; his hair was of a lustrous black, and flowing; his teeth of a pearly whiteness; but these luxuriances only formed a more horrid contrast with his watery eyes, that seemed almost of the same color as the dun white sockets in which they were set, his shriveled complexion and straight black lips.

The different accidents of life are not so changeable as the feelings of human nature. I had worked hard for nearly two years, for the sole purpose of infusing life into an inanimate body. For this I had deprived myself of rest and health. I had desired it with an ardor that far exceeded moderation; but now that I had finished, the beauty of the dream vanished, and breathless horror and disgust filled my heart. Unable to endure the aspect of the being I had created, I rushed out of the room, and continued a long time traversing my bedchamber, unable to compose my mind to sleep. At length lassitude succeeded to the tumult I had before endured; and I threw myself on the bed in my clothes, endeavoring to seek a few moments of forgetfulness. But it was in vain: I slept, indeed, but I was disturbed by the wildest dreams. I thought I saw Elizabeth, in the bloom of health, walking in the streets of Ingolstadt. Delighted and surprised, I embraced her; but as I imprinted the first kiss on her lips, they became livid with the hue of death; her features appeared to change, and I thought that I held the corpse of my dead mother in my arms; a shroud enveloped her form, and I saw the graveworms crawling in the folds of the flannel. I started from my sleep with horror; a cold dew covered my forehead, my teeth chattered, and every limb became convulsed: when, by the dim and yellow light of the moon, as it forced its way through the window shutters, I beheld the wretch—the miserable monster whom I had created. He held up the curtain of the bed; and his eyes, if eyes they may be called, were fixed on me. His jaws opened, and he muttered some inarticulate sound, while a grin wrinkled his cheeks. He might have spoken, but I did not hear; one hand was stretched out, seemingly to detain me, but I escaped, and rushed down stairs. I took refuge in the courtyard belonging to the house which I inhabited; where I remained during the rest of the night, walking up and down in the greatest agitation, listening attentively, catching and fearing each sound as if it were to announce the approach of the demoniacal corpse to which I had so miserably given life.

from Frankenstein, pp. 56–57.

Fashioning a Soul
Isabelle Eberhardt, French-Moroccan adventurer, 1877–1904

Geneva, Wednesday 27 June 1900

I would like to go to Ouargla, settle there and *make a home, something I miss more and more*. A little mud house close to some date palms, a place to cultivate the odd vegetable in the oasis, a servant and companion, a few small animals to warm my lonely heart, a horse perhaps, and books as well.

Lead two lives, one that is full of adventure and belongs to the Desert, and one, calm and restful, devoted to thought and far from all that might interfere with it.

I should also want to travel now and then, to visit Augustin, and go to Paris, only to return to my solitary, silent retreat.

Fashion a soul for myself out there, an awareness, an intelligence and a will.

I have no doubt that my attraction to the Islamic faith would blossom magnificently over there.

Should anyone happen to take the trouble to read this diary one day, it would be a faithful mirror of the fast pace of my life which, for all I know, may already be in its final stages.

from The Passionate Nomad: The Diary of Isabelle Eberhardt,
translated by Nina de Voogd, p. 11.

The Soul of the Work
Ferndand Pouillon, French architect and author

Courage lies in being oneself, in showing complete independence, in loving what one loves, in discovering the deep roots of one's feelings.

Creation happens when boldness is released at the very moment that something brilliant is done. Timidity produces nothing of value, and the timid are legion. They think of themselves, of other people, and of what people might say. They wonder if they are sufficiently original or sufficiently with the trend. They do not do what they like. The pusillanimous creator with a critical eye says:

"No, that's not enough," or "No, that's too much." That "too much," that "not enough" has to satisfy and flatter and *be* the soul of the work; it is a great deal to ask of it. Drawing with the right hand and holding back with the left, keeping an eye on one's own eye—that's too many eyes. Courage lies in being oneself, in showing complete independence, in loving what one loves, in discovering the deep roots of one's feelings. A work must not be a copy, one of a group, but unique, sound and untainted, springing from the heart, the intelligence, the sensibility. A real work is truth, direct and honest. It is simply a declaration of one's knowledge to the world. In architecture, the only guides are craftsmanship and experience; all the rest is instinct, spontaneity, decision, the release of all one's accumulated energy. Never is one's courage courageous enough, never is one's sincerity sincere enough nor one's frankness frank enough. You have to take the greatest possible risks; even recklessness seems a bit halfhearted. The best works are those that are at the limits of real life; they stand out among a thousand others when they prompt the remark: "What courage that must have taken!" Enduring work follows from a leap into the void, into unknown territory, icy water or murderous rock.

from *The Stones of the Abbey,*
translated by Edward Gillot, p. 80.

Journal of a Solitude
May Sarton, American novelist and poet

Once more poetry is for me the soul-making tool. Perhaps I am learning at last to let go, and that is what this resurgence of poetry is all about.

October 8th
I don't know whether the inward work is achieving something or whether it is simply the autumn light, but I begin to see my way again, which means to resume *myself.* This morning two small miracles took place. When, still in bed, I looked out of my window (it is a soft misty morning), it happened that "light was on half the rock" out in the meadow. I understand now why that line of Gogarty's has haunted me for years, for when I saw light on half that granite boulder, I felt a stab of pure joy. Later on when I was wandering around watering flowers, I was stopped at the threshold of my study by a ray on a Korean chrysanthemum, lighting it up like a spotlight, deep red petals and Chinese yellow center, glowing, while the lavender aster back of it was in shadow with a

salmon-pink spray of peony leaves and the barberry Eleanor picked
for me. Seeing it was like getting a transfusion of autumn light
right to the vein.

Arnold came to begin work on a new barn floor. It is all rot
under the big boards and going to be a more expensive job than we
thought at first, but that is the way it always is.

Yesterday Anne and I had two beautiful excursions, the first to
the Ledges where there are still fringed gentians in the field. That
vivid blue standing up in the cut stubble is extravagantly exciting.
I can never quite believe the gentians will be there and for a time
we couldn't see one; but as we walked on, they began to appear,
one by one, three or four flowers on a stem. Afterward we sat for
a while by Silver Lake, perfectly still, a mirror with the mountain
like a pale blue ghost at the end, light through the brilliant red
rock maple. Perfect peace.

I never see Anne without learning something I didn't know.
There are still monarch butterflies floating about. We looked long
at one, the slow pulse, as it sucked sweetness from an autumn crocus here in the garden. Anne told me the monarchs are migrating
now to Brazil. Is it Brazil? Anyway, thousands of miles to the
south.

She brought two paintings—one an illustration of my sonnet
"The Light Years," the other the conjunction of red shirley poppies
greatly enlarged, with one of the ancient slate gravestones from
our cemetery. Memento Mori in the midst of our fragile lives, the
poppy's. Anne is using a flat technique and the danger, of course,
is that the painting may end by being merely "decorative," without
nuance. But this one seems to me successful. Anne's genius is in
this kind of poetic synthesis, a vision of things as they are.

Once more poetry is for me the soul-making tool. Perhaps I am
learning at last to let go, and that is what this resurgence of poetry
is all about.

October 9th

Has it really happened at last? I feel released from the rack, set
free, in touch with the deep source that is only *good,* where poetry
lives. We have waited long this year for the glory, but suddenly the
big maple is all gold and the beeches yellow with a touch of green
that makes the yellow even more intense. There are still nastur-
tiums to be picked, and now I must get seriously to work to get the
remaining bulbs in.

It has been stupidly difficult to let go, but that is what has been
needed. I had allowed myself to get overanxious, clutching at what
seemed sure to pass, and clutching is the surest way to murder

love, as if it were a kitten, not to be squeezed so hard, or a flower to fade in a tight hand. Letting go, I have come back yesterday and today to a sense of my life here in all its riches, depth, freedom for soul making.

It's a real break-through. I have not written in sonnet form for a long time, but at every major crisis in my life when I reach a point of clarification, where pain is transcended by the quality of the experience itself, sonnets come. Whole lines run through my head and I cannot *stop* writing until whatever it is gets said.

Found three huge mushrooms when I went out before breakfast to fill the bird feeder. So far only jays come, but the word will get around.

from *Journal of a Solitude*, pp. 35–37.

Farming the Soul
Robert Bly, American poet and translator

The soul truth assures the young man or woman that if not rich, he or she is still in touch with truth; that his inheritance comes not from his immediate parents but from his equals thousands of generations ago.

Thoreau was sure that we could have an original love affair with the universe, but only if we decline to marry the world, and he suspected that the divine man is the man uncontrolled by social obligation. He believed that the young man or young woman should give up tending the machine of civilization and instead farm the soul. We can sense the boundaries of our soul, whose stakes are set thousands of miles out in space, only if we disintegrate property boundaries here on earth. When we fight for the soul and its life, we receive as reward not fame, not wages, not friends, but what is already in the soul, a freshness that no one can destroy, that animals and trees share.

The most important word is *soul*. All of the ideas referred to above are really a single idea, one massive truth, and we can call that truth the Truth of Concord, the Green Mountain Truth, the truth believed in the Bronze Age, the truth of the soul's interior abundance.

To many Americans in the generation of the 1840s it felt as if the United States had fallen into mesmeric attention to external forces, and a shameless obedience to them. The swift development of the Northeast, with its numerous factories, its urban workshops for immigrants, its network of free-acting capitalists, its centralized industry, showed that external forces can and do overwhelm forces of soul and conscience, changing everyone's life for the worse. To many in New England it felt as if some sort of Village King had been killed; the ancient, grounded religious way was passing; a new dispensation had arrived. The sovereign of the new administration was not a king or a human being, but what Blake called "a ratio of numbers," and this ominous, bodiless king lived in the next country, the next state, the next planet. Living under the power of a bodiless king is a bad way to live. . . .

The direction could not be clearer. We don't expect this man [Emerson] to urge the establishment of vocational schools, or to praise the trickle-down philosophy of heavy industry, or to believe that amassing wealth is evidence of divine favor. These words move toward the soul, not toward manipulation of matter, and when we have arrived within the soul the motion is not lateral, but downward and upward:

"Standing on the bare ground,—my head bathed by the blithe air and uplifted into infinite space,—all mean egotism vanishes. I become a transparent eyeball. ("Nature")

The metaphor, though well known, remains astonishing: the transparent eyeball. The emphasis on transparency tells us that Emerson does not intend to occupy the castle of sorrow and the kingdom of melancholy, nor to descend into the dungeon of the body, but that he wants to recruit an army for a charge into the infinite, desperate as the Light Brigade's. He wants inside him an army disciplined, ascetic, single-minded; an army with few baggage trains, living in floorless tents on dried food. His quest will be to marry nature for vision, rather than for possession. His aim is not to live more but to see more. . . .

Many young men and women want to marry nature for vision, not possession. Some, having accomplished by their late twenties no deed worth praise, feel insignificant and scorned. The world scorns football players who make no yardage, writers who do not publish, fishermen who catch no fish. But the soul truth, which young people, when lucky, pick up from somewhere—perhaps in Emerson's phrasing, perhaps in someone else's—sustains them. If the world doesn't feed them, they receive some nourishment from this truth. The substance of the truth goes to their paws, and they live through the winter of scorn and despicability in the way hibernating bears were once thought to live, by sucking their own paws.

The soul truth assures the young man or woman that if not rich, he or she is still in touch with truth; that his inheritance comes not from his immediate parents but from his equals thousands of generations ago; that the door to the soul is unlocked; that he does not need to please the doorkeeper, but that the door in front of him is his, and intended for him, and the doorkeeper obeys when spoken to. It implies that nature is not below the divine, but is itself divine, "perpetual youth." Most important of all, the soul truth assures the young man or woman that despite the Industrial Revolution certain things are as they have always been, and that in human growth the road of development goes through nature, not around it.

I think one reason the Thoreau-Melville-Hawthorne generation wrote so much great literature is that this fundamental soul truth, well phrased by Emerson, Horace Bushnell, and other writers, and untainted yet by mockery, came through freshly to mind and body.

from *The Winged Life: The Poetic Voice of Henry David Thoreau,*
pp. 3–4.

Soul and the Art of Memory
Francis A. Yates, English historian

The soul's remarkable power for remembering things is proof of its divinity.

Cicero was not only the most important figure in the transfer of Greek rhetoric to the Latin world; but was also probably more important than anyone else in the popularizing of Platonic philosophy. In the *Tusculan Disputations,* one of the works written after his retirement with the object of spreading the knowledge of Greek philosophy among his countrymen, Cicero takes up the Platonic and Pythagorean position that the soul is immortal and of divine origin. A proof of this is the soul's possession of memory "which Plato wishes to make the recollection of a previous life." After proclaiming at length his absolute adherence to the Platonic view of memory, Cicero's thought runs towards those who have been famous for their powers of memory:

> For my part I wonder at memory in a still greater degree. For what is it, or what is its origin? I am not inquiring into the powers of memory which it is said, Simonides possessed, or Theodectes, or the powers of Cineas, whom Pyrrhus sent as ambassador to the Senate, or the powers in recent days of the average memory of man, and chiefly of those who are engaged in some higher branch of study and art, whose mental capacity it is hard to estimate, so much do they remember.

He then examines the non-Platonic psychologies of memory, Aristotelian and Stoic, concluding that they do not account for the prodigious powers of the soul in memory. Next, he asks what is the power in man which results in all his discoveries and inventions, which he enumerates; the man who first assigned a name to everything; the man who first united the scattered human units and formed them into social life; the man who invented written characters to represent the sounds of the voice in language; the man who marked down the paths of the wandering stars. Earlier still, there were "the men who discovered the fruits of the earth, dwellings, and ordered way of life, protection against wild creatures—men under whose civilizing and refining influence we have gradually passed on from the indispensable handicrafts to the finer arts." To the art, for example, of music and its "due combinations of musical sounds." And to the discovery of the revolution of the heavens, such as Archimedes made when he "fastened on a globe the movements of moon, sun, and five wandering stars." Then there are still more famous fields of labor; poetry, eloquence, philosophy.

> A power able to bring about such a number of important results is to my mind wholly divine. For what is memory of things and words? What further is invention? (*Quid est enim memoria rerum et verborum? Quid porro inventio?*) Assuredly nothing can be apprehended even in God of greater value than this . . . Therefore the soul is, as I say, divine, as Euripides dares say, God. . . .

Memory for things; memory for words! It is surely significant that the technical terms of the artificial memory come into the orator's mind when, as philosopher, he is proving the divinity of the soul. That proof falls under the heads of the parts of rhetoric, *memoria* and *inventio*. The soul's remarkable power of remembering things and words is a proof of its divinity; so also is its power of invention, not now in the sense of inventing the arguments or things of a speech, but in the general sense of invention or discovery. The things over which Cicero ranges as inventions represent a history of human civilization from the most primitive to the most highly developed ages. (The ability to do this would be in itself evidence of the power of memory; in the rhetorical theory, the things invented are stored in the treasure house of memory.) Thus *memoria* and *inventio* in the sense in which they are used in the *Tusculan Disputations* are transposed from parts of rhetoric into divisions under which the divinity of the soul is proved, in accordance with the Platonic presuppositions of the orator's philosophy.

In this work, Cicero probably has in mind the perfect orator as defined by his master Plato in the *Phaedrus*, the orator who knows the truth and knows the nature of the soul, and so is able to persuade souls of the truth. Or we may say that the Roman orator when he thinks of the divine powers of memory cannot but also be reminded of the orator's trained memory, with its vast and roomy architecture of places on which the images of things and words are stored. The orator's memory, rigidly trained for his practical purposes, has become the Platonic philosopher's memory in which he finds his evidence of the divinity and immortality of the soul.

from *The Art of Memory*, pp. 44–46.

The Soul of Poetry and Painting
Gaston Bachelard, French philosopher, 1884–1962

The dialectics of inspiration and talent become clear if we consider their two poles: soul and mind.

The poet, in the novelty of his images, is always the origin of language. To specify exactly what a phenomenology of the image can be, to specify that the image comes *before* thought, we should have to say that poetry, rather than being a phenomenology of the mind, is a phenomenology of the soul. We should then have to collect documentation on the subject of the *dreaming consciousness*.

The language of contemporary French philosophy—and even more so, psychology—hardly uses the dual meaning of the words soul and mind. As a result, they are both somewhat deaf to certain themes that are very numerous in German philosophy, in which the distinction between mind and soul (*der Geist und die Seele*) is so clear. But since a philosophy of poetry must be given the entire force of the vocabulary, it should not simplify, not harden anything. For such a philosophy, mind and soul are not synonymous, and by taking them as such, we bar translation of certain invaluable texts, we distort documents brought to light thanks to the archeologists of the image. The word "soul" is an immortal word. In certain poems it cannot be effaced, for it is a word born of our breath. The vocal importance alone of a word should arrest the attention of a phenomenologist of poetry. The word "soul" can, in fact, be poetically spoken with such conviction that it constitutes a commitment for the entire poem. The poetic register that corresponds to the soul must therefore remain open to our phenomenological investigations.

In the domain of painting, in which realization seems to imply decisions that derive from the mind, and rejoin obligations of the world of perception, the phenomenology of the soul can reveal the first commitment of an oeuvre. René Huyghe, in his very fine preface for the exhibition of Georges Roualt's works in Albi, wrote, "If we wanted to find out wherein Roualt explodes definitions . . . we should perhaps have to call upon a word that has become rather outmoded, which is the word, 'soul.'" He goes on to show that in order to understand, to sense and to love Roualt's work, we must "start from the center, at the very heart of the circle from where the whole thing derives its source and meaning: and here we come back again to that forgotten, outcast word, the soul." Indeed, the soul—as Roualt's painting proves—possesses an inner light, the light that an inner vision knows and expresses in the world of brilliant colors, in the world of sunlight, so that a veritable reversal of psychological perspectives is demanded of those who seek to understand, at the same time that they love Roualt's painting. They must participate in an inner light which is not a reflection of a light from the outside world. No doubt there are many facile claims to the expressions "inner vision" and "inner light." But here it is a painter speaking, a producer of lights. He knows from what heat source the light comes. He experiences the intimate meaning of the passion for red. At the core of such painting, there is a soul in combat—the fauvism, the wildness, is interior. Painting like this is therefore a phenomenon of the soul. The oeuvre must redeem an impassioned soul.

These pages by René Huyghe corroborate my idea that it is reasonable to speak of a phenomenology of the soul. In many circumstances we are obliged to acknowledge that poetry is a commitment of the soul. A consciousness associated with the soul is more relaxed, less intentionalized, than a consciousness associated with the phenomena of the mind. Forces are manifested in poems that do not pass through the circuits of knowledge. The dialectics of inspiration and talent become clear if we consider their two poles: the soul and the mind. In my opinion, soul and mind are indispensable for studying the phenomena of the poetic image in their various nuances, above all, for following the evolution of poetic images from the original state of reverie to that of execution. [In fact, in a future work, I plan to concentrate particularly on poetic reverie as a phenomenology of the soul.] In itself, reverie constitutes a psychic condition that is too frequently confused with dream. But when it is a question of poetic reverie, of reverie that derives pleasure not only from itself, but also prepares poetic pleasure for other souls, one realizes that one is no longer drifting into somnolence. The mind is able to relax, but in poetic reverie the soul keeps watch, with no tension, calmed and active. To compose a finished, well-constructed poem, the mind is obliged to make projects that prefigure it. But for a simple poetic image, there is no project; a flicker of the soul is all that is needed.

And this is how a poet poses the phenomenological problem of the soul in all clarity. Pierre-Jean Jouve writes: "Poetry is a soul inaugurating a form." The soul inaugurates. Here it is the supreme power. It is human dignity. Even if the "form" was already well known, previously discovered, carved from "commonplaces," before the interior poetic light was turned upon it, it was a mere object for the mind. But the soul comes and inaugurates the form, dwells in it, takes pleasure in it. Pierre-Jean Jouve's statement can therefore be taken as a clear maxim of a phenomenology of the soul.

from *Poetics of Space*,
translated by Maria Jolas, pp. xv–xviii.

On the Vibration of Art in the Soul
Wassily Kandinsky, Russian artist, 1866–1944

There is nothing on earth so curious for beauty or so absorbent of it, as a soul.

Generally speaking, colour is a power which directly influences the soul. Colour is the keyboard, the eyes are the hammers, the soul is the piano with many strings. The artist is the hand which plays, touching one key or another, to cause vibrations in the soul.

It is evident therefore that colour harmony must rest only on a corresponding vibration in the human soul; and this is one of the guiding principles of the inner need . . .

Painting is an art, and art is not vague production, transitory and isolated, but a power which must be directed to the improvement and refinement of the human soul—to, in fact, the raising of the spiritual triangle.

If art refrains from doing this work, a chasm remains unbridged, for no other power can take the place of art in this activity. And at times when the human soul is gaining greater strength, art will also grow in power, for the two are inextricably connected and complementary one to the other. Conversely, at those times when the soul tends to be choked by material disbelief, art becomes purposeless and talk is heard that art exists for art's sake alone. Then is the bond between art and the soul, as it were, drugged into unconsciousness. The artist and the spectator drift apart, till finally the latter turns his back on the former or regards him as a juggler whose skill and dexterity are worthy of applause. It is very important for the artist to gauge his position aright, to realize that he has a duty to his art and to himself, that he is not king of the castle but rather a servant of a nobler purpose. He must search deeply into his own soul, develop and tend it, so that his art has something to clothe, and does not remain a glove without a hand.

The artist must have something to say, for mastery over form is not his goal but rather the adapting of form to its inner meaning.

The artist is not born to a life of pleasure. He must not live idle; he has a hard work to perform, and one which often proves a cross to be borne. He must realize that his every deed, feeling, and thought are raw but sure material from which his work is to arise, that he is free in art but not in life.

The artist has a triple responsibility to the nonartist: (1) He must repay the talent which he has. (2) His deeds, feelings, and thoughts, as those of every man, create a spiritual atmosphere which is either pure or poisonous. (3) These deeds and thoughts are materials for his creations, which themselves exercise influence on the spiritual atmosphere. The artist is not only a king, as Peladan says, because he has great power, but also because he has great duties.

If the artist be priest of beauty, nevertheless this beauty is to be sought only according to the principle of the inner need, and can be measured only according to the size and intensity of that need.

That is beautiful which is produced by the inner need, which springs from the soul.

Maeterlinck, one of the first warriors, one of the first modern artists of the soul, says: "There is nothing on earth so curious for beauty or so absorbent of it, as a soul. For that reason few mortal souls withstand the leadership of a soul which gives them beauty."

And this property of the soul is the oil, which facilitates the slow, scarcely visible but irresistible movement of the triangle, onwards and upwards.

from *Concerning the Spiritual in Art*,
translated by M. T. H. Sadler, pp. 25–26, 54–55.

Story as Soul-Journey
Paul Zweig, American author, 1935–1984

In short, the soul-journey resembles very much the sort of adventure one encounters in folklore and myth. According to archaic view, all men apparently had the chance to become a sort of Odysseus, whether they liked it or not.

When someone is "ravished" by a strong emotion, or is absorbed in a story, or daydreams "absentmindedly," it seems as if that person were no longer here. A hole has gaped open in the continuum of the visible reality. When he returns, our idiomatic speech asks the right question: Where you have been? The shaman answers this question when he wakes up from his ecstatic trance, by telling the story of his visit to the spirit world. To be "absent" is to be in some other place: *dans la lune,* perhaps, as the French say, or in some aimless nook of time, as when we say "the mind wanders." Apparently the two meanings of "transport" are not as contradictory as they seemed. Both refer to modes of traveling, both describe ways of getting elsewhere.

But where is elsewhere in the case of storytelling? Is it the same as the elsewhere of daydreams, or trance? Do transports of emotion take one to the same place? Is "tripping" with drugs a way of getting there, too? Another more difficult question suggests itself: Does the adventurer, by extravagantly different means, travel to the same elsewhere?

In short, the soul-journey resembles very much the sort of adventure one encounters in folklore and myth. According to the archaic view, all men apparently had the chance to become a sort of Odysseus, whether they liked it or not.

Two remarks are called for at this point. Soul-loss or the soul-journey unites in a remarkable way the experience of physical adventure and that of psychic adventure. It establishes between them a relationship in which the adventure story is called upon to describe the experience of a "soul" unstuck from its attachments to conventional reality. For modern readers this is a familiar connection. Since the early nineteenth century, we have learned to respond to the ramifications of "inward" adventure. Romantic and modern literature have supplied a variety of idioms to describe the spirit plunging into its own depths: reviving the older conventions of dream narrative, as in Gerard de Nerval's *Aurelia;* ransacking the language of insanity for literary effect; adapting themes from mythology, as in Joyce's *Ulysses*. The Romantic view of the artist as hero reflects our sense of the encounters sustained by the artist in the secrecy of his mind, to bring "home" the forms of artistic truth.

Such inward traveling was perfectly understood by archaic cultures, with this difference: The reality of the trip, and the realism of the tale it gave rise to, were unquestioned. The soul-journey, and the central importance of the stories told about it, expressed a belief that the principal reality was to be found in the meanders of the invisible world. The mysterious ground of life itself could be known only by the traveler.

A resemblance exists between the adventurer exploring the countries of the marvelous and the "absent" one: each finds his way to the "other" world and returns to tell the story. For each, the story is what he brings back; it is all he brings back, suggesting an essential connection between adventure and storytelling: a connection which becomes all the more complex, if we recognize the "transport" of the listener, the self-abandonment which it is the story's business to create, as a form of soul-journey. By entering the story, the listener not only allows himself to be transported into a particular narrative, he crosses the elusive barrier which divides the worlds. He makes a controlled excursion into the "elsewhere" of life itself.

from *The Adventurer*, pp. 85–89.

Cultivating the Soul
Thomas Moore, American psychologist

Everyone should know that you can't live in any other way than by cultivating the soul.

Care of the soul speaks to the longings we feel and to the symptoms that drive us crazy, but it is not a path away from shadow or death. A soulful personality is complicated, multifaceted, and shaped by both pain and pleasure, success and failure. Life lived soulfully is not without its moments of darkness and periods of foolishness. Dropping the salvational fantasy frees us up to the possibility of self-knowledge and self-acceptance which are the very ground of soul.

Several classical phrases describing care of the soul are relevant in the modern world. Plato used the expression *techne tou biou*, which means "the craft of life." When *techne* is defined with sufficient depth, it refers not just to mechanical skills and instruments but to all kinds of artful managing and careful shaping. For now, we can say that care of the soul requires a special crafting of life itself, with an artist's sensitivity to the way things are done. Soul doesn't pour into life automatically. It requires our skill and attention . . .

The later Roman writer Apuleius said, "Everyone should know that you can't live in any other way than by cultivating the soul." Care can also mean cultivation, watching, and participating as the seed of soul unfolds into the vast creation we call character or personality, with a history, a community, a language, and a unique mythology. Cultivation of the soul implies a lifelong husbanding of raw materials. Farmers cultivate their fields, all of us cultivate our souls. The aim of soul work, therefore, is not adjustment to accepted norms or to an image of the statistically healthy individual. Rather, the goal is a richly elaborated life, connected to society and nature, woven into the culture of family, nation, and globe. The idea is not to be superficially adjusted, but to be profoundly connected in the heart to ancestors and to living brothers and sisters in all the many communities that claim our hearts . . .

. . . Soul is nothing like ego. Soul is closely connected to fate, and the turns of fate almost always go counter to the expectations and often to the desires of the ego. Even the Jungian idea of Self, carefully defined as a blend of conscious understanding and unconscious influences, is still too personal and too human in contrast to the idea of soul. Soul is the font of who we are, and yet it is far beyond our capacity to devise and control. We can cultivate, tend, enjoy, and participate in the things of the soul, but we can't outwit it or manage it or shape it to the designs of a willful ego.

Care of the soul is inspiring. I like to think that it was the theology of soul worked out so painstakingly and so concretely in Renaissance Italy that gave rise to the extraordinary art of that period. The act of entering into the mysteries of the soul, without sentimentality or pessimism, encourages life to blossom forth according to its own designs and with its own unpredictable beauty. Care of the soul is not a solving of the puzzle of life; quite the opposite, it is an appreciation of the paradoxical mysteries that blend light and darkness into the grandeur of what human life and culture can be . . .

Let us imagine care of the soul, then, as an application of poetics to everyday life. What we want to do here is to re-imagine those things we think we already understand . . .

from Care of the Soul, pp. 5–8.

Stretching Our Souls

Alan Jones, American author and dean of Grace Cathedral in San Francisco

When we begin working on our own souls, we discover that we are not self-made. Our identity depends on Another. We cannot make ourselves . . . but fortunately a wild card has been announced. . . .

The making of a soul, which is another way of talking about learning what love is, requiring what the poet John Keats called "Negative Capability . . . that is, when a man is capable of being in uncertainties, mysteries, doubts, without any irritable reaching after fact and reason." Playing cards with God requires the grace of negative capability. Without it, there would be no room for the unpredictable, the unexpected. There would be no room for love (the wild card); no room for the soul. The development of the gift of negative capability is difficult and painful. Yet without the nourishment provided by the ability to rest in uncertainties, mysteries, and doubts, the soul begins to starve. . . .

. . . Here is the basic paradox of soul making: In order for me to be myself, I need to be able to be alone; in order to be myself, I need to be with others. The question is, how can I be at one with another and yet remain myself? How can we be truly formed into a community without our swallowing or dominating one another? All questions concerning the making of a soul revolve around issues of identity (that's *me*) and unity (that's *you*).

When we begin working on our own souls, we discover that we are not self-made. Our identity depends on Another. We cannot make ourselves . . . but fortunately a wild card has been announced, only we were too preoccupied to notice it. In the end, the making of a soul, like love, requires a miracle, and the appropriation of miracles requires faith; and faith leads us back into the muddy question of "God" and all that nonsense that often surrounds that word. But I am ahead of myself. Let us look more closely at the "wild card."

Most of us have something of the romantic in us. As we grow older, skepticism and even cynicism take over; but it must be a mean and dried-up spirit who has not at least the dregs of some romance in his or her soul. We long for love. No one seems to be able to get enough of it. We are all deprived to some degree, and when we cannot get what we need we try neurotic solutions to the soul's craving.

Religion is often made into a comprehensive neurotic solution. There are those who think that they love God because they don't love anyone else. This seems to be an occupational hazard for religious people. Loving is hard and perilous, and there are many counterfeits. Part of soul making involves the willingness to sort out the true from the false and to face those inner cravings for control, security, and affection, that masquerade for love. . . .

Soul making, then, has something to do with paying attention to the Things Invisible, things which do not lend themselves to manipulation and control. Things which contribute to the making of a soul will not succumb to being treated as problems to be solved. If we are concerned about those neurotic and destructive forces that try to abort the soul (often associated with mere problem solving), we will have to switch our whole style of thinking away from an overdeveloped analytical one to one that is more contemplative, more concerned for the Invisible Things. Soul making requires a move away from the need and desire to control to a waiting on the mystery at the heart of things. Negative capability is the key. It means cultivating a readiness for wonder and being ready for the special kind of pain that contemplative availability to reality always brings.

The kind of special wisdom for soul making is not "out there" to be had. The wisdom of the saints and mystics comes to us only after we have placed ourselves in a position of waiting and receptivity. This wisdom is what the medieval theologians called "connatural knowledge": a kind of knowing that is not so much intellectual as interior and intuitive. For example, to know what holiness really is, one must (in some small sense) *be* holy. To know what love really is one must have some experience of it.

This isn't to say that one must have some experience of it in order to know about these things. The seeds of holiness and love have to be there; or, better, the longing for them must be acknowledged if the soul is to grow. Longing and desire play a great part in soul making. It is as if God has deliberately put unfulfilled desires into our hearts so that our hearts may be stretched beyond their present capacity. Soul making requires this kind of stretching. It is not enough to know *about* soul making, although there are some who like to dabble in a kind of psychic horticulture. It should be clear by now that such dabbling is merely a device to avoid the genuine birth of the soul. It is an invidious form of resistance to the very life for which the soul longs.

We become more and more who we are (that, after all, is another way of talking about soul making) when we struggle with the "four last things," the Things Invisible: love, death, power, and time. To be a soul (to be fully nature and alive as a person) is to struggle in hope with love, because we know that at our deepest we are loved. To be a soul is to know what it is to be a terminal case—to have come to terms, however minimally, with the fact that we are going to die. To be a soul means to know what it is to struggle for, to achieve, and to be denied power. To be a soul is to live in time, with all its opportunities and limitations. Our life is a story that slowly unfolds in time. . . .

from *Soul Making: The Desert Way of Spirituality,*
pp. 130–32, 135–36.

What Is Soul Music?

Peter Guralnick, American journalist

Over and over again the soul singer, like his gospel counterpart, begs for complicity. "Let me hear you say yeah," he implores, taking directly from the church. "There's just one more thing I want to say," he declares, just waiting to be invited to say it. "Can I get a witness?"

This is what I mean today when I am talking about soul music. Soul music is Southern by definition if not by actual geography. Like the blues, jazz, and rock 'n' roll, both its birth and inspiration stem from the South, so that while Solomon Burke, one of the very greatest of soul singers, is a native of Philadelphia, and Garnet Mimms, a little appreciated but nearly equally talented vocalist, made many of his recordings there, the clear inspiration for the styles of both is the Southern revivalism that fueled such diverse figures as Elvis Presley and Hank Williams on the one hand, Little Richard and Ray Charles on the other. I do believe there's a regional philosophy involved here, too, whether it's the agrarian spirit cited by Jerry Wexler ("There was always this attitude, 'Oh, man, we're gonna lose our soul if we do that. We're not gonna let machinery kill our natural Southern thing.'"), or simply the idea that Dan Penn, the renegade white hero of this book, has frequently expressed: "People down here don't let nobody tell them what to do." Unquestionably the racial turmoil of the South was a factor, and the rapid social upheaval which it foreshadowed; in fact, the whole tangled racial history of the region, the intimate terms on which it lived with its passions and contradictions, played a decisive role in the forging of a new culture, one which the North's polite lip service to liberalism could never have achieved. Ultimately soul music derives, I believe, from the Southern dream of freedom.

It is not, however (contrary to most received opinion), a music of uninhibited emotional release—though at times it comes close. What it offers, rather, is something akin to the "knowledgeable apprehension," in Alfred Hitchcock's famous definition of suspense, that precedes the actual climax, that everyone knows is coming— it's just nobody is quite sure when. Soul music is a music that keeps hinting at a conclusion, keeps straining at the boundaries— of melody and convention—that it has imposed upon itself. That is where it is to be differentiated from the let-it-all-hang-out rock 'n' roll of a cheerful charismatic like Little Richard, who for all the brilliance of his singing and the subtleties of which he is capable, basically hits the ground running and accelerates from there. It is to be differentiated, too, from the cultural refinements of Motown, which, with equal claim to inspiration from the church, rarely uncorks a full-blooded scream, generally establishes the tension without ever really letting go, and only occasionally will reveal a flash of raw emotion. This is not because Motown singers were not equally talented or equally capable of revealing their true feelings; it is simply that Motown was an industry aimed specifically at reaching the white market, and every aspect of that industry was controlled, from the grooming and diction of its stars to the subtlest interpolations on its records. Southern soul music, on the other hand, was a haven for free-lancers and individualists. It was a musical mode in which the band might be out of tune, the drummer out of time, the singer off-key, and yet the message could still come across—since underlying feeling was all. Feeling dictated the rhythm, feeling dictated the pace; that is why soul remains to this day so idiosyncratic a domain. One of the most common fallacies of a postapocalyptic age such as ours is that there is no room for anything *but* the dramatic gesture; modulation is something as unheard-of as self-restraint. Soul music, which might in one sense be considered a herald of the new age, knew differently in the 1960s, and among the most surprising aspects of going back and listening to the music today—among its most enduring qualities— are the quiet moments at the center, the moments of stillness where action stops and "knowledgeable" anticipation takes over. Think of the great screams you've heard from everyone from James Brown to Wilson Pickett; think of the fervor of Solomon Burke's or Joe Tex's preaching on subjects as far removed in substance and seriousness as "skinny legs and all" or the price that love can exact. In gospel music, the progenitor of the style, a singer is often described as "worrying" the audience, teasing it, working the crowd until it is on the verge of exploding, until strong men faint and women start speaking in tongues. This is commonly referred to as "house wrecking." In soul music, perhaps the last of the great vocal arts, there is this same sense of dramatic structure, even if the message does not always provide the same unambiguous release. "I feel like I want to scream," James Brown announces over and over again, borrowing an age-old gospel technique. "I feel so good I want to scream," he declares testing the limits to which the tension can be extended and in one famous recorded passage going past them as a voice from the crowd yells back, "James, you're an asshole." Over and over again the soul singer, like his gospel counterpart, begs for complicity. "Let me hear you say yeah," he implores, taking directly from the church. "There's just one more thing I want to say," he declares, just waiting to be invited to say it. "Can I get a witness?" becomes the rhetorical question—secular and ecclesiastical—of the age.

All this is merely testimony to the indisputable bond between technique and feeling. Southern soul music and the church. What is not so readily appreciated, perhaps, is the extent to which soul, once its gospel origins are gotten past, is a self-invented music—not so much in its form (which, like that of every great American folk music, is an amalgam, a hybridization of various strains that have gone before) as in its evolution on record.

from *Sweet Soul Music: Rhythm and Blues and the Southern Dream of Freedom*, pp. 6–8.

PART SIX

THE
WORLD
SOUL

That which oppresses me, is it my soul
trying to come out in the open,
or the soul of the world knocking
at my heart for its entrance?
　　　　　—Rabindranath Tagore

It is only logical that the pauperization of our soul and the soul of society
coincide with the pauperization of the environment. One is the cause and
the reflection of the other.
　　　　　　　　　　　　　—Paolo Soleri

First of all the twinkling stars vibrated, but remained motionless in space,
then all the celestial globes were united into one series of movements. . . .
Firmament and planets both disappeared, but the mighty breath which gives
life to all things and in which all is bound up remained.
　　　　　　　　　　　　　—Vincent Van Gogh

Introduction

When the explorer Robert Byrd wrote his cold bones account of the winter he spent alone at the Bolling Advance Weather Base at the South Pole, he said he needed the time and the solitude and the long white silence to "sink his roots in a replenishing philosophy." What Byrd found in the bitter loneliness of his ordeal was a grueling blend of forced personal contemplation and close observation of the world roaring around him. "Nothing—and yet," he wrote early on in his journal, "there must be countless things to write about, if I had the will to look." Only, after months of what he called the "obs" of both his inner and outer worlds, could he finally say, "This indeed was the world advancing to meet me."

What waits for those who have the will to look? What advances to meet us? Why do our souls need constant replenishing from places, things where one can breathe in the spirit of the world?

A deeper awareness of the sacredness of the world is required of us because, as ecology writer Harold Gilliam has written, "If you don't know *where* you are, you don't know *who* you are." Since we're suffering from a serious overdose of individuality, a stubborn refusal to see soul and spirit anywhere but in ourselves, it can seem more difficult than ever to get our bearings. The ancient view is that we share a common consciousness with nature and that acknowledging the vital forces circulating through the world—and us—allows us to move beyond the imperialism of the exclusively personal soul. "For many people the individual self does not end with the skin," as nature writer Barry Lopez reminds us, people whose experience transcends the exclusive personal soul for experience of the circulating vital force constantly re-creating the world and us.

For Part 6, "The World Soul," I have chosen a number of passages that offer a creative response to this peculiarly modern problem of "people losing the capacity to fathom any nature but their own," as travel writer Edward Hoagland has labeled it. These selections explore a soul wisdom that lies in the conjunction of self-knowledge and world-knowledge, an awareness of the inner qualities of the outer world. For it's not until we hear the world call forth its own soul that we understand that "everything has a secret soul, which is silent more often than it speaks," as the Russian artist Wassily Kandinsky wrote.

What the Greeks called *psyche tou kosmou*, the soul of the universe, and the Neoplatonists *anima mundi*, the soul of the world, the Eskimos called *Sila*, an overarching power that asks us not to be afraid, to be respectful of the spirit, the genius, the intangible forces hidden beneath the surface of all things. To appreciate this poetic truth we must learn to sense what is divine in the world, to use René Dubos's elegant phrase, with what is divine within us: the god within, the eye of the soul.

The reenchantment of the world occurs for some in the encounters of the numinous shadows of sacred groves, canyons, or the remote reaches of the poles, the silencing sanctuaries that heal us; for others it is the realm of the ordinary things of our world as they surround us: the objects in our attics and basements, the animals in our backyards. Still others, like Emerson with his vision of the "Over-Soul," or John Steinbeck, as my Uncle Dave pointed out to me shortly before he died, see the big picture, understand the overview, that we are but part of "one great big soul," as Tom Joad says to Ma near the end of *The Grapes of Wrath*.

In this section I've tried to represent sensibilities that have granted the world a wide spectrum of consciousness, as portrayed by philosophers, cooks, musicians, and even a baseball commissioner. Soul seen with sidelong glances at the secret life force in all things: the building of a stone tower, the hearth, the night sky, fossils, espresso, computer, letters.

A poet from fifteenth-century India, the mystic Kabir, admonishes us to look in our own houses for soul, posing the question of his and every day, "If you can't find it in the world, then where?" For the Melanesians, we learn from a paper by R. H. Codrington, all the world is alive and pulsing. They conceive of the life force common to stones, plants, and chiefs as *mana,* an energy that pervades all of nature, even, as Hawaiian scholar Herb Kane defines it, "the spiritual power that motivates the universe." Barbara Kirksey's wonderful essay on the goddess Hestia is an exploration of the ancient Roman belief in the *focus* (Latin for hearth), the point in the home "where psyche and world meet." Without Hestia, she writes, the deep respect for the home fires, there is no focus, no place for the soul to dream.

Astronomer Chet Raymo focuses on the silent turning of stars, and in the silence to be explored there discovers the soul of the night sky. In a provocative piece from his clarion call of a book, *Facing the World with Soul,* psychologist Robert Sardello reminds us that the ancient seers saw magic in the world. But he makes a careful and useful distinction between animism and what I'd like to call "soulism." Whereas the former is a projection, the latter is a recognition of the actual power of the world soul. Soul is then less a thing or theory than a way of seeing the world through its *qualities* and as a source for true wisdom.

The common human desire to believe in things that last forever is a prime clue to the puzzling need to believe in the soul. In his essay "The Green Fields of the Mind," former baseball commissioner and Yale president A. Bartlett Giamatti nostalgically evokes the soul of a young ballplayer, a challenging illustration of James Joyce's adage that "anything deeply regarded is gateway to the gods." For Giamatti, the game's eternal aspects are "meant to break my heart" because of its ever-alluring promise of an "abiding pattern and impulse" in a world of unpredictable change. Seen this way, the game is engrained in our soul because of its timeless, changeless rituals played out in a "field of dreams."

In an excerpt from their underground classic, *The Secret Life of Plants*, Peter Tompkins and Christopher Bird provide us with the philosophical background from Aristotle to Goethe and Fechner for the belief in the sentience of the botanical world. Their contention is that belief in the biological world's essential vitality affects the possibility of our having any insights into an experience of nature's unified web of forces.

Taking on the question heard in many a boardroom and therapist's office, "How do I stay in business and not lose my soul?" Gary Zukav, in a speech on "Evolution and Business," urges a sense of we "immortal souls learning together that we might help the business world heal rather than exploit the world because it allows individuals to see life wherever they look and revere it where they see it." Speaking of finding soul in unlikely places, in his study of Data General's Eagle Project, *The Soul of a New Machine*, Tracy Kidder takes the reader down into a computer's silicon chips to learn a veritable fable of the industry. Soul is Kidder's metaphor for the attitude, the dedication, the depth of commitment, the "infusing of the self into the machine" that must happen in the building of something that will last if work is to give any sense of meaning to life.

One of the last pieces in this section is an excerpt from *We've Had a Hundred Years of Psychotherapy—And the World's Getting Worse*, the refreshingly irreverent dialogue book between Michael Ventura and James Hillman, where Hillman confesses that he's recently been startled to discover that Keats made a "major mistake" with his sole emphasis on individual soul making. Rather than perpetuating the Romantic fascination with individual soul, which can take soul *out of* the world, what's direly needed, he writes, is to revive the point of view that says we can't separate the soul in me from the soul in other people or the environment. Instead, Hillman reaches for a polytheistic psychology that recognizes soul in everything from doorknobs to beercans as a way of re-specting, re-viewing, re-souling the world. But when in doubt, read Rumi:

> Let the beauty we love be what we do
> There are hundreds of ways to kneel and kiss the ground.

The Hidden Soul
Kabir, fifteenth-century Sufi master

I laugh when I hear that the fish in the water is thirsty.
You don't grasp the fact that what is most alive of all is inside your
*   own house;*
and so you walk from one holy city to the next with a confused look!
Kabir will tell you the truth: go wherever you like, to Calcutta or
*   Tibet,*
if you can't find where your soul is hidden,
for you the world will never be real!

from *The Kabir Book: Forty-Four of the Ecstatic Poems of Kabir,*
translated by Robert Bly, p. 9.

Lure
Orpingalik, Netskilik Eskimo, early twentieth century

Reindeer,
earth-louse,
long-legged,
large-eared,
bristly-neck,
don't run away
from me!
If I kill you,
I will offer
handsome presents
to your soul:
hides for kamiks,
moss for wicks.
Come happily,
towards me!
Come!

from *Eskimo Poems from Canada and Greenland,*
translated by Tom Lowenstein, p. 96.

Hestia: The Soul of the Hearth

Barbara Kirksey, American psychologist

Without Hestia, there can be no focusing on the image, and there are no boundaries to differentiate the intimacy of the inner dwelling and the outer world . . . There can be no joyous feasts, no celebrations of life, no food for the soul. . . .

In order to reflect further on Hestia's psychological significance two unique aspects of her character require elaboration. The first is her peculiar lack of personified images: She resists personification as a humanlike figure. This is not to say that she has no personal quality, rather she resists becoming an object of imagining in a bodily way as occurs with other mythic personae. But when imagined, Hestia appears as the hearth and the contained fire upon it. She is the domestic fire without which there could be no feasts for men, as Homer stated. Hestia appears as a particular aspect of the world which is 'nobody' (without body) but which gathers men together and enables soul to have a place. It is as if when we gather we are in her body and so cannot see her *as* a body; place becomes her body. . . .

Hestia's value in psychological life is her ability to mediate soul by giving a place to congregate, a gathering point. And through this point the psyche and world merge. Hestia allows *spaciality* to be a form of *psychological reality*. The Greeks never forsook this truth for a purely geometric view of space. Spaciality had a divine aspect. According to Rollo May, "We Americans have very little sense of sacredness of space." May quotes De Toqueville as saying, "In the United States, a man builds a house in which to spend his old age, and he sells it before the roof is on. . . ."

But the ancients knew that the circularity of the hearth was the expression of sacred space, in accordance with the nature of a specific goddess. The space echoed the roundness of the earth, but this roundness was domestic and tied to man's cities and homes in a way that nature's circularity was not. It is through the mediumistic presence of Hestia that the abode of man's world is psychological. Imagining, which is the psychological activity *par excellence,* is not severed from the world and retained within an individual body. The imaginal does not equal a literal interior space; and the world, especially the dwelling spaces, reflects back to us an indication of our soul condition. The dwellings we create and in which we abide (interiorly and exteriorly) manifest an aspect of our soul. The "places" of dreams and fantasies, the dwellings—high-rise apartments, old haunted mansions, basements, hallways, and bedrooms—tell us much about where our soul is at the moment. To quote Bachelard, "All great simple images reveal a psychic state. The house, even more than the landscape, is a 'psychic state' and even when reproduced as it appears from the outside, it bespeaks intimacy." The day-world dwellings speak of our soul's place: They reveal an intimate side of one's psyche.

Because the psychology of Hestia is a revisioning of soul in terms of spatial metaphors, the pathology of the soul through Hestia's language contains phrases related to space. "Off-base," "off-center," "unable to find a place," "can't settle down," "spaced out," and "off the wall" are related to Hestian values and remind the wanderer of her power to bring the soul into a space of dwelling. Ever since antiquity, pathology has been fantasized as a "wandering" phenomenon (e.g., delirium, deviate). Cicero proclaimed that a sick soul was one which could not attain or endure and was always astray, The soul, gone astray, is a soul without psychic connection to this goddess and her centeredness. The soul can't come home for there is no place for the homecoming. This specific lack of having a place is not equal to being an abandoned child or to the wanderings of the puer. The child may still find a home and a place to nurse its abandonment within other dwelling places. But the loss of Hestia is a more severe threat to the total psyche with its multitude of images and their influence. Without Hestia, there can be no focusing on the image, and there are no boundaries to differentiate the intimacy of the inner dwelling and the outer world, for there is no psychic house to give protective walls. There can be no joyous feasts, no celebrations of life, no food for the soul. . . .

What is the quality of Hestia's illumination? From the original image of her we gain a clue to her specific lightbringing power. Hestia's illumination is the light from the hearth and its flame. Ovid tells us that the word for hearth in Latin is *focus* and "the hearth (*focus*) is so named from the flames, and because it fosters (*fovet*) all things." Because this word exists unchanged in the English language as it appeared in Latin, a discussion of the usage of this word can amplify the quality of Hestia's guardianship of images. . . .

The word "focus" alludes to a foundational principle of life. Hestia, found as Earth, promotes fantasies of underlying foundational structures and central disturbances. This continues in medical fantasies where the focus of disease is the "principle seat [in the body], also a point where its activity is manifest." (In German, the word *Herd* refers to hearth, as well as to focus and seat of disease.) Whatever is "focal" is also principal, manifest and central. Conversely, when the word "focus" is used, this word hints at the special value of the occasion for soul. . . .

As part of the archetype of the journey home to the hearth, focusing is the experience of and connection to Hestia, builder of the house, so that the soul may dream in peace.

from Facing the Gods,
edited by James Hillman, pp.104–8, 110–12.

The Melanesian Concept of Mana

R. H. Codrington, English anthropologist, 1830–1922

If a stone is found to have a supernatural power, it is because a spirit has associated itself with it . . .

The Melanesian mind is entirely possessed by the belief in a supernatural power or influence, called almost universally *mana*. This is what works to effect everything which is beyond the ordinary power of men, outside the common processes of nature: It is present in the atmosphere of life, attaches itself to persons and things, and is manifested by results which can only be ascribed to its operation. When one has got it he can use it and direct it, but its force may break forth at some new point; the presence of it is ascertained by proof. A man comes by chance upon a stone which takes his fancy; its shape is singular, it is like something, it is certainly not a common stone, there must be some *mana* in it, so he argues with himself, and he puts it to the proof; he lays it at the root of a tree to the fruit of which it has a certain resemblance, or he buries it in the ground when he plants his garden; and abundant crop on the tree or in the garden shows that he is right, the stone is *mana* to other stones. In the same way certain forms of words, generally in the form of a song, have power for certain purposes; a charm of words is called a *mana*. But this power, though itself impersonal, is always connected with some person who directs it; all spirits have it, ghosts generally, some men. If a stone is found to have a supernatural power, it is because a spirit has associated itself with it; a dead man's bone has with it *mana*, because the ghost is with the bone; a man may have so close a connection with a spirit or ghost that he has *mana* in himself also, and can so direct it as to effect what he desires; a charm is powerful because the name of a spirit or ghost or spirit exercises through it. Thus all conspicuous success is a proof that a man has *mana;* his influence depends on the impression made on the people's mind that he has it: He becomes a chief by virtue of it. Hence a man's power, though political or social in its character, is his *mana;* the word is naturally used in accordance with the native conception of the character of all power and influence as supernatural. If a man has been successful in fighting, it has not been his natural strength of arm, quickness of eye, or readiness of resource that has won success; he has certainly got the *mana* of a spirit or of some deceased warrior to empower him, conveyed in an amulet of a stone round his neck, or a tuft of leaves in his belt, in a tooth hung upon a finger of his bow hand, or in the form of words with which he brings supernatural assistance to his side. If a man's pigs multiply, and his gardens are productive, it is not because he is industrious and looks after his property, but because of the stones full of *mana* for pigs and yams that he possesses. Of course a yam naturally grows when planted, that is well known, but it will not be very large unless *mana* comes into play; a canoe will not be swift unless *mana* be brought to bear upon it, a net will not catch many fish, nor an arrow inflict a mortal wound.

from *Essential Sacred Writings from Around the World,*
edited by Mircea Eliade, pp. 194–95.

His Soul Lies Naked in Letters
Samuel Johnson, English man of letters, 1709–1784

Is not my soul laid open in these veracious pages? Do you not see me reduced to my first principles?

October 27, 1777
Dearest Madam [Thrale],
You talk of writing and writing, as if you had all the writing to yourself. If our correspondence were printed, I am sure posterity, for posterity is always the author's favorite, would say that I am a good writer too. To sit down so often with nothing to say: to say something so often, almost without consciousness of saying, and without any remembrance of having said, is a power of which I will not violate my modesty by boasting, but I do not believe everybody has it.

Some, when they write to their friends, are all affection: some wise and contentious: some strain their powers for efforts of gaiety: some write news, and some write secrets: but to make a letter without affection, without wisdom, without gaiety, without news, and without a secret is, doubtless, the great epistolick art.

In a man's letters, you know, Madam, his soul lies naked, his letters are only the mirror of his heart: Whatever passes within him is shown undisguised in its natural process: nothing is inverted, nothing distorted: you see systems in their elements: you discover actions in their motives.

Of this great truth, sounded by the knowing to the ignorant, and so echoed by the ignorant to the knowing, what evidence have you now before you? Is not my soul laid open in these veracious pages? Do you not see me reduced to my first principles? Is not this the pleasure of corresponding with a friend, where doubt and distrust have no place, and everything is said as it is thought? . . . These are the letters by which souls are united, and by which minds naturally in unison move each other as they are moved themselves. I know, dearest Lady, that in the perusal of this, such is the consanguinity of our intellects, you will be touched as I am touched. I have concealed nothing from you, nor do I expect ever to repent of having thus opened my heart. I am, etc.

cited in *A Treasury of the World's Great Letters,*
selected and edited by M. Lincoln Schuster, pp. xvi–xvii.

The Vale of Soul-Making
John Keats, English poet, 1795–1821

Call the world if you Please "The vale of Soul-making" Then you will find out the use of the world . . .

To the George Keatses, 21 April 1819
. . . The most interesting question that can come before us is, How far by the most persevering endeavours of a seldom appearing Socrates Mankind may be made happy – I can imagine such happiness carried to an extreme – but what must it end in? – Death – and who could in such a case bear with death – the whole troubles of life which are now frittered away in a series of years, would the[n] be accumulated for the last days of a being who instead of hailing its approach, would leave this world as Eve left Paradise – But in truth I do not at all believe in this sort of perfectibility – the

nature of the world will not admit of it – the inhabitants of
the world will correspond to itself – Let the fish philosophise
the ice away from the Rivers in winter time and they shall be
at continual play in the tepid delight of summer. Look at the
Poles and at the sands of Africa, Whirlpools and volcanoes –
Let men exterminate them and I will say that they may arrive
at earthly Happiness – The point at which Man may arrive is
as far as the paral[l]el state in inanimate nature and no further – For instance suppose a rose to have sensation, it
blooms on a beautiful morning it enjoys itself – but there
comes a cold wind, a hot sun – it can not escape it, it cannot
destroy its annoyances – they are as native to the world as
itself: no more can man be happy in spite, the world[l]y elements will prey upon his nature – The common cognomen of
this world among the misguided and superstitious is 'a vale
of tears' from which we are to be redeemed by a certain arbi-
trary interposition of God and taken to Heaven – What a little circumscribe[d] straightened notion! Call the world if you
Please "The vale of Soul-making" Then you will find out the
use of the world (I am speaking now in the highest terms for
human nature admitting it be immortal which I will here
take for granted for the purpose of showing a thought which
has struck me concerning it) I say *'Soul making'* Soul as
distinguished from an Intelligence – There may be intelle-
gences or sparks of the divinity in millions – but they are not
Souls till they acquire identities, till each one is personally itself. I[n]telligences are atoms of perception – they know and
they see and they are pure, in short they are God – how then
are Souls to be made? How then are these sparks which are
God to have identity given them – so as ever to possess a
bliss peculiar to each ones individual existence? How, but by
the medium of a world like this? This point I sincerely wish
to consider because I think it a grander system of salvation
than the chrystain religion – or rather it is a system of Spirit-
creation – This is effected by three grand materials acting
the one upon the other for a series of years – These three
Materials are the *Intelligence* – the *human heart* (as distinguished from intelligence or Mind) and the *World* or *Ele-
mental space* suited for the proper action of *Mind and Heart*
on each other for the purpose of forming the *Soul* or *Intelligence destined to possess the sense of Identity.* I can scarcely
express what I but dimly perceive – and yet I think I perceive
it – that you may judge the more clearly I will put it in the
most homely form possible – I will call the *world* a School

instituted for the purpose of teaching little children to read –
I will call the *human heart* the *horn Book* used in that School
– and I will call the *Child able to read, the Soul* made from
that *school* and its *hornbook*. Do you not see how necessary a
World of Pains and troubles is to school and Intelligence and
make it a soul? A Place where the heart must feel and suffer
in a thousand diverse ways! Not merely is the Heart a Hornbook, It is the Minds Bible, it is the Minds experience, it is
the teat from which the Mind or intelligence sucks its identity – As various as the Lives of Men are – so various become
their souls, and thus does God make individual beings,
Souls, Identical Souls of the sparks of his own essence –
This appears to me a faint sketch of a system of Salvation
which does not affront our reason and humanity – I am convinced that many difficulties which christians labour under
would vanish before it – There is one wh[i]ch even now
Strikes me – the Salvation of Children – In them the Spark
or intelligence returns to God without any identity – it having had no time to learn of, and be altered by, the heart – or
seat of the human Passions – It is pretty generally suspected
that the chr[i]stian scheme has been coppied from the
ancient persian and greek Philosophers. Why they may
not have made this simple thing even more simple for common apprehension by introducing Mediators and Personages
in the same manner as in the hethen mythology abstrac-
tions are personified – Seriously I think it probable that this
System of Soul-making – may have been the Parent of all the
more palpable and personal Schemes of Redemption, among
the Zoroastrians the Christians and the Hindoos. For as one
part of the human species must have their carved Jupiter; so
another part must have the palpable and named Mediator
and saviour, their Christ their Oromanes and their Vishnu –
If what I have said should not be plain enough, as I fear it
may not be, I will but [*for* put] you in the place where I
began in this series of thoughts – I mean, I began by seeing
how man was formed by circumstances – and what are circumstances? – but touchstones of his heart–? and what are
touch stones?–but proovings of his heart? – and what are
proovings of his heart but fortifiers or alterers of his nature?
and what is his altered nature but is soul? – and what was his
soul before it came into the world and had These provings
and alterations and perfectionings? – An intelligence – without Identity – and how is this Identity to be made? Through
the medium of the Heart? And how is the heart to become
this Medium but in a world of Circumstances? – There now

I think what with Poetry and Theology you may thank your
Stars that my pen is not very long winded. . . .

from *The Complete Poems of John Keats*,
edited by John Barnard, pp. 549–51.

The Soul of the Night
Chet Raymo, American astronomer

The silence of the stars is the silence of creation and re-creation.

The physical silence of the universe is matched by its moral silence. A child flies through the air toward injury, and the galaxies continue to whirl on well-oiled axes. But why should I expect anything else? There are no Elysian Fields up there beyond the seventh sphere where gods pause in their revels to glance down aghast at our petty tragedies. What's up there is just one galaxy after another, magnificent in their silent turning, sublime in their huge indifference. The number of galaxies may be infinite. Our indignation is finite. Divide any finite number by infinity and you get zero.

Only a few hundred yards from the busy main street of my New England village, the Queset Brook meanders through a marsh as apparently remote as any I might wish for. To drift down that stream in November is to enter a primeval silence. The stream is dark and sluggish. It pushes past the willow roots and the thick green leaves of the arrowhead like syrup. The wind hangs dead in the air. The birds have fled south. Trail bikes are stacked away for the winter, and snowmobiles are still buried at the backs of garages. For a few weeks in November the marsh near Queset Brook is as silent as the space between the stars.

How fragile is our hold on silence. The creak of a wagon on a distant highway was sometimes noise enough to interrupt Thoreau's reverie. Thoreau was perceptive enough to know that the whistle of the Fitchburg Railroad (whose track lay close by Walden Pond) heralded something more than the arrival of the train, but he could hardly have imagined the efficiency with which technology has intruded upon our world of natural science. Thoreau rejoiced in owls; their hoot, he said, was a sound well suited to swamps and twilight woods. The interval between the hoots was a deepened silence suggesting, said Thoreau, "a vast and undeveloped nature which men have not recognized." Thoreau rejoiced in that silent interval, as I rejoice in the silence of the November marsh.

As a student, I came across a book by Max Picard called *The World of Silence*. The book offered an insight that seems more valuable to me now than it did then. Silence, said Picard, is the source from which language springs, and to silence language must constantly return to be re-created. Only in relation to silence does sound have significance. It is for this silence, so treasured by Picard that I turn to the marsh near Queset Brook in November. It is for this silence that I turn to the stars, to the ponderous inaudible turning of galaxies, to the clanging of God's great bell in the vacuum. The silence of the stars is the silence of creation and re-creation. It is the silence to be explored alone. Along the shores of Walden Pond the owl hooted a question whose answer lay hidden in the interval. The interval was narrow but infinitely deep, and in that deep hid the soul of the night.

I drift in my canoe down the Queset Brook and I listen, ears alert, like an animal that sniffs a meal or a threat on the wind. I am not sure what it is that I want to hear out of all this silence, out of this palpable absence of Wallace Stevens: "A scrawny cry from outside . . . a chorister whose cry preceded the choir . . . still far away." Is that too much to hope for? I don't ask for the full ringing of the bell. I don't ask for a clap of thunder that would rend the veil in the temple. A scrawny cry will do, from far off there among the willows and the cattails, from far off there among the galaxies.

from *The Soul of the Night*, pp. 7–9.

The Spirit of Place in the Western World
J. Donald Hughes, American author

Of course, individual trees were inhabited by spirits called dryads, and naiads dwelt within streams, springs, and waterfalls.

A sacred precinct, called *hieros temenos* in Greek and *templum* in Latin, was an area set aside and often walled to mark the boundary between holy and ordinary space. These usually contained groves of trees and springs or other water, though often mountaintops or other prominent features were so treated. Within them the environment was preserved in its natural state. The presence of spirit was often recognized in the quality of the environment itself, which called forth an inner response. As the Roman philosopher Seneca remarked, "If you came upon a grove of old trees that have lifted their crowns up above the common height and shut out the light of the sky by the darkness of their interlacing boughs, you feel that there is a spirit in the place, so lofty is the wood, so lone the spot, so wondrous the thick unbroken shade." Of course, indi-

vidual trees were inhabited by spirits called dryads, and naiads
dwelt within streams, springs, and waterfalls. But it was always
the place itself that was the temple, originally; the forest, not the
structure erected to protect an image of the god. Worship was in
the out-of-doors. It was illegal to disturb the place and the living
things in it by hunting, fishing, polluting the water, tree-cutting,
removing wood or leaves, plowing, sowing, pasturing domestic animals, setting fires, or erecting unauthorized buildings. Suppliants
who sought protection in holy places were granted asylum and
could not be killed. Punishments for violating these rules were
severe and enforced by city governments. However, the spirits
themselves were thought to be perfectly capable of exacting their
own revenge. When Erysichthon ignored the protests of a dryad
and cut down her tree, he was stricken with hunger that could
never be satisfied. Hunger seems a particularly appropriate punishment for a crime against the land.

Some of the *temene* were therapeutic sanctuaries, where those
suffering from illness would come to pray to Asclepius and other
spirits of healing. Various forms of treatment, including dream in-
cubation, were used to find cures. Modern experts on environmental medicine who have studied ancient healing sites such as
Epidaurus and Kos have remarked that their climate and exposure
are conducive to the treatment of respiratory and other ailments.
Hippocrates, the founder of medicine, recognized that some localities had healing properties, especially for certain diseases, while
others had bad effects. He advised the founders of cities to take
these factors into account.

The philosophers also had something to say about place (*topos*
in Greek). Theophrastus maintained that every living thing has
an *oikeios topos* or "favorable place," where all the energies and
conditions are suitable to its flourishing. Aristotle made a similar
point in regard to animals. The Greek word used here to charac-
terize a harmonious relationship between an organism and its
environment is *oikeios,* which shares a root with the modern word
"ecology." Plato commented directly on the spirit of place in his
dialogue, the *Laws.* "Some localities have a more marked tendency
than others to produce better or worse men, and we are not to
legislate in the face of the facts," he remarks, implying that *nomos,*
human culture, must be altered to accord with the natural environment in a particular *topos.* "Some places, I conceive, owe their
propitious or ill-omened character to variations in wind and sunshine, others to the waters, and yet others to the products of the
soil, which not only provide the body with better or worse sustenance, but equally affect the mind for good or ill." Plato continues, "Most markedly conspicuous of all, again, will be localities

which are the homes of some supernatural influences, or the haunts of spirits who give a gracious or ungracious reception to successive bodies of settlers. A sagacious legislator will give these facts all the considerations a person can, and do the best to adapt legislation to them." Here Plato has the beginnings of a theory for geomancy. But he went even further. Following Pythagoras, he extended the idea of a spirit inhabiting a place to the entire universe, which he envisioned as a living body inhabited by a world soul in vast organic unity. In this view every place forms a meaningful part of the whole, although some have more vital functions than others. Plutarch adds that certain parts of the earth's surface (the ones least inhabited by human beings) are essential to the health and vitality of the rest. Thus respected philosophers would agree that proper relationship with spirit of place is necessary to the well-being of the whole world.

from *The Power of Place,* edited by James Swan, pp. 18–20.

Facing the World with Soul
Robert Sardello, American psychotherapist

On the contrary, soul inheres within the world and creates our psyches.

By soul wisdom I mean the development of a capacity for self-knowledge in conjunction with an objective sense of the inner qualities of the outer world. The capacity for this conjunction leads to a new image of consciousness that "sees through" events, both inner and outer, finding a circulation going on between them in which a constant re-creation of both the human being and the world takes place. This circulating force or power I shall call soul, and to make clear that what I am calling soul has little to do with individual life alone, by soul I shall always imply *the soul of the world* as a way of referring to the inseparable conjunction of individual and world; and further, this is always a conjunction in depth . . .

When the ancient seers looked upon the world, what did they see? They saw magic. One can still see that today if one knows how to look. The seer might be walking in a forest and see among all the trees a birch—because the birch is such a conspicuous tree. It is unbelievably supple. With her beautiful white trunk she stands, yielding to the slightest movement of air, swaying amongst the more woody and unbending trees such as the oaks and beeches. No matter how old a big birch becomes, the suppleness is retained. And she does not allow herself to be overgrown. Drawing up enormous amounts of water through her roots, the birch effectively drains the ground. The seer sees these qualities and thus sees the gifts of the birch. She is wonderful medicine; since she is able to keep at bay all hardening tendencies, the birch can assist in keeping body tissues soft and supple. Because the birch drains as well she offers an effective diuretic. But we need not conclude from this example that the way to Sophia is the return to nature. It is not so much the birch that is important as it is the way of seeing the birch, seeing the magic in the birch, its soul qualities. Magic, then, is the soul of the world creating itself, according to its own laws . . .

Now, there is magic and there is the magic of the soul of the world. Christopher Marlowe's *Faust* presents the archetypal image of individual magic, the usurpation of the realm of the magic of the world by the need for control. Faust reveals an image of elitism, of one who sought special privileges for himself and the means to obtain them. Magic here becomes the way to power, to accomplishment without responsibility, the degradation of soul wisdom to individual omnipotence . . .

The magical tradition, when not corrupted, never concerns an interest in personal power, but rather the passage through three gateways leading to the capacity for perception of the world soul. The first gateway concerns remembering the ancestors, passing into living relation with the ancestors. The second gateway concerns passing into a living relation with archetypal beings, and the third gateway gives passage into the soul substance of the land. Rather than coming to personal power, through these activities humans become mediators between the ancestral and archetypal beings and the archetypal substance of the land. Earth here—the land—does not carry the connotation of nature or of inert matter. The physical being of the planet is composed from numerous worlds that in the magical tradition are called the inner worlds. The inner worlds are not worlds within our imagination, but are imaginal worlds, populated by the composing beings of the fabric of the physical planet. Our imagination is the organ by which we know these composing beings. The magical world, the inner world, the psychic world is this world of the physical planet and none other. The magical tradition sustains the feeling we all have but never acknowledge, that everything is animated. Such feeling is not animism, for animism is a theory that says soul life is projected onto an inanimate world from within the human psyche. On the contrary, soul inheres within the world and creates our psyches.

from *Facing the World with Soul*, pp. 20–22.

The Green Fields of the Mind

A. Bartlett Giamatti, American lawyer, baseball commissioner, and president
of Yale, 1938–1989

*It broke my heart because it was meant to, because it was meant to foster in
me again the illusion that there was something abiding, some pattern and
some impulse that could come together to make a reality that would resist
the corrosion. . . .*

It breaks your heart. It is designed to break your heart. The game
begins in the spring, when everything else begins again, and it
blossoms in the summer, filling the afternoons and evenings, and
then as soon as the chill rains come, it stops and leaves you to face
the fall alone. You count on it, rely on it to buffer the passage of
time, to keep the memory of sunshine and high skies alive, and
then just when the days are all twilight, when you need it most, it
stops. Today, October 2, a Sunday of rain and broken branches
and leaf-clogged drains and slick streets, it stopped, and summer
was gone.

Somehow, the summer seemed to slip by faster this time. Maybe
it wasn't this summer, but all the summers that, in my fortieth
summer, slipped by so fast. There comes a time when every summer will have something of autumn about it. Whatever the reason,
it seemed to me that I was investing more and more in baseball,
making the game do more of the work that keeps time fat and slow
and lazy. I was counting on the game's deep patterns, three strikes,
three outs, three times three innings, and its deepest impulse, to
go out and back, to leave and to return home, to set the order of
the day and to organize the daylight. I wrote a few things this last
summer, this summer that did not last, nothing grand but some
things, and yet that work was just camouflage. The real activity
was done with the radio—not the all-seeing, all-falsifying television—and was the playing of the game in the only place it will last,
the enclosed, green field of the mind. There, in that warm, bright
place, what the old poet called Mutability does not so quickly
come.

But out here on Sunday, October 2, where it rains all day, Dame
Mutability never loses. She was in the crowd at Fenway yesterday,
a grey day full of bluster and contradiction, when the Red Sox
came up in the last of the ninth trailing Baltimore 8–5, while the
Yankees, rain-delayed against Detroit, only needing to win one or
have Boston lose one to win it all, sat in New York washing down

cold cuts with beer and watching the Boston game. Boston had won two, the Yankees had lost two, and suddenly it seemed as if the whole season might go to the last day, or beyond, except here was Boston losing 8–5, while New York sat in its family room and put its feet up. Lynn, both ankles hurting now as they had in July, hits a single down the right field line. The crowd stirs. It is on its feet. Hobson, third baseman, former Bear Bryant quarterback, strong, quiet, over 100 RBIs, goes for three breaking balls and is out. The goddess smiles and encourages her agent, a canny journeyman named Nelson Briles.

Now comes a pinch hitter, Bernie Carbo, one-time Rookie of the Year, erratic, quick, a shade too handsome, so laid back he is always, in his soul, stretched out in the tall grass, one arm under his head, watching the clouds and laughing; now he looks over some low stuff unworthy of him and then, uncoiling, sends one out, straight on a rising line, over the center field wall, no cheap Fenway shot, but all of it, the physics as elegant as the arc the ball describes.

New England is on its feet, roaring. The summer will not pass. Roaring, they recall the evening, late and cold, in 1975, the sixth game of the World Series, perhaps the greatest baseball game played in the last fifty years, when Carbo, loose and easy, had uncoiled to tie the game that Fisk would win. It is 8–7, one out, and school will never start, rain will never come, sun will warm the back of your neck forever. Now Bailey, picked up from the National League recently, big arms, heavy gut, experienced, new to the league and the club; he fouls off two and then, checking, tentative, a big man off balance, he pops a soft liner to the first basemen. It is suddenly darker and later, and the announcer doing the game coast to coast, a New Yorker who works for a New York television station, sounds relieved. His little world, well-lit, hot-combed, split-second-timed, had no capacity to absorb this much gritty, grainy, contrary reality.

Cox swings a bat, stretches his long arms, bends his back, the rookie from Pawtucket, who broke in two weeks earlier with a record six straight hits, the kid drafted ahead of Fred Lynn, rangy, smooth, cool. The count runs two and two, Briles is cagey, nothing too good, and Cox swings, the ball beginning toward the mound and then, in a jaunty, wayward dance, skipping past Briles, feinting to the right, skimming the last of the grass, finding the dirt, moving now like some small, purposeful marine creature negotiating the green deep, easily avoiding the jagged rock of second base, traveling steady and straight now out into the dark, silent recesses of center field.

The aisles are jammed, the place is on its feet, the wrappers, the programs, the Coke cups and peanut shells, the detritus of an afternoon; the anxieties, the things that have to be done tomorrow, the regrets about yesterday, the accumulation of a summer: all forgotten, while hope, the anchor, bites and takes hold where a moment before it seemed we would be swept out with the tide. Rice is up, Rice whom Aaron had said was the only one he'd seen with the ability to break his records, Rice the best clutch hitter in the club, with the best slugging percentage in the league, Rice, so quick and strong he once checked his swing halfway through and snapped the bat in two, Rice the Hammer of God sent to scourge the Yankees, the sound was overwhelming, fathers pounded their sons on the back, cars pulled off the road, households froze, New England exulted in its blessedness, and roared its thanks for all good things, for Rice and for a summer stretching halfway through October. Briles threw, Rice swung, and it was over. One pitch, a fly to center, and it stopped. Summer died in New England and like rain sliding off a roof, the crowd slipped out of Fenway, quickly, with only a steady murmur of concern for the drive ahead remaining of the roar. Mutability had turned the seasons and translated hope to memory once again. And once again, she had used baseball, our best invention to stay change, to bring change on. That is why it breaks my heart, that game—not because in New York they could win because Boston lost; in that, there is a rough justice, and a reminder to the Yankees of how slight and fragile are the circumstances that exalt one group of human beings over another. It breaks my heart because it was meant to, because it was meant to foster in me again the illusion that there was something abiding, some pattern and some impulse that could come together to make a reality that would resist the corrosion; and because after it had fostered again that most hungered-for illusion, the game was meant to stop, and betray precisely what it promised.

Of course, there are those who learn after the first few times. They grow out of sports. And there are other others who were born with the wisdom to know that nothing lasts. These are the truly tough among us, the ones who can live without illusion, or without even the hope of illusion. I am not that grown-up or up-to-date. I am a simpler creature, tied to more primitive patterns and cycles. I need to think something lasts forever, and it might as well be that state of being that is a game; it might as well be that, in a green field, in the sun.

from Baseball I Gave You All the Best Years of My Life,
edited by Kevin Kerrane and Richard Grossinger,
pp. 320–21.

The Soul-Spark

James Hillman, American author and psychotherapist

. . . our imaginative recognition, the childlike act of imagining the world, animates the world and returns it to soul.

Let us imagine the anima mundi as that particular soul-spark, that seminal image, which offers itself through each thing in its visible form. Then anima mundi indicates the animated possibilities presented by each event as it is, its sensuous presentation as a face bespeaking its interior image—in short, its availability to imagination, its presence as a psychic reality. Not only animals and plants ensouled as in the Romantic vision, but soul is given with each thing, God-given things of nature and man-made things of the street.

The world comes with shapes, colors, atmospheres, textures—a display of self-presenting forms. All things show faces, the world not only a coded signature to be read for meaning, but a physiognomy to be faced. As expressive forms, things speak; they show the shape they are in. They announce themselves, bear witness to their presence: "Look, here we are." They regard us beyond how we may regard them, our perspectives, what we intend with them, and how we dispose of them. This imaginative claim on attention bespeaks a world ensouled. More—our imaginative recognition, the childlike act of imagining the world, animates the world and returns it to soul. . . .

The improvement of the quality of life depends on a restoration of a language which notices the properties of bodies, the qualities of life. Our way back to the bus thus leads back to the Renaissance insistence on rhetoric, incorporating along the way the poetic methods of Imagism, Concretism, Objectivism, Projective Verse— modes of language that do not dwell in 'experience' and which instead enliven things, giving them back their animated faces.

Second, that unspoken religious fervor in psychotherapy would shift its focus from saving the soul in the personal patient to saving the soul of the world, the resurrection of the world rather than the resurrection of man, the celebration of creation before the redemption of creativity in the individual . . . to Ficino: "Creation is a more excellent act than illumination," so that the task of "raising of consciousness" (as redemption of the soul is now disguised in modern therapy) becomes a raising of consciousness of created things, a therapy of the constructed world's psychic reality.

A world without soul offers no intimacy.

We will not be able to move in this direction until we have made radical shifts of orientation, so that we can value soul before mind, image before feeling, each before all, aisthesis and imagining before logos and conceiving, thing before meaning, noticing before knowing, rhetoric before truth, animal before human, anima before ego, what and who before why. We would have to let fall such games as subject-object, left-right, inner-outer, masculine-feminine, immanence-transcendence, mind-body—the game of oppositions altogether. A great deal of what we now hold dear would break down so that the emotion held by these cherished relics could break those vessels and flow back into the world.

Breaking the vessels is the return, the turn again to the world, giving back what we have taken from it by storing inside ourselves its soul. By this return we regard the world anew, having regard for it as it shows its regard for us and to us in its face. We pay respect to it simply by looking again, re-specting, that second look with the eye of the heart.

from The Thought of the Heart and the Soul of the World,
pp. 101–2, 128–29.

The Secret Soul of Plants
Peter Tompkins and Christopher Bird, American author, American biologist

In addition to souls which run and shriek and devour might there not be souls which bloom in stillness, exhale fragrance and satisfy their thirst with dew and their impulses by their burgeoning?

Aristotle's dogma that plants have souls but no sensation lasted through the Middle Ages and into the eighteenth century, when Carl von Linné, grandfather of modern botany, declared that plants differ from animals and humans only in their lack of movement, a conceit which was shot down by the great nineteenth-century botanist Charles Darwin, who proved that every tendril has its power of independent movement. As Darwin put it, plants "acquire and display this power only when it is of some advantage to them.". . .

Goethe's poetic notion that a spiritual essence lies behind the material form of plants was put on a firmer basis by a medical doctor and a professor of physics at the University of Leipzig. Credited with over forty papers on such subjects as the measurement of electrical currents and the perceptions of colors, Gustave Theodor Fechner came to his profound understanding of plants in a totally unexpected way. In 1839 he began to stare at the sun in the hope of discovering the nature of afterimages, those strange pictures which seem to persist on the retina of the eye even after the cessation of normal visual stimulus.

A few days later, Fechner was horrified to realize that he was going blind. Exhausted from overwork, and unable in his new affliction to face his friends and colleagues, he retired to a darkened room with a mask over his face, to live in solitude praying for recovery.

One spring morning three years later, sensing that his sight had been restored, he emerged into the light of day. Joyously walking along the Mulde River he instantly recognized that flowers and trees along its banks were what he called be-souled. "As I stood by the water and watched a flower, it was as though I saw its soul itself from the bloom and, drifting through the mist, become clearer until the spiritual form hung clearly above it. Perhaps it wanted to stand on the roof of its budding house in order better to enjoy the sun. Believing itself invisible, it was quite surprised when a little child appeared."

While still in semiseclusion Fechner began setting down a series of similar remarkable impressions. The result was *Nanna, or the Soul-Life of Plants,* published in Leipzig in 1848, which though scathingly rejected by his fellow academicians, became so popular that it was still being printed in Germany three-quarters of a century later.

In his introduction, Fechner explained that he happened on the title by accident. At first he thought of calling his new book *Flora,* after the Roman goddess of flowers, or *Hamadryas,* after the wood nymphs which the Hellenes recognized as living only as long as the trees of which they were the spirit. But he rejected the first as too botanical, the second as too classically stiff and antiquarian. One day, while reading Teutonic mythology, Fechner learned that Baldur, god of light, had, like Actaeon peeping at Diana, secretly gazed upon the naked form of the flower princess Nanna as she bathed in a stream. When her natural loveliness was enhanced by the energy over which Baldur ruled, his heart, said the legend, was pierced, and the marriage of Light and Flowers became a foregone conclusion.

Fechner's awakening to the soul life of plants turned him from professing physics to professing philosophy, of which branch of knowledge he was given a chair at Leipzig the same year that *Nanna* appeared. . . .

Fechner introduced *Nanna* with the concept that believing whether plants have a soul or not changes one's whole insight into nature. If man admitted to an omnipresent, all-knowing, and almighty god who bestowed animation on all things, then nothing in the world could be excluded from this munificence, neither plant nor stone nor crystal nor wave. Why would universal spirit, he asked, sit less firmly in nature than in human beings, and not be as much in command of nature's power as it is of human bodies?

Anticipating Bose's work, Fechner further reasoned that if plants have life and soul, they must have some sort of nervous system, hidden perhaps in their strange spiral fibers. Going beyond the limitation of today's mechanistic physiology. Fechner referred to "spiritual nerves" in the universe, one expression of which was the interconnection of celestial bodies, not with "long ropes," but with a unified web of light, gravity, and forces as yet unknown. The soul, said Fechner, receives sensations, in a manner analogous to that of a spider which is alerted to outside influences by its web. It seemed reasonable to Fechner to accept the idea that plants have nerves, their purported absence being due to man's ignorance rather than to any innate vegetal deficiency.

According to Fechner, the psyche of plants is no more linked to their nervous system than is the soul of man to a human body. Both are diffused throughout, yet separated from all the organs which they direct. "None of my limbs anticipates anything for itself," wrote Fechner, "only I, the spirit of my whole, sense everything that happens to me."

Fechner created a new branch of learning called *psychophysics,* which abolished the artificial separation between mind and body and held the two entities to be only different sides of one reality, the mind appearing subjectively, the body objectively, as a circle is either concave or convex depending on whether the observer stands inside it or outside. The confusion resulted, said Fechner, because it was difficult to hold both points of view simultaneously. To Fechner all things express in different ways the same *anima mundi,* or cosmic soul, which came into existence with the universe, is its conscience, and will die when and if the universe dies. Basic to his animate philosophy was the axiom that all life is *one* and simply takes up different shapes in order to divert itself. The highest good and supreme end of all action is the maximum pleasure not of the individual but of all, said Fechner, and on this he based all his rules for morals. . . .

from *The Secret Life of Plants,* pp. ix, 120–24.

The Soul of Community
Eliezer Shore, Israeli writer and teacher

The contemplative is to the community what the soul is to the body.

So important is community that Kabbalistic writings consider *Knesset Yisrael,* the body of the People of Israel, as synonymous with the Shekinah, the Divine Presence on earth. For they are both understood to share the same purpose, that of revealing God in the world, being "a light to the nations," in the words of the prophet. The Shekinah is the feminine element of creation, for it receives God's light, nurtures it, and reveals it in the world. Thus the union of God and the Shekinah, of the transcendent and the immanent, is not a static act. It is constantly bringing to birth a new and ever increasing awareness of God. Every single act, performed according to the laws of the Torah, brings about a greater revelation of God in the world, greater union between the Soul of Creation and the physical. Every act becomes a prayer. And as the *Zohar* says, "prayer without intention is like a body without a soul."

This, then, is the role of mankind: to lift back up to God that which is furthest away. It is the reason why the soul leaves its pristine abode to come down into the body, why God descends to create a world, and why the contemplative must eventually leave his retreat and unite with humanity. The contemplative is to the community what the soul is to the body. He gives it life, inspiration, and leads its members to a higher level. Then, if he finds that he must retreat to his solitary path, it is because the final rectification has not yet been accomplished. He retreats, to draw from the source of inspiration, and he returns again to water the garden of souls. This back and forth movement will continue until peace is finally made between body and soul, and God's presence so fills the earth that there is no place empty of him. "When will the Messiah come?" the Talmud asks. "When all the souls have come out in the body." Then there will be no need for solitude, for the whole world will reveal His glory. The duality of God and the world will no longer exist. And the words of the prophet will be fulfilled: "On that day God will be one, and His name one" (Zechariah 14:9).

from *Parabola*, vol. XVII, no. 1, 1992, pp. 20–21.

Soul and Business
Gary Zukav, American philosopher

As the human species awakens to itself as a collection of immortal souls learning together, care for the environment and the earth will become a matter of the heart, the natural response of souls moving toward their full potential.

By placing itself at the pinnacle of the hierarchy of life from the point of view of the five senses, and assigning maximal value to that position, humanity has created a world in which exploitation of the environment appears natural. The results of this orientation now confront us in every aspect of our environment—air, water, soil, and everything that grows.

This is the learning domain of the five senses at work: We are facing the consequences of what we have chosen in the past, and, simultaneously, being given the opportunity to choose again. Each choice that we make now determines our experiences in the future, and so on. This process is continual, we are surrounded by what we have created, and, through our responses, creating anew.

The lack of reverence for all of life that allows the CEO to be more important than his driver, the physician to be more important than her receptionist, and the engineer to be more important than the welder also allows the needs of humanity to be more important than the needs of the species with which it shares the earth, and more important than the environment.

As individuals begin to recognize themselves and others as immortal souls, and as they begin to function as multisensory rather than five-sensory humans, they begin to see life wherever they look, and to revere it where they see it. This leads naturally to an attitude of care and protection for the environment that is based not only upon the realization that our physical survival depends upon it, but upon the desire of the soul to care for life, to contribute to it, and to value it in all its forms.

As businesses and employees awaken to the deep bonds of life that connect them to each other, they awaken also the deep bonds that connect all life. The environment and the world—our tiny precious planet—become important not as resources, but as the home that we as immortal souls have chosen for our learning and that now terribly needs care and healing. As the human species awakens to itself as a collection of immortal souls learning together, care for the environment and the earth will become a matter of the heart, the natural response of souls moving toward their full potential. Businesses will strive to heal the earth, rather than to exploit it, because business will no longer reflect the pursuit of external power, but the authentic power of each of the individuals within the business community, now expanded to include all souls that the business touches through its activities, products, and services.

From "Evolution and Business," a chapter from
a forthcoming book by Gary Zukav.

The Soul of the Road
Jack Kerouac, American novelist, 1922–1969

The whole mad swirl of everything that was to come began then; it would mix up all my friends and all I had left of my family in a big

dust cloud over the American night. Carlo told him of Old Bull
Lee, Elmer Hassel, Jane: Lee in Texas growing weed, Hassel on
Riker's Island, Jane wandering on Times Square in a benzedrine
hallucination, with her baby girl in her arms and ending up in
Bellevue. And Dean told Carol of unknown people in the West like
Tommy Snark, the clubfooted poolhall rotation shark and card-
player and queer saint. He told him of Roy Johnson, Big Ed
Dunkel, his boyhood buddies, his street buddies, his innumerable
girls and sex-parties and pornographic pictures, his heroes, hero-
ines, adventures. They rushed down the street together, digging
everything in the early way they had, which later became so much
sadder and perceptive and blank. But then they danced down the
streets like dingledodies, and I shambled after as I've been doing
all my life after the people who interest me, because the only people for me are the mad ones, the ones who are mad to live, mad to
talk, mad to be saved, desirous of everything at the same time, the
ones who never yawn or say a commonplace thing, but burn, burn,
burn like fabulous yellow roman candles exploding like spiders
across the stars and in the middle you see the blue centerlight pop
and everybody goes "Awww!: What did they call such young people
in Goethe's Germany? Wanting dearly to learn how to write like
Carlo, the first thing you know, Dean was attacking him with a
great amorous soul such as only a con-man can have. "Now, Carlo,
let *me* speak—here's what *I'm* saying . . . " I didn't see them for
about two weeks, during which time they cemented their relationship to fiendish allday-allnight-talk proportions. . . .

Then came spring, the great time of traveling, and everybody in
the scattered gang was getting ready to take one trip or another.
I was busily at work on my novel and when I came to the halfway
mark, after a trip down South with my aunt to visit my brother
Rocco, I got ready to travel West for the very first time. . . .

My first ride was a dynamite truck with a red flag, about thirty
miles into great green Illinois, the truck driver pointing out the
place where Route 6, which we were on, intersects Route 66 before they both shoot west for incredible distances. Along about
three in the afternoon, after an apple pie and ice cream in a roadside stand, a woman stopped for me in a little coupe. I had a
twinge of hard joy as I ran after the car. But she was a middle-aged
woman, actually the mother of sons my age, and wanted somebody
to help her drive to Iowa. I was all for it. Iowa! Not so far from
Denver, and once I got to Denver I could relax. She drove the first
few hours, at one point insisted on visiting an old church somewhere, as if we were tourists, and then I took over the wheel and,
though I'm not much of a driver, drove clear through the rest
of Illinois to Davenport, Iowa, via Rock Island. And here for the

first time in my life I saw my beloved Mississippi River, dry in the
summer haze, low water, with its big rank smell that smells like the
raw body of America itself because it washes it up. Rock Island—
railroad tracks, shacks, small downtown section; and over the
bridge to Davenport, same kind of town, all smelling of sawdust in
the warm Midwest sun. Here the lady had to go on to her Iowa
hometown by another route, and I got out.

The sun was going down. I walked, after a few cold beers, to the
edge of town, and it was a long walk. All the men were driving
home from work, wearing railroad hats, baseball hats, all kinds of
hats, just like after work in any town anywhere. One of them gave
me a ride up the hill and left me at a lonely crossroads on the edge
of the prairie. It was beautiful there. The only cars that came by
were farmer-cars; they gave me suspicious looks, they clanked
along, the cows were coming home. Not a truck. A few cars zipped
by. A hotrod kid came by with his scarf flying. The sun went all the
way down and I was standing in the purple darkness. Now I was
scared. There weren't even any lights in the Iowa countryside; in a
minute nobody would be able to see me. Luckily a man going back
to Davenport gave me a lift downtown. But I was right where I
started from.

I went to sit in the bus station and think this over. I ate another
apple pie and ice cream; that's practically all I ate all the way
across the country, I knew it was nutritious and it was delicious, of
course. I decided to gamble. I took a bus in downtown Davenport,
after spending a half hour watching a waitress in the bus-station
cafe, and rode to the city limits, but this time near the gas stations.
Here the big trucks roared, wham, and inside two minutes one of
them cranked to a stop for me. I ran for it with my soul whoopee-
ing. And what a driver—a great big tough truck driver with pop-
ping eyes and a hoarse raspy voice who just slammed and kicked at
everything and got his rig under way and paid hardly any attention
to me. So I could rest my tired soul a little, for one of the biggest
troubles hitchhiking is having to talk to innumerable people, make
them feel that they didn't make a mistake picking you up, even entertain them almost, all of which is a great strain when you're
going all the way and don't plan to sleep in hotels. The guy just
yelled above the roar, and all I had to do was yell back, and we relaxed. And he balled that thing clear to Iowa City and yelled me
the funniest stories about how he got around the law in every town
that had an unfair speed limit, saying over and over again, "Them
goddam cops can't put no flies on *my* ass!" Just as we rolled into
Iowa City he saw another truck coming behind us, and because he
had to turn off at Iowa City he blinked his tail lights at the other

guy and slowed down for me to jump out, which I did with my bag, and the other truck, acknowledging this exchange, stopped for me, and once again, in the twink of nothing, I was in another big high cab, all set to go hundreds of miles across the night, and was I happy! And the new truck driver was as crazy as the other and yelled just as much, and all I had to do was lean back and roll on. Now I could see Denver looming ahead of me like the Promised Land, way out there beneath the stars, across the prairie of Iowa and the plains of Nebraska, and I could see the greater vision of San Francisco beyond like jewels in the night. He balled the jack and told stories for a couple of hours, then, at a town in Iowa where years later Dean and I were stopped on suspicion in what looked like a stolen Cadillac, he slept a few hours in the seat. I slept too, and took one little walk along the lonely brick walls illuminated by one lamp, with the prairie brooding at the end of each little street and the smell of the corn like dew in the night.

from *On the Road*, pp. 8, 14–16.

Espresso
Tomas Transtromer, Swedish poet

Black coffee at sidewalk cafes
with chairs and tables like gaudy insects.

It is a precious sip we intercept
filled with the same strength as Yes and No.

It is fetched out of the gloomy kitchens
and looks into the sun without blinking.

In daylight a dot of wholesome black
quickly drained by the wan patron . . .

Like those black drops of profundity
sometimes absorbed by the soul

that give us a healthy push: Go!
The courage to open our eyes.

from *Windows and Stones: Selected Poems*,
translated by May Swenson and Leif Sjöberg,
edited by Robert Hass, p. 55.

Soul Food

Sheila Ferguson, African-American singer and author

. . . When you taste good soul food then it'll take ahold of your soul and hang your unsuspecting innards out to dry.

Ah, soul food. Soul is just what the name implies. It is soulfully cooked food or richly flavored foods good for your ever-loving soul. But soul food is much more than a clever name penned by some unknown author. It is a legacy clearly steeped in tradition; a way of life that has been handed down from generation to generation, from one black family to another, by word of mouth and sleight of hand. It is rich in both history and variety of flavor.

To cook soul food you must use all of your senses. You cook by instinct but you also use smell, taste, touch, sight, and, particularly, sound. You learn to hear by the crackling sound when it's time to turn over the fried chicken, to smell when a pan of biscuits is just about to finish baking, and to feel when a pastry's just right to the touch. You taste, rather than measure, the seasonings you treasure; and you use your eyes, not a clock, to judge when that cherry pie has bubbled sweet and nice. These skills are hard to teach quickly. They must be felt, loving, and come straight from the heart and soul.

Ah, but when you taste good soul food then it'll take hold of your soul and hang your unsuspecting innards out to dry. It's that shur-'nuf everlovin' down-home stick-to-your-ribs kinda food that keeps you glued to your seat long after the meal is over and done with, enabling you to sit back, relax, and savor the gentle purrings of a well satisfied stomach, feeling that all's right with the world. Yes suh! As the good Baptist minister says every Sunday morning. Yes suh!

Let me give you a for instance. Say you fry up a batch of fresh chicken to a golden-brown crispness, but you keep the insides so moist, so tender, that all that good juice just bursts forth with the first crunchy bite. Then maybe you bake up some cornbread and buttermilk biscuits, ready to smother with freshly churned butter, and you cook up a big pot of collard greens and pot likka seasoned with ham hocks, onion, vinegar, red pepper flakes, and just enough hot sauce to set fire to your palate. Just a little fire though! Now you pile on a mound of slightly chilled home-made potato salad and fill a pitcher full of ice-cold lemonade ready to cool out that fire. And when you've eaten your way through all of that, you finish it off with a healthy hunk of pecan pie topped with a scoop of home-made vanilla ice cream. Now, tell me the truth—do you think you could move after a meal like that? Only for second helpings, of course!

But that's just the fun-loving, toe-tapping, belly-busting, knee-slapping, thirst-quenching, foot-stomping side of a cuisine that has its more serious side too. For the basic framework of this style of cooking was carved out in the deep South by the black slaves, in part for their white masters and in part for their own survival in the slave quarters. As such, it is, like the blues or jazz, an inextricable part of the black Americans' struggle to survive and to express themselves. In this sense it is a *true* American cuisine, because it wasn't imported into America by immigrants like so many other ethnic offerings. It is the cuisine of the American, if you like. Because what can't be cured must be endured. As John Egerton so aptly puts it in *Southern Food,*

> In the most desolate and hopeless of circumstances, blacks caught in the grip of slavery often exhibited uncommon wisdom, beauty, strength, and creativity. The kitchen was one of the few places where their imagination and skill could have free rein and full expression, and there they often excelled. From the elegant breads and meats and sweets of plantation cookery to the inventions of Creole cuisine, from beaten biscuits to bouillabaisse, their legacy of culinary excellence is all the more impressive, considering the extremely adverse conditions under which it was compiled.

Rations were usually once a week, on Saturday nights, and then the righteous jubilation would commence in the slave quarters. The slaves pretty much insisted on having Sundays as their day to worship. Of course, no alcohol was allowed. Don't be ridiculous! It was alright for white folk, but bad for African and American Indian blood. However, that didn't matter. The slaves had their own way to lift up their souls. They would pray, they would sing, and they would eat! They would throw pork skins into the fire until they crackled, bake up some cornpones nice and brown using bacon fat, and cook up any game or eggs that had been found and hadn't been confiscated.

Then they would sing and dance. . . . The songs were unsophisticated, but they fulfilled their purpose: The slaves could let go of their souls and find solace in the little they had.

from *Soul Food*, pp. 1–2.

The Soul of the Computer

Tracy Kidder, American journalist

"Ninety-eight percent of the thrill comes from knowing that the thing you designed works, and works almost the way you expected it would. If that happens, part of you is in that machine."

Adopting a remote, managerial point of view, you could say that the Eagle Project was a case where a local system of management worked as it should: competition for resources creating within a team inside a company an entrepreneurial spirit, which was channeled in the right direction by constraints sent down from the top. But it seems more accurate to say that a group of engineers got excited about building a computer. Whether it arose by corporate bungling or by design, the opportunity had to be grasped. In this sense, the initiative belonged entirely to West and the members of his team. What's more, they did the work, both with uncommon spirit and for reasons that, in a most frankly commercial setting, seemed remarkably pure.

In *The Nature of Gothic*, John Ruskin decries the tendency of the industrial age to fragment work into tasks so trivial that they are fit to be performed only by the equivalent of slave labor. Writing in the nineteenth century, Ruskin was one of the first, with Marx, to have raised this now-familiar complaint. In the Gothic cathedrals of Europe, Ruskin believed, you can see the glorious fruits of free labor, given freely. What is usually meant by the term *craftsmanship* is the production of things of high quality; Ruskin makes the crucial point that a thing may also be judged according to the conditions under which it was built.

Presumably the stonemasons who raised the cathedrals worked only partly for their pay. They were building temples to God. It was the sort of work that gave meaning to life. That's what West and his team of engineers were looking for, I think. They themselves liked to say they didn't work on their machine for money. In the aftermath, some of them felt that they were receiving neither the loot nor the recognition they had earned and some said they were a little bitter on that score. But when they talked about the project itself, their enthusiasm returned. It lit up their faces. Many seemed to want to say that they had participated in something quite out of the ordinary. They'd talk about the virtues of the machine—"We built it right"—and how quickly they had done it— "No one ever did it faster; at least, Data General never did"—and of the experience they had gained—"Now I can do in two hours what used to take me two days." One of the so-called kids—kids no longer, but veterans now—remarked, "This'll make my resume look real good." But, he quickly added, that wasn't what it was all about.

Many looked around for words to describe their true reward. They used such phrases as "self-fulfillment," "a feeling of accomplishment," "self-satisfaction." Jim Guyer struggled with those terms awhile with growing impatience. Then he said: "Look, I don't have to get official recognition for anything I do. Ninety-eight percent of the thrill comes from knowing that the thing you designed works, and works almost the way you expected it would. If that happens, part of *you* is in that machine." On this project, he had reached a pinnacle the day when he finally expunged the "last known bug" from the board that he'd designed. . . .

Maybe in the late 1970s designing and debugging a computer was inherently more interesting than most other jobs in industry. But to at least some engineers, at the outset, Eagle appeared to be a fairly uninteresting computer to build. Yet more than two dozen people worked on it overtime, without any real hope of material rewards, for a year and a half; and afterward most of them felt glad. That happened largely because [project leader Tom] West and the other managers gave them enough freedom to invent, while at the same time guiding them toward success. . . .

Now it was done. The Eclipse Group and the many others who had worked on the machine—including, especially, Software and Diagnostics—had created 4096 lines of microcode, which fit into a volume about eight inches thick; diagnostic programs amounting to thousands of lines of code; over 200,000 lines of system software; several hundred pages of flowcharts; about 240 pages of schematics; hundreds and hundreds of engineering changes from the debugging; twenty hours of videotape to describe the new machine; and now a couple of functioning computers in blue-and-white cases, plus orders for many more on the way. Already, you could see that the engineers who had participated fully would be looking back on this experience a long time hence. It would be something unforgettable in their working lives. All this, at last, was no canard.

from The Soul of a New Machine, pp. 272–76.

Waiting for Tyler
Keith Thompson, American author

The way you would whimper and tremble during dreams. The deep breezy soul-breath that came each time we reached for you. Your animal warmth joining ours.

Each memory brings you closer, as if we could touch. Familiar hopes return, with their inevitable enticements. Maybe this time they are telling the truth. If we open our hearts once again to the myriad images pressing to come in—if we let your still vivid presence cross into the hollows we haven't returned to for so long— surely we'll get to feel your warm body sleeping next to us like before, the slow full pulse of your breath one with ours all through the night.

This is the promise of remembering: You'll be here, with us, and the world will not have broken.

That extraordinary spring day, three years ago; the day you were born, it turns out. Strolling in a quiet neighborhood of Mill Valley, Kathryn and I, delighting in our growing love affair. Talking about you, Tyler. Indirectly. The idea of you.

For weeks we've been talking about what breed of puppy to get when we move in together next month. As we walk along today Kathryn has made up her mind: a golden retriever. I answer, yes, that seems right to me too. A baby golden.

A few minutes of gratifying silence, then: magic. Around a bend in the road, like out of a dream, appears a pack of magnificent dogs organized around the presence of a particularly beautiful golden retriever. Honey-blond. Stately. Massive. Elegant. Playful. Exuding affection, yet wonderfully calm, clearly well-trained.

His name is Logan, we learn from the woman at the other end of his lead, Ellen. Logan is proud, she tells us, because that very day, Sophie, Logan's bitch, will deliver a litter of puppies.

Kathryn's eyes meet mine. As the dogs surround and include us, there's only one question: How can we get one? Ellen gives us a phone number to call that night.

We don't wait; we call within the hour. Ann, the breeder, puts us on a list for a baby Logan. That night, Sophie whelps three females, one male. The boy is yours, Ann calls back to say, if you want him. Do we ever.

Six weeks pass. Pickup day. Late June, so hot and humid. The long drive north to Napa.

There they all are, stumbling around the lawn in their tentative mammal bodies, to my eye equal parts dog, bear, lion, cub seal. Sophie watchful, Logan regal.

That's him, Ann tells us, pointing to a small blond ball of angora busily delighting himself with the sheer astonishment of being: closing in on a tall shoot of grass, edging fatefully toward a spectacular pounce.

"Tyler," we call. You look up, for an instant transcending yourself and taking us in. In that moment, our life together began:

Your delirious sigh as I cooled your baby belly with ice cubes during the hot drive home.

How I'd put one end of the rubber chew-toy ring in my mouth and coax you to take the other in yours. How tug became our best game.

Your sharp squeal (alarm? pleasure? both?) when you made your first mess on the bedroom rug.

That dolphin-smile you flashed each time Kathryn sang to you.

How I'd throw stick after stick into the reservoir as you barked and squealed, bit and pawed at the muddy edge. That immortal moment you pushed away from the shore and collapsed into the water. Your startled "but where's the ground?" terror giving way to amphibious ecstasy.

The way you learned to track gophers through their mazes of underground tunnels, always meeting them at the end.

How after midnight you'd leave the cold tile floor, step up onto our bed and fall asleep sprawled—luxuriously, aristocratically—on your back. The way you would whimper and tremble during dreams. The deep breezy soul-breath that came each we reached for you. Your animal warmth joining ours.

Your soft brown eyes, so sad, so knowing. What did you know, Tyler? Did you tell us? Did we seem to hear? Did you think we understood?

The day we brought you two-month Yoshi, your Great Pyrenees companion. How you welcomed him dog-to-pup, showing him every part of the five acres, including your best hiding place; how he outgrew you in size so quickly. The gorgeous sight of you running together, biting ankles, charging like bulls, colliding like elk; retreating, returning and falling exhausted; stampeding through the tall grass near the creek and beyond; showing up on the porch drenched with the black mud of eons.

Our life had become full. Whole.

All of this, and more, returns each time I say your name. As do the fast, heavy shadows of the last morning.

The delivery man was supposed to have been watching, especially in our driveway. He was supposed to know where you and Yoshi were as you barked alongside his truck. He said he didn't notice; he should have.

Yoshi nudging your writhing body as I ran to you; his baby brother confusion unbearable to watch. Holding you and pleading with God.

The uncountable ways I've tried to play the tape backward, to keep that day from happening.

So you would be here today for our afternoon walks through the orchard, to watch and smell the pippins whispering ripeness, enjoined by the rhythms of some larger alchemy.

You and Yoshi and Kathryn and me together.

Do you see?

All day and night at the vet hospital. The songs we sang, the prayers we murmured. *Tyler don't go.* The moment we knew we had to let you. No more injections, tubes, heroics. How we held you as your body quieted to silence. The unspoken, unspeakable holiness of that moment.

The weekend vigil we kept at home. Your muscular form so still on the makeshift platform, surrounded by daisies. Clearly, certainly, you would get up again *any moment now.*

Friends arriving and leaving. The incense, the candles, the chants, the countless rounds of last words, separate streams of laughter and tears coming together. Your blond fur still soft, your body getting harder, cold.

The sound, the sense, the feeling of earth calling for you, and you for earth.

It's time.

Sunday, early dusk. Securing you on the platform, we begin the dead march into the woods, slowed by weight: your body, our hearts. Each step an image from some ancient lucid dream. *Muffled drum. Taps. Dirge. Death bell. Funeral ring. Tolling of the knell. Requiem. Pallbearers. Last rites. Raven. "Weeping and gnashing of teeth." Crepe. Black. Cypress. Sackcloth and ashes.*

Yoshi keeping his distance, as he has these slow days, watching intently as we approach the grave we dug at dawn, "the lone couch of his everlasting sleep," said the poet. Yoshi simply attending as we lay you *down below* with your ball, a bunch of your favorite cookies, a print of our first Christmas family photo, so you'll remember us on the Other Side. And your first chew-toy.

Your soul all around. Everywhere.

Good-bye, sweetest boy.

One year has come and gone since that day. Afternoon air warm in some patches, cool in others. Wind says fog coming back to the valley. Everything has changed. Nothing has changed.

Tonight Kathryn and I will sit on the porch with your brother Yoshi and look down the long driveway. We'll talk, and we'll be silent. Yoshi will catch sight of a deer and take off, barking in the translucent dusk.

Neither of us will say so, but we'll expect to see you come bounding back up the road with Yoshi. The road to this house that was ours together.

How we miss you, golden Tyler. How we wait.

An original essay by Keith Thompson, 1993.

The Soul Hunger of Children
Valerie Andrews, American author

There is, and will forever be, a link between the innocence of childhood and the soul of the land.

As a child I had a secret place. Everyday at sunset I visited a grove of birches surrounded by a hedge of sweet-smelling privet. At the center was a mound where I would lie down and listen to the steady rhythmic heartbeat of the earth. For seven years I performed this daily ritual; even in winter I could feel this pulse as though I were connected by a rootlike umbilicus to the dark core of the land.

The grove faced west and formed a kind of kiva or womblike container. This enclosure had all the power of an ancient shrine; as the sun left the sky awash in crimson flames, I learned a way of being in the world and in transition. Something in my soul changed as the earth underwent its own transfiguration and the day's activity gave way to the long slow respiration of the night.

In the beginning of my life, I received my teachings directly from the natural world. I understood the rhythms of existence through the interplay of light and shadow, the subtle changes of the air and climate. I learned that for every mood there is a corresponding season and that our lives are seamlessly linked to the great life of the earth.

When I withdrew in winter and found myself in dark and inaccessible regions, I came to know that darkness is a time for the migration of the soul. I saw then that what we hold in common with the roots and seeds—a stage of mute and invisible growth.

My inner changes were always triggered by the changes in the land: I would feel the first breakthrough of spring as the windswept sky and swollen streams brought forth a new round of activity. I would become like the hard, insistent shoots sprouting upward from the earth, and something in me would be heartened and encouraged as I stretched my spirit upward toward the light.

The eruptions of the crocus and the daffodil still remind me that in the days ahead I will know the exhilaration of opening that belongs to the buds and flowers. By such observations, we discover that life is not static or fixed. Indeed, we are standing in the midst of it, wide-eyed and innocent.

There is, and will forever be, a link between the innocence of childhood and the soul of the land. Our innocence allows us to perceive the magic of creation. We remain under its spell until the onset of adulthood; then the bond is broken, the intimacy lost, as we surrender to a world of our own making, where everything is quantified and known. The poet Sven Birkerts describes childhood and the soul of nature this way:

> I had a happy childhood. Back then it was not one thing or another, just a way things had of happening natural and unquestioned. I was full to the brim, with nothing lacking; space and time were not yet separate concepts at all. "Weren't you ever bored?" Dear God, I was in ecstasy of boredom! I was so bored that time would back up on itself and start flowing in a new direction. And yet, it wasn't like the trivial boredom which afflicts me now. It was a dream, a plenitude. . . .

Our souls are formed in the idleness of youth and it is then when our time is unstructured and unmeasured, that we know ourselves to be at one with the essential wisdom of the land. When I was seven, I roamed the hillsides and the meadows, aware that the world around me was engaged in an endless cycle of renewal. I went to my birch grove certain that it would accept all my loves and disappointments, my childhood joys and tragedies. It was this place, then, that gave me my first sense of communion, that fueled my erotic bond with nature, my hunger for soul in other living things.

adapted by the author from *A Passion for This Earth*, pp. 15–17.

But What About the World's Soul?

James Hillman, American author and psychotherapist

. . . Keats's phrase, which has sustained my therapy for so long, contains a major mistake! It actually neglects the world, even while finding a soul use for it. You go through the world for your own sake, making your own soul. But what about the world's soul, Michael?

Dear Michael,
Surprise! I want to defend therapy, your basic kind—inward-searching, long-term, insight therapy—and its goal of individuation.

To my mind, there is clearly a price for the skills and knowledge acquired during the one hundred years of solitude—knowledge about the solitude, its significance, its imaginative richness, its relation to death, and its education in love. Also, the value of staying with tough stuff in a time of the fast fix and quick buck. There is a place for the strength of character and subtlety of insight that the investigation of interiority produces. I've called this psychological engagement "soul making," a term and an idea taken from the Romantics: Keats, Blake, and D. H. Lawrence. A long-term, soul-focused, depth analysis provides a discipline—a religious devotion with rituals, symbols, teachings, kind submissions, obediences, sacrifices—that is truly a care of soul. There are individual patients and individual therapists whose work, whose love, whose calling is clearly in this area, but—and this is crucial—the calling does not have to be away from the world or rest upon a theory of self-enclosed individuals. Soul making and care of soul do not have to be identified with introversion and the spiritual denial of the world of matter, objects, things.

Keats said, "Call the world if you please, 'the vale of Soul-making.' Then you will find out the use of the world." This was my motto for therapy for fifteen years, longer.

The motto imagines the tribulations of life as contributions to soul. I found Wallace Stevens saying something similar: "The way through the world/Is more difficult to find than the way beyond it." Simply said, you make soul by living life, not by retreating from the world into "inner work" or beyond the world in spiritual disciplines and meditation removes.

This way through the world was a hugely satisfying insight, a great step for me. No longer was I trapped in the usual program of, first, retreat into deep inner work and, then, return to the world. Instead, I began to value every ongoing engagement for the sake of soul. It doesn't matter where the stimulus of distraction comes from, how lofty or how cheap, one simply feels it and reflects on it in terms of soul. You ask yourself: How does this event bear on soul making? This insight from Keats—a puer, by the way, who died before he was twenty-six—also separated me from my classical colleagues who, I believe, never really left the Cartesian split between inner and outer—good soul inside and the world, the flesh, and the devil outside—reformulated as introversion and extraversion.

Horribile dictu, now I see that even the Keatsian solution is inadequate. Why? Because it is self-centered. It still focuses on one's personal destiny or, as they now call it, "journey." The exterior world's value is simply utilitarian, for the sake of soul making. It provides obstacles, pitfalls, monsters to be met in order to make one's interior soul.

So, I want to clear this up here, because Keats's phrase, which has sustained my therapy for so long, contains a major mistake! It actually neglects the world, even while finding a soul use for it. You go through the world for your own sake, making your own soul. But what about the world's soul, Michael? What about the *anima mundi* and making that? The plight of the world, suffering of its oceans and its rivers, its air and its forests, the ugliness of its cities, and depletion of its soils have certainly forced us to feel that we cannot go through the world for our own benefit and that we are actually destroying our souls by an attitude that pretends to save them. The ship of death [D. H.] Lawrence says we must each build is no longer a private ark that can take the storms; the ship of death is the world soul sinking like an overloaded garbage barge. That's why I say therapy—even the best deep therapy—contributes to the world's destruction.

We have to have new thinking—or much older thinking than Lawrence, Blake, and Keats—to find roots for therapy's deep interiorizing work. Soul making must be reimagined. We have to go back before romanticism, back to medieval alchemy and Renaissance Neoplatonism, back to Plato, back to Egypt, and also especially out of Western history to tribal animistic psychologies that are always mainly concerned, not with individualities, but with the soul of things ("environmental concerns," "deep ecology," as it's now called) and propitiatory acts that keep the world on its course.

As Sendivogius, an alchemist, said, "The greater part of the soul lies outside the body." (*Mens sana in corpore sano*) today means "the body of the world"; if it is not kept healthy, we go insane. The neglect of the environment, the body of the world, are part and parcel of our personal "insanity." The world's body must be restored to health, for in that body is also the world's soul. I don't think spiritual disciplines take the world enough into account; they're always set on transcending, that is, denying it with spiritual practices. That's why therapy is still so important—once it makes the effort of rethinking its base—because therapy stays here on earth, in the mess of life, truly concerned with soul.

The only way I can justify still using the term *individuation* today is by extending it to mean the individuation of each moment in life, each action, each relationship, and each thing. The individuation of things. Not merely my individuation with its belief in an interior self that draws my care from the world to my "process," my "journey."

Our focus could be on the soul potential of the object—as we are trying to do with this book we are writing. *Aren't we trying for a well-made book rather than trying to express or realize our subjective personalities?* This means individuating each act we do and thing we live with, actualizing *its* potential (the human potential movement turned outward beyond the human) so that the innate dignity, beauty, and integrity of any act and any thing from doorknob to desk chair to bed sheet may become fully present in its uniqueness. I am inviting us to think again of the morality of craft, the value of rhetoric, and the truth of the body's gestures. Let's make things "well"—which means both well made and also healthy. For this, we need the individuating eye that can see what Wallace Stevens called "the poem in the heart of things," that innate imaginal essence I called an acorn. So, individuating begins with noticing, paying attention to the specifics of what is actually there so that it can become fully what it is. This is simply what therapy has been doing all along, only that its attention has been held exclusively to humans.

Curiously, just as humans show the first inklings of their uniqueness in their pathologies, so a thing's *pathology* may show its specific essence, its raison d'être. The hard light from a fluorescent tube says that light is not "well," but it also says that the tube's essential purpose is light making. The tear-off tab on an aluminum can says that its job is to make the contents easily available, yet that tab cuts our fingers. Like with human pathology, the pathology of things is where the noticing eye first alights, despite the glossy cover-up ads.

Michael, if we don't begin speculating and experimenting with extending individuation into the world of things, the idea remains captured by private capitalism, an enterprise of developing my own private property, "myself," my very own soul, my personal journey, and my locked-away journal, the gesture for which points away from the world and toward the recesses of the chest. Me oh my.

The Neoplatonic idea I am pursuing in this book and everywhere I go to talk cannot separate soul in me from soul in others—others being not just people but environment. You could also say what I am reaching for by bringing in door-knobs and beer cans is shifting the ideas of depth from the psychology of the inner person to a psychology of things, a depth psychology of extraversion.

I look forward to your answer to this essay. Fondly, as usual,

Jim

from *We've Had a Hundred Years of Psychotherapy—And the World's Getting Worse,* by James Hillman and Michael Ventura, pp. 50–53.

The wind, one brilliant day, called
Antonio Machado, Spanish poet, 1875–1939

*The wind, one brilliant day, called
to my soul with an aroma of jasmine.
"In return for this jasmine odor,
I'd like all the odor of your roses."
"I have no roses; I have no flowers left now
in my garden. . . . All are dead."
"Then I'll take the waters of the fountains,
and the yellow leaves and the dried-up petals."
The wind left. . . . I wept. I said to my soul,
"What have you done with the garden entrusted to you?"*

from *Times Alone: Selected Poems of Antonio Machado,*
translated by Robert Bly, p. 57.

PART SEVEN

SOUL AND DESTINY

Arise, soul, arise. Ascend to your ancient home.
—Ginza III

Shall we believe that the soul, which is invisible, and which goes hence to a place that is like herself, glorious, and pure, and invisible, to Hades, which is rightly called the unseen world to dwell with the good and wise God (whither, if it be the will of God, my soul too must shortly go)—shall we believe that the soul, whose nature is so glorious, and pure, and invisible, is blown away by the winds and perishes as soon as she leaves the body, as the world says?
—Socrates, *The Phaedo*

Immortality is like trying to carve your initials in a block of ice in the middle of July.
—Arthur Miller

Introduction

It is said of the traditional Ik society of East Africa that the ceremonies of the elders can no longer be performed. As their culture disintegrates around them the old people must strain to recall the old ways. Then, the bodies of the dead were buried with rituals handed down by the gods themselves to remind the survivors of the good things in life, but also, at the moment when the night stood still, to speed the soul on its journey to the stars.

For many traditional societies the universe itself is a womb for the soul's development and a passageway to eternity. The Maya conception of the soul gives people confidence that their lives partake of a greater reality extending far beyond the visible realm. The Vietnamese believe cranes carry souls to the afterworld. Moslems believe that the souls of the faithful assume forms of snowwhite birds and nestle under the throne of Allah until the resurrection. Catholics believe that on November 2, All Souls Day, there should be solemn repose for the faithfully departed. In medieval England soul bells were rung during funerals, and soul cakes baked and distributed at churches to the poor, who went a-souling, crying for soul cakes: "Soul, soul, for soul-cake/Pray you, good mistress, a soul cake."

The principle of immortality must have been a "momentous discovery," as Georg Feuerstein describes it elsewhere in his essay on soul. He speculates that the belief in an immaterial, immortal soul may have come from the transpersonal experiences of those in trance, out-of-body experiences, the so-called soul retrievals of shamans. In turn, this may have inspired the earliest philosophies based on life in metamorphosis, that all is flux, all is constant renewal, regeneration; that all things return to their source. Today's cosmologists must imagine the unimaginable stretches of the universe; poets must wrap words around the indescribable; so too, our ancestors had to flex their imaginations to encompass the invisible possibilities after visible death.

For this last section of my anthology I have chosen passages that bring us full circle in our exploration of the soul's origins, manifestations, and destiny. Like the Tibetan and Egyptian Books of the Dead, ancient guidebooks for the souls departing for the netherworld, these selections attempt to unriddle life by unraveling the afterlife. They ask: How do we reconcile the unknown? Are there any patterns in the belief of life after death?

We begin this section with the magnificent prison dialogues of Socrates with his friends Cebes and Simmias, and a sixth-century "riddling song" about the shape-changing soul of the poet, attributed to the Welsh poet Taliesin, the traditional inspiration for the Merlin character in the King Arthur legends. Following them in turn is the death scene of Beowulf, the earliest extant poem in modern English.

Reincarnation, the belief that each individual is imbued with an immortal essence, independent of the physical body, and may be reborn into another body after death, is a worldwide conviction of the long journey of soul. This vastly complex philosophical idea is interpreted quite differently from East to West. Continual rebirth has sobering implications in the East, so the emphasis is on an eventual eternal departure from the natural realm, which is nirvana, the mystic merging with the One. The Western emphasis on individual identity and its insatiable hunger for life interprets reincarnation as a desire for ever more incarnations. My selections on what the Druids called metempsychosis range from the sublime dialogues of Sri Ramakrishna to theosophist Rudolf Steiner, who spoke of the two streams of the soul—past and present—that flow eternally, seeking to draw nearer to the divine. "This intimation is the first awakening of a feeling of God within us," he writes, "a feeling of something greater than all our will-power dwelling within us." Joseph Campbell's retelling of a Siberian shaman soul journey gives us the origin of the half-drum as well as a hint of the beliefs of the northern people into the immortality of the soul.

In rather dramatic contrast with the literal belief of the soul's full-bodied survival after death, I've chosen from filmmaker and ethnographer Maya Deren's account of Haitian death rituals an excerpt that should puncture any remaining stereotypes from Saturday matinees. The Western ideal of harmony between mind, body, and soul is juxtaposed here with the Haitian belief in dead bodies without souls, the zombie tradition that reveals a certain terror of immortality because of the implicit ambiguity of being embodied in a soulless zombie.

Turning to the realm of science fiction, I've chosen a dreamlike excerpt from a fine story by Alan Brennert, where a scientist is startled to find a "pilgrim soul" in a column of deep violet light in his laboratory. "Do you suppose," he gingerly asks his partner, "a human soul has been reincarnated inside that computer?" Out of the labyrinthine world of recent Latin American literature I've chosen an excerpt from the enchanting magical realism of Juan Bosch's "The Beautiful Soul of Don Damian." This reeling tale has a vertiginous perspective in which we see death from the perspective of the soul fluttering away—uncertain about its own departure.

Finally, Emily Dickinson encapsules the entire anthology in her poem about the "Soul's distinct connection" as a flash, a click, a moment of sudden awareness.

And then? As Homer describes the *immortalizing* moment in the *Odyssey*. ". . . the soul dream-like, flitters, and is gone."

The Last Hours of Socrates
Plato, Greek philosopher, ca. 470–399 B.C.E.

For I do nothing but go about persuading you all, old and young alike, not to take thought for your persons or your properties, but first and chiefly to care about the greatest improvements of the soul.

Tell me, then, what is that of which the inherence will render the body alive?

The soul, he replied.

And is this always the case?

Yes, he said, of course.

Then whatever the soul possesses, to that she comes bearing life?

Yes, certainly.

And is there any opposite to life?

There is, he said.

And what is that?

Death.

Then the soul, as has been acknowledged, will never receive the opposite of what she brings.

Impossible, replied Cebes.

And now, he said, what did we just now call that principle which repels the musical or the just?

The unmusical, he said, and the unjust.

And what do we call that principle which does not admit of death?

The immortal, he said.

And does the soul admit of death?

Yes, he said.

And may we say that has been proven?

Yes, abundantly proven, Socrates, he replied.

Supposing that the odd were imperishable, must not three be imperishable?

Of course.

And if that which is cold were imperishable, when the warm principle came attacking the snow, must not the snow have retired whole and unmelted—for it could never have perished, nor could it have remained and admitted the heat.

True, he said.

Again, if the uncooling or warm principle were imperishable, the fire when assailed by cold would not have perished or have been extinguished, but would have gone away unaffected?

Certainly, he said.

And the same may be said of the immortal: If the immortal is also perishable, the soul when attacked by death cannot perish; for the preceding argument shows that the soul will not admit of death, or even be dead, any more than three or the odd numbers will admit of the even, or fire, or the heat in the fire, of the cold. Yet a person may say: 'But although the odd will not become even at the approach of the even why may not the odd perish and even take the place of the odd?' Now to him who makes this objection, we cannot answer that the odd principle is imperishable; for this has not been acknowledged, but if this had been acknowledged, there would have been no difficulty in contending that at the approach of the even the odd principle and the number three took their departure; and the same argument would have held good of fire and heat and any other thing.

Very true . . .

But then, O my friends, he said, if the soul is really immortal, what care should be taken of her, not only in respect of the portion of time which is called life, but of eternity! And the danger of neglecting her from this point of view does indeed appear to be awful. If death had only been the end of all, the wicked would have had a good bargain in dying, for they would have been happily quit not only of their body, but of their own evil together with their souls. But now, inasmuch as the soul is manifestly immortal, there is no release or salvation from evil except the attainment of the highest virtue and wisdom. For the soul when on her progress to the world below takes nothing with her but nurture and education; and these are said greatly to benefit or greatly to injure the departed, at the very beginning of this journey thither.

For after death, as they say, the genius of each individual, to whom he belonged in life, leads him to a certain place in which the dead are gathered together, whence after judgment has been given they pass into the world below, following the guide, who is appointed to conduct them from this world to the other: and when they have there received their due and remained their time, another guide brings them back again after many revolutions of ages. Now this way to the other world is not, as Aeschylus says in the Telephus, a single and straight path—if that were so no guide would be needed, for no one could miss it; but there are many partings of the road, and windings, as I infer from the rites and sacrifices which are offered to the gods below in places where three ways meet on earth. The wise and orderly soul follows in the straight path and is conscious of her surroundings; but the soul which desires the body, and which, as I was relating before, has long been fluttering about the lifeless frame and the world of sight, is after many struggles and many sufferings hardly and with violence carried away by her attendant genius; and when she arrives at the place where the other souls are gathered, if she be impure and have done impure deeds, whether foul murders or other crimes which are the brothers of these, and the works of brothers in crime—from that soul every one flees and turns away; no one will be her companion of evil until certain times are fulfilled, and when they are fulfilled, she is borne irresistibly to her own fitting habitation; as every pure and just soul which has passed through life in the company and under the guidance of the gods has also her own proper home.

from *The Phaedo: The Trial and Death of Socrates,*
translated by Benjamin Jowett, pp. 256–61.

The Shape-Shifter
Taliesin, sixth-century Welsh bard

Knowest thou what thou art
In the hour of sleep—
A mere body, a mere soul—
Or a secret retreat of light?. . .
I marvel that in their books
They know not with certainty
The properties of the soul;
Of what form are its members;
In what part, and when, it takes up its abode,
Or by what wind or stream it is supplied.

I have been in many shapes before I attained a congenial form . . .
There is nothing in which I have not been.

I was with my Lord in the highest sphere
On the fall of Lucifer into the depth of hell;
I have borne a banner before Alexander. . . .
I am a wonder whose origin is not known.
I have been in Asia with Noah in the ark,
I have seen the destruction of Sodom and Gomorrah. . . .
I shall be until the doom on the face of the earth. . . .
I was originally little Gwion,
And at length I am Taliesin.

from *Reincarnation: An East-West Anthology,* compiled and edited
by Joseph Head and S. L. Cranston, pp. 42–43.

The Death of Beowulf

Anonymous Anglo-Saxon singer, eighth century

Fate has swept our race away,
Taken warriors in their strength and led them
To the death that was waiting.

Then Wexstan's son went in, as quickly
As he could, did as the dying Beowulf
Asked, entered the inner darkness
Of the tower, went with his mail shirt and his sword.
Flushed with victory he groped his way,
A brave young warrior, and suddenly saw
Piles of gleaming gold, precious
Gems, scattered on the floor, cups
And bracelets, rusty old helmets, beautifully
Made but rotting with no hands to rub
And polish them. They lay where the dragon left them;
It had flown in the darkness, once, before fighting
Its final battle. (So gold can easily
Triumph, defeat the strongest of men,
No matter how deep it is hidden!) And he saw,
Hanging high above, a golden
Banner, woven by the best of weavers
And beautiful. And over everything he saw
A strange light, shining everywhere,
On walls and floor and treasure. Nothing
Moved, no other monsters appeared;
He took what he wanted, all the treasures
That pleased his eye, heavy plates

And golden cups and the glorious banner,
Loaded his arms with all they could hold.
Beowulf's dagger, his iron blade, traitors,
Had finished the fire-spitting terror
That once protected tower and treasures
Alike; the gray-bearded lord of the Geats
Had ended those flying, burning raids
Forever.
   Then Wiglaf went back, anxious
To return while Beowulf was alive, to bring him
Treasure they'd won together. He ran,
Hoping his wounded king, weak
And dying, had not left the world too soon.
Then he brought their treasure to Beowulf, and found
His famous king bloody, gasping
For breath. But Wiglaf sprinkled water
Over his lord, until the words
Deep in his breast broke through and were heard.
Beholding the treasure, he spoke, haltingly:
"For this, this gold, these jewels, I thank
Our Father in Heaven, Ruler of the Earth—
For all of this, that His grace has given me,
Allowed me to bring to my people while breath
Still came to my lips. I sold my life
For this treasure, and I sold it well. Take
What I leave, Wiglaf, lead my people,
Help them; my time is gone. Have
The brave Geats build me a tomb,
When the funeral flames have burned me, and build it
Here, at the water's edge, high
On this spit of land, so sailors can see
This tower, and remember my name, and call it
Beowulf's tower, and boats in the darkness
And mist, crossing the sea, will know it."
Then that brave king gave the golden
Necklace from around his throat to Wiglaf,
Gave him his gold-covered helmet, and his rings,
And his mail shirt, and ordered him to use them well:
"You're the last of all our far-flung family.
Fate has swept our race away,
Taken warriors in their strength and led them
To the death that was waiting. And now I follow them."
The old man's mouth was silent, spoke
No more, had said as much as it could;

He would sleep in the fire, soon. His soul
Left his flesh, flew to glory.

from *Beowulf*, translated by Burton Raffel,
pp. 108–10.

When I Have Sacrificed My Angel Soul
Jalal-Uddin Rumi, twelfth-century Sufi master, 1207–1275

I died a mineral, and became a plant.
I died a plant and rose an animal.
I died an animal and I was a man.
Why should I fear? When was I less by dying?
Yet once more I shall die as man, to soar
With the blessed angels; but even from angelhood
I must pass on. All except God perishes.
When I have sacrificed my angel soul,
I shall become that which no mind ever conceived.
O, let me not exist! for Non-Existence proclaims,
"To Him we shall return."

from *The Perennial Philosophy*, Aldous Huxley, p. 213.

The Soul-Searcher
A Siberian Shaman Journey
retold by Joseph Campbell, American mythologist, 1904–1989

Erlen Khan, the Lord of the Dead, complained to the great god
Tengri, on high, that because of Moron-Kara he was no longer able
to hold the souls brought to him by his Messengers; and so Tengri
himself determined to make trial of the shaman with a test. He
took possession of the soul of a certain man, slipped it into a bottle, and then, sitting with the bottle in hand, his thumb covering
its opening, he waited to see what the mighty Burian would do.

The man whose soul had been taken fell ill, and his family sent
for Morgon-Kara. The shaman immediately recognized that the
soul of the man had been taken, and riding on his wonderful
drum, he searched the forests, the waters, the mountain gorges,
indeed the earth, and then descended to the Underworld. The soul
being nowhere in any of these, there remained but one domain to
be searched: High Heaven. So, sitting on his drum, he flew aloft.

And he cruised the heavens for some time before noticing that the radiant High God was sitting there with a bottle in his hand, over the top of which the ball of his thumb was pressed. Studying the circumstance, Morgon-Kara perceived that within the bottle was the very soul he had come to retrieve. So he transformed himself into a wasp, flew at the god, and gave him such a hot sting on the forehead that his thumb jerked from the opening and the soul escaped. The next thing Tengri knew was that the shaman, together with his prize, was on his drum again, sailing back to earth. He reached for a thunderbolt, let it fly, and the drum was split in half. And that is why shaman drums today have but one head.

from *The Way of the Animal Powers,* Joseph Campbell,
vol. I, part 2: *Mythologies of the Great Hunt,* p. 176.

The Celtic Doctrine of Immortality
Stuart Piggott, British archaeologist

The item of Druidic belief which struck the classical writers most forcibly was that of literal personal immortality. In Posidonius as quoted by Diodorus, the Celts held that "the souls of men are immortal, and that after a definite number of years they live a second life when the soul passes to another body." Strabo puts this in the form of a belief of the Druids "as well as other authorities" that "men's souls and the universe are indestructible, although at times fire and water may prevail." Caesar makes the chief point of doctrine "that souls do not suffer death, but after death pass from the one to the other," *ab aliis . . . transire ad alios.* Ammianus quotes Timagenes to the effect that the Druids "with grand contempt for mortal lot . . . professed the immortality of the soul," while Mela names as the best-known dogma of the Druids "that souls are eternal and there is another life in the infernal regions," and like Caesar rationalizes this as an incentive to pointless bravery in war. Lucan, in the rhetorical address to the Druids already quoted goes on:

> But you assure us, no ghosts seek the silent kingdom
> of Erebus, nor the pallid depths of Dis 'realm, but with a new
> body the spirit reigns in another world—if we understand
> your hymns death's halfway through a long life.

Diodorus, Ammianus, and Valerius Maximus associate the belief in immortality with the Pythagorean theory of metempsychosis, equating the Celtic doctrine with the "belief of Pythagoras" or idealizing this by making Druids "members of the intimate fellowship of the Pythagorean faith." This leads us to the Alexandrian sources, where Hippolytus not only makes the Druids to have "profoundly examined the Pythagorean faith" but to have been instructed in it by the mythical Thracian Zalmoxis, said to have been a pupil of Pythagoras himself. With such writers as Clement and Cyril we are in a world where the Druids are not only wholly Pythagorean, but where the invention of that school of philosophy is even attributed to them. We are hardly surprised to find too that Anacharsis the Scythian sage, and the vegetarian Hyperboreans, as well as Zalmoxis, are all brought together in this dream-world of barbarian philosophers.

It has been pointed out on more than one occasion that the Celtic doctrine of immortality, as set out in the sources just quoted, is not in fact Pythagorean in content at all, in that it does not imply a belief in the transmigration of souls through all living things—"that the soul of our grandma might haply inhabit a bird"—but only a naive, literal and vivid reliving of an exact counterpart of earthly life beyond the grave. Despite the Greek influence on Celtic culture from the time of Pythagoras (in what was archaeologically the Hallstatt D phase of barbarian Europe), we need hardly look to outside sources for this simple concept, corroborated not only by the tales of the classical writers, such as that of Celts offering to pay off debts in the afterlife, and by the inferences to be drawn from the earlier Irish literature, but also by the archaeological evidence. . . . What is surely significant is the very real contrast between the Celtic and the classical vision of eternity and the afterlife, which would render the former so strange as to be necessary of explanation in some familiar philosophical terms: This is the contrast explicitly stressed by Lucan, though in Pythagorean terms.

from *The Druids*, pp. 102–4.

The Aboriginal Death—Expanding into the Dreamtime
Robert Lawlor, Australian author and artist

The higher the initiation, the more an individual lives in the awareness of this Dreamtime reality and the stronger the ancestral soul will be at the time of death.

The first and most fundamental concept of death in the Aboriginal tradition is the doctrine of three worlds, the unborn, the living and the dying, and the Land of the Dead . . . *Each individual spirit passes through these three domains only once.* After death, it is the profound responsibility of the living to ensure that the spiritual component of the dead person is separated from this world and can proceed to the next. There is no rebirth for the individual spirit aspect of consciousness. The Aborigines believe, as do Native Americans, that the notion of reincarnation is based on two factors: (1) the obsession with the illusion of individuality extends into the belief that the ego survives death and remains intact in the afterlife; (2) such cultures have lost the knowledge of burial practices that assist the spiritual energy of the deceased to separate from the earthly sphere, and so the spiritual atmosphere is polluted with fragmented, disembodied energies of the dead. Fragments of spirit from the dead can interact with the living, sometimes inhabiting, shadowing, or controlling conscious behavior and destiny. People may mistakenly refer to these influences as remembrances of past lives or "channeling." The Aborigines say that the earthly atmosphere is now saturated with dead spirits and that this pollution of the spiritual atmosphere parallels the physical pollution of the biosphere—both of which contribute to the self-destructive course of our civilization.

The second universally held Aboriginal belief about death is that at the moment of death, the spiritual component of the individual splits into three distinct parts. The first aspect of spirit is the totemic center of being, or the *totemic soul.* This soul is related to the sources of the life of the body: the earthly location of birth and the spirit of the animal and plant species to which the person's bloodlines are connected and from which he or she has derived nourishment through life. After death, the totemic soul essence, once incorporated in the psychic and physical makeup of the person, is returned in ceremonial ritual to the spirits of nature, to the animals, plants, rocks, water, sunlight, fire, trees, and wind that have contributed their life and substance to the person's bodily existence. The realm of the unborn is the domain of the totemic soul of each of earth's forms and species. Returning spiritual energy to the animating forces of the totemic species reciprocates the debt to all those living things that were sacrificed for the sake of humans. In other words, they give back spiritual animation to that which has physically animated our bodily existence. In this exchange, the spiritual development of the tribal person contributes to the deepening spiritual unfolding of the entirety of the natural world.

The second aspect of an individual's spirit force that is released at death resonates with the great Creative Ancestors of the Dreamtime and can be called the *ancestral soul*. The domain of the unchanging metaphysical archetypes, the Dreamtime Ancestors, is the Land of the Dead, which is in the sky. The aspect of the deceased's soul that emanates from the Ancestors' journeys to the constellations in a particular region of the sky. Each region of the starry heavens has not only a pictorial constellation (usually an animal) but also a particular pattern of invisible energy. These patterns are symbolized in the geometric clan designs painted on the abdomen of the corpse during burial rites. The same clan design was painted on the person at the time of his or her first initiation. At the person's initiation and at death the celebrants chant, "May from here your spirit reach to the stomach of the sky."

The energy of the celestial field resonates with the geometry of the painted design and acts as a guide for the spirit in its journey to the heavens. Throughout life, the successive initiations encourage a person to identify his or her character and destiny increasingly with the primary patterns of the mythic creative beings. In this way the individual soul gradually merges with the archetypal ground of creation. The higher the initiation, the more an individual lives in the awareness of this Dreamtime reality and the stronger the ancestral soul will be at the time of death.

The third aspect of the human soul is referred to by the Aborigines as the Trickster. It is the spiritual source of the individualized ego and can be characterized as the *ego soul*. This spirit force is bound to locality; to relationships with wives, husbands, and kin relatives; and to material things such as tools and items of apparel. It is the spirit force that bonds us to the finite and the particular and to the responsibilities, relationships, and pleasures of our individual existence. At the time of death the Trickster or ego soul is the most dangerous to deal with. It resents death, because this change of status removes contact from the material or local world in which it functions. It may get stuck in this world, so to speak, after the other aspects of the soul have departed. . . .

In a sense, the Aboriginal concept of ego soul is related to the trickster figure in Greek mythology, Hermes. Hermes is the archetypal force that makes the temporal world appear to be the eternal. We all have had the experience of Hermes, when a transitory thing or event appears to be all-important, or a fleeting disguise appears as reality. . . .

Artists in our society are often positively imbued with a type of Hermes or trickster spirit. Through paintings, sculpture, architecture, books, or films, the artist implants designs for an earthly immortality. The very presence of a work of art acts like a relic, perpetuating the memory and force of the deceased artist. Eventually, however, this trickster soul fades and its traces in earth and memory disintegrate. Every soul ultimately must proceed to find true immortality in identifying itself with the enduring energy emanating from the celestial realms of the Dreamtime Ancestors.

from *Voices of the First Day,* pp. 343–45.

The Two Streams of Soul
Rudolf Steiner, German anthroposophist, 1861–1925

Thus there are these two streams, one from the past and one from the future, which come together in the soul—will anyone who observes himself deny that?

Anyone who looks deeply into the life of the soul will see that these two streams, one from the past and one from the future, are continually meeting there. The fact that we are influenced by the past is obvious: Who could deny that our energy or idleness of yesterday has some effect on us today? But we ought not to deny the reality of the future, either, for we can observe in the soul the intrusion of future events, although they have not yet happened. After all, there is such a thing as fear of something likely to happen tomorrow, or anxiety about it. Is that not a sort of feeling or perception concerned with the future? Whenever the soul experiences fear or anxiety, it shows by the reality of its feelings that it is reckoning not only with the past but in a very lively manner with something hastening towards it from the future. These, of course, are single examples, but they will suffice to suggest that anyone who surveys the soul will find numerous others to contradict the abstract logic which says that since the future does not yet exist, it can have no present influence.

Thus there are these two streams, one from the past and one from the future, which come together in the soul—will anyone who observes himself deny that?—and produce a kind of whirlpool, comparable to the confluence of two rivers. Closer observation shows that the impressions left on us by past experiences, and in which we have dealt with them, have made the soul what it is. We bear within ourselves the legacy of our doing, feeling, and thinking in the past. If we look back over these past experiences, especially those in which we played an active part, we shall very often be impelled to an assessment of ourselves. . . .

We need only to remember the feelings of fear and anxiety that gnaw at our soul-life in face of the unknown future. Is there any-

thing that can give the soul a sense of security in this situation?
Yes, there is. It is what we may call a feeling of humbleness towards anything that may come towards the soul out of the darkness of the future. But this feeling will be effective only if it has
the character of prayer. Let us avoid misunderstanding. We are not
extolling something that might be called humbleness in one sense
or another; we are describing a definite form of it—humbleness to
whatever the future may bring. Anyone who looks anxiously and
fearfully towards the future hinders his development, hampers the
free unfolding of his soul-forces. Nothing, indeed, obstructs this
development more than fear and anxiety in face of the unknown
future. But the results of submitting to the future can be judged
only by experience. What does this humbleness mean?

Ideally, it would mean saying to oneself: Whatever the next hour
or day may bring, I cannot change it by fear or anxiety, for it is not
yet known. I will therefore wait for it with complete inward restful-
ness, perfect tranquility of mind. Anyone who can meet the future
in this calm, relaxed way, without impairing his active strength and
energy, will be able to develop the powers of his soul freely and in-
tensively. It is as if hindrance after hindrance fall away, as the soul
comes to be more and more pervaded by this feeling of humbleness towards approaching events.

from *Metamorphoses of the Soul*, vol. 2,
translated by C. Davy and C. von Arnim, pp. 43–45.

The Soul of the Fierce People

Napoleon A. Chagnon, American anthropologist

*One has a noreshi within his being, a sort of spirit or portion of the soul,
and, in addition, an animal that lives in the jungle and corresponds to the
soul.*

[Yąnomamö] concepts of the soul are elaborate and complicated.
The true or real portion of living man is his "will" or "self" (*buhii*).
At death, this changes into a *no borebö* and travels from this layer
to *hedu*, the place above where the souls of the departed continue
to exist in an ethereal state, much in the same fashion as do the
people on earth: gardening, hunting, and practicing magic.

The trail along which the *no borebö* travel forks after it reaches
hedu. Sometimes, the Yąnomamö will point to the sky and explain
that such and such a cloud is the *no borebö* of a Yąnomamö who is
just reaching *hedu*. After the soul reaches the fork in the trail, a
spirit, the son of Thunder (Yąru), Wadawadariwä, asks the *no*

borebö if it had been generous during its life on earth. If it had been stingy, Wadawadariwä directs the soul along the path that leads to *shobari waka,* a place on *hedu* where souls of stingy Yąnomamö burn eternally. Most of the Yąnomamö I questioned on this asserted that they planned to lie to Wadawadariwä and avoid going to *shobari waka.* In general, they did not fear this place and were convinced that they would not be sent there. They expect Wadawadariwä to direct them to the trail that leads into *hedu* proper.

Another portion of the soul, the *no uhudi* or *bore,* is released at cremation. This part of the soul remains on earth and wanders about in the jungle. The children who die always change into this, as they do not have the *no borebö* portion that goes to *hedu:* It must be acquired. The reason that children do not change into the *no borebö* is that their "wills" (*buhii*) are ignorant or innocent (*mohode*). Thus, one has a character only after a certain amount of knowledge and experience are gained; with this, one develops a knowledgeable "will" and can expect to enter *hedu* in the form of a *no borebö.* Apart from this, one is born with an *uhudi* (bore), which is invariably released at cremation and wanders eternally in the jungle after death. Some of these wandering *uhudi* are malevolent and attack travelers in the jungle at night. When they do so, they use sticks and clubs. The Yąnomamö usually use the name *bore* when describing the attacks of these malevolent spirits, although this is just an alternate name for the *no uhudi.*

Finally, each individual has a *noreshi.* This is a dual concept: One has a *noreshi* within his being, a sort of spirit or portion of the soul, and, in addition, an animal that lives in the jungle and corresponds to this soul. The *noreshi* animals are inherited patrilineally for men and matrilineally for women. Kąobowa, for example, inherited his *noreshi* animal, the black monkey, from his father, and transmitted it to his son. All male kinsmen have the black monkey as their *noreshi.* Bahimi, Kąobowa's wife, has the dog for her *noreshi* animal, as does her mother and her daughter by Kąobowa. The *noreshi* animal of a woman always travels on the ground below the animal of the husband. . . .

The soul aspect of the *noreshi,* however, can leave the human body at will and wander. Sickness results when the *noreshi* has left the body; unless it is brought back soon, the person will die. The *noreshi* is the vulnerable portion of the complete being, the part that is the target of witchcraft and harmful magic. The shamans (*shabori*) wage constant war against the evil demons (*hekura*) of enemy groups who have been sent to capture the *noreshi* parts of children. They, in turn, send their own *hekura* to capture the *nore-*

shi of enemy children; the wars that take place between men who raid to kill are likewise carried over into the domain of the supernatural. . . .

The vulnerability of the *noreshi* to magical spells is best exemplified by the fact that the shamans of every village spend most of their time chanting to the *hekura* (demons) with the intention of persuading them either to attack the *noreshi* of other (enemy) children or to drive off the *hekura* sent by enemy shamans. Again, the Yąnomamö used two of their concepts of the soul to describe photographs and tape recordings. They were very hostile to me when I attempted to take photographs, especially of children, because I, in effect, was capturing the *noreshi* of the child: A photograph was called *noreshi*. Tape recordings, in contrast, were not considered to be harmful. If anything, they enjoyed having me record their music and discussions, and always demanded that I play them back for everyone to hear. The word used to describe a recording was *no uhudibö*, the part of the soul that wanders in the jungle after the body is cremated. In short, only the *noreshi* aspect of the soul is vulnerable.

from *Yąnomamö: The Fierce People*, pp. 48–50.

The Sioux Soul-Releasing Ceremony
Black Elk, nineteenth-century Oglala Sioux medicine man

Before the soul is released, all the people gather together, for everybody participates in this great rite, which can best be called The Making of Sacredness. As this time approaches, all the men go hunting for the buffalo, and when many are killed the bones are cracked and boiled, and from this tallow *wasna* is made. The women dry the best part of the meat, which is then called *papa*, and all this is contributed to the rites.

After first consulting with the other holy men of the band, the keeper of the soul appoints the special day, and when this time arrives, the helpers make a large ceremonial lodge from several small tipis and cover the earth inside with sacred sage.

The helper of the keeper of the soul then takes a pipe, and holding it up to the heavens, he cries: "Behold, O *Wakan-Tanka!* [Great Mystery, The Supreme Being] We are now about to do Thy will. With all the beings of the universe, we offer to You this pipe!"

The helper then takes a pinch of the sacred tobacco *kinnikinnik*, and holding it and the stem of the pipe towards the west, he cries: "With this *wakan* [sacred, mysterious] tobacco, we place

You in the pipe. O winged Power of the west. We are about to send our voices to *Wakan-Tanka*, and we wish You to help us!

"This day is *wakan* because a soul is to be released. All over the universe there will be happiness and rejoicing! O You sacred Power of the place where the sun goes down, it is a great thing we are doing in placing You in the pipe. Give to us for our rites one of the two sacred red and blue days which You control!"

[When the sacred pipe has been filled and offered to the directions and the earth, the keeper of the soul smokes it and leads the rites for releasing the soul and the sacred prayers. Then the pipe is passed around sun-wise and all the gathered people smoke.]

After the pipe has been offered up to *Wakan-Tanka*, the keeper begins to cry, and soon all the people are crying.

I should, perhaps, explain to you, here, that it is good to cry at this moment, for it shows that we are thinking of the soul and of death, which must come to all created beings and things; and it is also a sign that we are humiliating ourselves before the Great Spirit, for we know that we are as dust before Him, who is everything, and who is all powerful . . .

A small bit of each food that has been brought for the soul is put into a wooden bowl, and this is placed in front of the two holy men who are seated at the west. Four pure virgins then enter and take their places at the north of the lodge, for the Power of this direction is purity. The keeper of the pipe then stands and speaks to the soul.

"You, O soul, are the *hokshichankiya* [spiritual influence, or seed]! You are as the root of the *wakan* tree which is at the center of our nation's hoop. May this tree bloom! May our people and the winged and the four-legged peoples flourish! O soul, your relatives have brought you this food which you will soon eat, and by this act, goodness will spread among the people. O soul, *Wakan-Tanka* has given to you four relatives who are sitting there at the north; they represent our true relatives: Grandfather and Father, *Wakan-Tanka*, and Grandmother and Mother *Maka*, the Earth. Remember these four relatives, who are all really One, and, with Them in mind, look back upon your people as you travel upon the great path!"

A small hole is dug at the foot of the "soul post," and the keeper of the pipe holds the wooden bowl, in which is the purified food, towards the hole, saying to the soul: "You are about to eat this *wakan* food. When it is placed in your mouth its influence will spread, and it will cause the fruits of our Mother, the Earth, to increase and prosper. Your Grandmother is *wakan*; look upon Her as we place this food in your mouth. Do not forget us when you go forth to *Wakan-Tanka,* but look upon us!"

The food is placed in the hole, and on top of it the juice of the wild cherry is poured, for this juice is the water of life. The hole is then covered over with dirt, for the soul has finished its last meal . . .

The keeper of the pipe then walks around to the south and, picking up the "soul bundle," says to it: "Grandchild, you are about to leave on a great journey. Your father and mother and all your relatives have loved you. Soon they will be happy."

The father then embraces the sacred bundle, by holding it to each shoulder, and after he has done this, the keeper says to him: "You loved your son, and you have kept him at the center of our people's hoop. As you have been good to this your loved one, so be good to all other people! The sacred influence of your son's soul will be upon the people; it is as a tree that will always bloom."

He then walks around to the north, and as he touches each virgin with the sacred bundle, he says: "The tree which was selected to be at the center of your sacred hoop is this! May it always flourish and bloom in a *wakan* manner!" Then, holding the bundle up towards the heavens, he cries: "Always look back upon your people, that they walk the sacred path with firm steps!"

This, the keeper cries four times as he walked towards the door of the lodge, and, as he stops the fourth time just outside the door, he cries with a very shrill voice: "Behold your people! Look back upon them!"

The moment the bundle passes out of the lodge, the soul is released; it has departed on the "spirit trail" leading to *Wakan-Tanka.*

Once the soul has left the bundle containing the lock of hair, it is no longer especially *wakan,* but it may be kept by the family, if they wish, as something of a remembrance. The four holy virgins are each given a buffalo robe, and then they leave the lodge immediately after the keeper of the pipe.

With this, the rite is finished, and then the people all over the camp are happy and rejoice, and they rush up to touch the four virgins who are *lela wakan,* and who will always bear with them this great influence, bringing great strength to the people. Gifts are given out to the poor and unfortunate ones, and everywhere there is feasting and rejoicing. It is indeed a good day. *Hetchetu welo!*

from *The Sacred Pipe: Black Elk's Account of the Seven Rites of the Oglala Sioux,* by Joseph Epes Brown, pp. 18–19, 26–30.

The Haitian Notion of the Zombie
Maya Deren, Russian-American filmmaker and author, 1917–1961

The dread zombie, the major figure of terror, is precisely this: the body without a soul, matter without mortality.

The death rituals relating to the body are, in sum, directed against physical resurrection—against, on the one hand, a false death, and, on the other, a false life. The initial act of those surviving is to determine that the death is real and not a false death brought about by magic. For, if the regular rituals that dissociate the soul from the body should be performed in ignorance of the fact that the death is false, the body would remain as a live but emptied vessel, subject to the direction of any alien psychic force (usually the malevolent one which engineered the magic precisely for such a purpose). The dread *zombie*, the major figure of terror, is precisely this: the body without a soul, matter without morality.

The popular notion—outside Haiti—pictures the zombie as an enormously powerful giant who, being soulless and incapable of moral judgment, is inaccessible to reason, entreaty, or any other dissuasion if he is directed to a malevolent purpose by his controlling force. This notion reflects a confusion as to the function of a zombie. Actually, the very essence of magic is *psychic*, rather than physical force, and it is by such relatively subtle means that a magician would attain his malevolent ends. The choice of physically powerful individuals for zombies is precisely because their major function is not as instruments of malevolence, but as a kind of uncomplaining slave—labor to be used in the fields, the construction of houses, and so on. While the Haitian does not welcome any encounter with a zombie, his real dread is that of being made into one himself. This is not because he fears hard work, for he is accustomed to this; besides, the characteristic insensibility of the zombie precludes any pain or suffering for him. The terror is of a moral nature, related to the deep-rooted value which the Haitian attaches to powers of consciousness and the attendant capacity for moral judgment, deliberation, and self-control. In the daily life of the Haitians, this value is reflected in his distaste for the confusions and the lack of self-control which may result from drunkenness, and it is extremely rare to see a Haitian in even the least stage of inebriation. The same value is reflected also in his prefer-ence for controlled, and even self-consciously formal behavior, and any departure from such codes of social conduct is censured by the epithet: "Malélevé!" (Ill-mannered! Uncouth!). In the soulless zombie the Haitian sees the ultimate extension of that which he despises in any context: the loss of one's powers of perception, evaluation, and self-control. Thus, the Haitian does not share the notion of the cultivated primitivist—that free, naive, and unself-conscious naturalness is a condition of essential goodness and-or that the exercise of the human intellect tends to run counter to the good direction of the divine essence in man. On the contrary, the Haitian conceives of goodness or morality as a function of man's consciousness, experience, information, understanding, and discipline; and he conceives of ritual as being a means by which men induce the essentially *amoral* forces of the universe towards moral ends. In the final analysis human consciousness, with all its attendant powers and potentials, holds the highest position in Voudoun metaphysics. It is this which the Haitian understands by esprit and which he separates from the matter of the body, rescues from the abyss, leaves as ancestral legacy to his descendants, and upon which, eventually, he confers the status of divinity. A zombie is nothing more than a body deprived of its conscious powers of cerebration; for the Haitian, there is no fate more terrible.

To avoid this development, all measures are taken to make certain that the body is truly lifeless and therefore physically useless. It may be killed again, with a knife through the heart; or its burial may be accompanied by any number of ruses to circumvent a possible resurrection. For example, a plant may be placed in the coffin containing so many seeds that anyone coming to raise the body, but being compelled to count the seeds first, could never accomplish his task before daybreak. Care is taken, as well, that no parts rightfully belonging to the dead matter should remain in circulation in the living world. Such precautions against a false life, which might also be put to magic and malevolent use, are numerous. The water in which the corpse is bathed is carefully poured into a hole. The three drops of fluid believed to be in a dead man's mouth, understood somehow as the final secretion, the residue of the body's life, must not spill out. The hair and nails are clipped and buried, with special care, alongside the corpse. Together with these precautions go certain efforts to purify the matter before its return to the earth. For the most part, these consist of rituals of cleansing. In the case of persons dying of leprosy and other such maladies, or from a stroke of lightning, however, a special kind of

"quarantine" is prescribed, as well as numerous other, compara-
tively complicated ritualistic measures . . .

from Divine Horsemen: The Living Gods of Haiti, pp. 42–44.

The Immortality of the Soul
Mircea Eliade, Romanian-American religious historian, 1907–1987

21 May, 1964

Last night, at Crossroads, a Catholic center for international
meetings, we talked, among other things, about the theories of
Teilhard de Chardin. I remember what he told me, in January
1950, about the necessity to renovate dogma. "The Church," he
said, "is like a crustacean; periodically, she must throw off her
shell in order to grow." His great confidence in "the progress of
science." (The electronic brain, all alone, in a few seconds, does
the work of a dozen mathematicians working for a century. Scientific instruments help man to "swallow time" and "conquer
time." Scientific progress also had a religious function for T. de
Ch. The entire cosmos—that of the galaxies, not that of the
Greco-Roman world—will have to come to know the Christologi-
cal mystery.)

What impressed me the most in my conversations with Teilhard
was his response to the question that I had asked him: What did
the immortality of the soul mean for him? Difficult to summarize.
Briefly: according to T. de Ch., everything that can be transmitted
and communicated (love, culture, politics, etc.) "does not pass
into the beyond" but disappears with the death of the individual.
But there remains an irreducible, incommunicable foundation, or,
more precisely, what is impossible to express or communicate—
and it is this mysterious, incalculable foundation that "passes into
the beyond" and survives the disappearance of the body. An interesting theory because it appears to imply that if we succeeded
some day in communicating and transmitting absolutely all human
experiences, immortality would become useless and would then
cease. What interested Father Teilhard was the principle of the
conservation of human experiences. Nothing must be lost. All experience must be expressed (by language by culture), and it is thus
recorded and kept in the noosphere.

from No Souvenirs, translated by Fred H. Johnson, Jr.,
p. 99-100.

Maya, Toltec, and Aztec Conceptions of Soul
Ptolemy Tompkins, American anthropologist

After four years of accompanying the sun on the pleasant portion of its daily journey, the soul of the fortunate warrior underwent a final transformation: It became a radiant bird . . .

By the fifteenth century of our era, a new strategy for recalling the disenchanted gods into communication with humanity was definitely in order. Humankind had spent the vast majority of its time on this planet as wanderers or simple village dwellers who over the eons had learned to see the universe as a womb for the soul's development. The heritage of that vision survived in America's first cities, which were built along lines dictated by the primordial shamanic mapping of the cosmos that these peoples rightly intuited as a legacy deserving fuller development. That something went wrong along the way is evident not only from the Mesoamerican equation of the rise of the city with the mythical fall of humanity out of a state of spiritual perfection, but from the actual course of historical events.

The notion that civilization is a necessary evil with unforeseen consequences is a very old idea, but its usefulness in understanding the often disastrous course of human history is perhaps not yet exhausted. In Mesoamerica we find this idea expressed in myth and enacted in history to the point where separating the two becomes all but impossible. But whether it is depicted as myth or history or both, its central implication for humankind—that cultural productions entail a loss of focus on spiritual realities that must be guarded against at every turn of human development—remains the same and demands to be taken into account. The Mesoamerican civilizations were struggling to do just that, and in the record of that struggle lie the first outlines of a conception of the soul resilient enough to withstand the confusions of meaning that occur with each increase in human cultural complexity.

In line with this, it is possible to interpret the brutal rites of war and kingship as practiced throughout the high period of Mesoamerican cultures as first fumblings at a new economy of the spirit: an economy based on the same warping and redefinition of the psyche that prehistory's shamanic teachers had intuited to be an essential experience in the lives of all men and women.

The details of this new economy are hinted at in Maya myth and ritual, in the tales of Quetzalcoatl Topilzin, the man-god of the Toltecs, and in the bizarre details of the Aztec sacrificial drama. A nascent redefinition of the shamanic initiatory scenario is evident even in the games practiced in these cities, especially the well-known Mesoamerican ball game. The court on which this game was played from Olmec up to Aztec times appears to have functioned as a model, not of the universe itself as did the pyramid, but of one particular part of it: the subterranean amphitheater where souls were torn to pieces and remade by the tutelary demons that shamans had been depicting in horrible detail on their stoneworks and funerary ceramics. Behind the evil appearance of these demons, as behind all the more onerous motifs of Middle American thought and culture, lay the promise of a fabulous kingdom of color and light—one for which the human soul is homesick whether it knows it or not but into the precincts of which it is only allowed after passing through a redefining and finishing process of sometimes fearful dimensions. This was the paradise that the architects of pyramid and temple had sought to mirror on earth but which in the end they succeeded only in obstructing, thanks to a series of intertwined confusions and misplaced emphases that arose in the minds of those who built these structures up around themselves. . . .

After four years of accompanying the sun on the pleasant portion of its daily journey, the soul of the fortunate warrior underwent a final transformation: It became a radiant bird singing forever in a fiery paradise set in some distant part of the sky exempt from that imminent catastrophe for which the rest of the Aztec universe is slated. The texts describing this paradise were taken down after the arrival of the Spaniards, who brought with them a heaven of their own, whose rules and attributes the subjected Aztecs were under tremendous pressure to adopt. But Paradise is not a Christian invention, and the version of it enjoyed by the winged spirits of the Aztec warriors bears a strong resemblance not only to the Christian Heaven but also to the flowering crown of the world tree that the shaman visits, and to which he or she conducts the souls of the newly departed once they have negotiated the maze of the underworld. It thus appears that at the time of the Conquest the Aztecs were in the process of reconstructing the shaman's ancient techniques and adapting them to the one religious practice—warfare—that could still give people the feeling that their souls partook in a reality greater than the one circumscribed by mundane, physical reality.

from *This Tree Grows Out of Hell*, pp. 28–29.

Is There Such a Thing as Reincarnation?

Sri Ramakrishna, nineteenth-century Hindu master

(To M.) "That which is Pure Atman [Surpreme soul] is un-attached. Maya, or avidya, is in It. In maya there are three gunas: sattva, rajas, and tamas. These three gunas also exist in the Pure Atman. But Atman Itself is unattached. If you throw a blue pill into the fire, you will see a blue flame. If you throw a red pill, you will see a red flame. But fire itself has no color of its own.

"If you put a blue pill in water, the water will turn blue. Again, if you put alum in water, it will regain its natural color.

"A butcher was carrying a load of meat when he touched Sankara. Sankara exclaimed: 'What! You have touched me!' The butcher replied, 'Venerable sir, neither have you touched me nor have I touched you. You are Pure Atman, unattached.' Jadabharata said the same thing to King Rahugana.

"The Pure Atman is unattached, and one cannot see It. If salt is mixed with water, one cannot see the salt with the eyes.

"That which is the Pure Atman is the Great Cause, the Cause of the cause. The gross, the subtle, the causal, and the Great Cause. The five elements are gross. Mind, bud-dhi, and ego are subtle. Prakriti, the Primal Energy, is the cause of all these. Brahman, Pure Atman, is the Cause of the cause.

"This Pure Atman alone is our real nature. What is jnana? It is to know one's own Self and keep the mind in It. It is to know the Pure Atman. . . "

MARWARI DEVOTEE: "Who is this 'I' that says, 'O Lord, I am Thy servant?'"

MASTER: "This is the lingasarira, or embodied soul. It con-sists of manas, buddhi, chitta, and ahamkara."

DEVOTEE: "Who is the embodied soul?"

MASTER: "It is the Atman bound by the eight fetters. And what is the chitta? It is the 'I-consciousness' that says, 'Aha!'"

DEVOTEE: "Revered sir, what happens after death?"

MASTER: "According to the *Gita*, one becomes afterwards
what one thinks of at the time of death. King Bharata
thought of his deer and became a deer in his next life.
Therefore one must practice sadhana in order to realize
God. If a man thinks of God day and night, he will have
the same thought in the hour of death."

from *The Gospel of Sri Ramakrishna,*
translated by Swami Nikhilananda, pp. 153–54, 416.

Why Do We Not Remember Our Past Lives?

H. B. Blavatsky, Russian Theosophist, 1831–1891

*Can you remember what you were or did when a baby? Have you preserved
the smallest recollection of your life, thoughts or deeds, or that you lived at
all during the first eighteen months or two years of your existence?*

ENQUIRER: Do you mean to infer that that which survives
is only the Soul-memory, as you call it, that Soul or Ego
being one and the same, while nothing of the personality
remains?

THEOSOPHIST: Not quite; something of each personality,
unless the latter was an *absolute* materialist with not even
a chink in his nature for a spiritual ray to pass through,
must survive, as it leaves its eternal impress on the incar-
nating permanent Self or Spiritual Ego. . . . The personality with its Skandhas [attributes of an incarnation] is ever
changing with every new birth. It is, as said before, only
the part played by the actor (the true Ego) for one night.
This is why we preserve no memory on the physical plane
of our past lives, though the *real* "Ego" has lived them over
and knows them all.

ENQ. Then how does it happen that the real or Spiritual
man does not impress his new personal "I" with this
knowledge?

THEO. How is it the servant-girls in a poor farm-house
could speak Hebrew and play the violin in their trance or
somnambulic state, and knew neither when in their normal condition? Because, as every genuine psychologist of
the old, not your modern school, will tell you, the Spiritual
Ego can act only when the personal Ego is paralyzed. The
Spiritual "I" in man is omniscient and has every knowledge innate in it; while the personal self is the creature of

its environment and the slave of the personal memory. Could the former manifest itself uninterruptedly, and without impediment, there would be no longer men on earth, but we should all be gods.

ENQ. Still there ought to be exceptions, and some ought to remember.

THEO. And so there are. But who believes in their report? Such sensitives are generally regarded as hallucinated hysterics, as crack-brained enthusiasts, or humbugs, by modern materialism. Let them read, however, works on this subject, preeminently *Reincarnation, a Study of Forgotten Truth* by E. D. Walker, F.T.S., and see in it the mass of proofs which the able author brings to bear on this vexed question. One speaks to people of soul, and some ask "What is Soul?" "Have you ever proved its existence?" Of course it is useless to argue with those who are materialists. But even to them I would put the question: "Can you remember what you were or did when a baby? Have you preserved the smallest recollection of your life, thoughts, or deeds, or that you lived at all during the first eighteen months or two years of your existence? Then why not deny that you have ever lived as a babe, on the same principle?" When to all this we add that the reincarnating Ego, or *individuality,* retains during the Devachanic period merely the essence of the experience of its past earth-life or personality, the whole physical experience involving into a state of *in potentia,* or being, so to speak, translated into spiritual formulae; when we remember further that the term between two births is said to extend from ten to fifteen centuries, during which time the physical consciousness is totally and absolutely inactive, having no organs to act through, and therefore *no existence,* the reason for the absence of all remembrance in the purely physical memory is apparent.

from *The Key to Theosophy,* pp. 131–33.

From "A Dialogue of Self and Soul"
William Butler Yeats, Irish poet and playwright, 1865–1939

> My Self. *A living man is blind and drinks his drop.*
> *What matter if the ditches are impure?*
> *What matter if I live it all once more?*
> *Endure that toil of growing up;*
> *The ignominy of boyhood; the distress*

Of boyhood changing into man;
The unfinished man and his pain
Brought face to face with his own clumsiness;

The unfinished man among his enemies?—
How in the name of Heaven can he escape
That defiling and disfigured shape
The mirror of malicious eyes
Casts upon his eyes until at last
He thinks that shape must be his shape?
And what's the good of an escape
If honor find him in the wintry blast?

I am content to live it all again
And yet again, if it be life to pitch
Into the frog-spawn of a blind man's ditch,
A blind man battering blind men;
Or into that most fecund ditch of all,
The folly that a man does
Or must suffer, if he woos
A proud woman not kindred to his soul.

I am content to follow to its source
Every event in action or in thought;
Measure the lot; forgive myself the lot!
When such as I cast out remorse
So great a sweetness flows into the breast
We must laugh and we must sing,
We are blest by everything
Everything we look upon is blest.

from *The Poems of W. B. Yeats: A New Edition*,
edited by Richard J. Finneran, pp. 132-33.

The Legend of St. Elmo's Fire
From the journal of an anonymous nineteenth-century sailor

. . . that fire, which resembles a glass of brandy that is alight, is the soul of a poor sailor who drowned in the sea in a storm.

During a stormy night one noticed on board fires that played at each end of our main yard. This bright and blue flame, like those that one lights on the punch that is served in cafes, aroused my curiosity for the first time.

"What on earth is that?" I asked a sailor in amazement.

"Saint Elmo's fire, sir."

"Ah, yes, it burns!"

"One had better say that is the sailor's friend. Do you see that kind of flame? Well, if the officer of the watch told me: 'Climb up by yourself, pull down the small topsail' [which is in fact quite heavy for just one man], I would pull it down on the double because that fire would go up with me up the rigging to help me, as it helps all sailors."

"But how can you take such a story seriously? It is quite simply, as I remember having read, a natural effect, an electrical discharge that, like a fluid of this kind, seeks points."

"How can I believe that story? An effect of *lubricity, electrical* discharge, as you please. But it is no less true that that fire, which resembles a glass of brandy that is alight, is the soul of a poor sailor who drowned in the sea in a storm. So you see, when the weather is about to get worse, the soul of the sailors who have taken one drink too many from the great pond, comes and warns their comrades that a danger-ous storm is approaching."

"My word, just in case it is true I want to see if I can touch the soul of a dead man, and I shall go straight to the running board of the yardarm to catch up with your Saint Elmo's fire."

I climbed to the end of the yardarm, as I had said I would, to the great surprise of my companion, who saw a kind of profanation in the intention that I had of going needlessly to bother what he called the sailor's friend.

As my hand gradually got closer to the Saint Elmo's fire, the fluid moved up and down and away and did not come back until I had withdrawn it. This sort of little war between it and myself greatly amused the men of the watch, and they said to me again and again:

"Oh, that one is meaner than you or us."

A sailor from Lower Brittany cried out to me:

"Do you want me to make it disappear?"

"Yes," I replied.

And he made the sign of the cross. The fire did indeed vanish at that very moment, and that instantaneous coincidence between the fire's disappearance and the sign of the cross made by the devout man helped to engrave a superstition even more profoundly in the imagination of those good people.

from *The Slave Trader*, by Edouard Corbière, 1832,
cited in *The Sky, Mystery, Magic, and Myth*,
translated by Anthony Zielonka, p. 148.

The Beautiful Soul of Don Damian
Juan Bosch, Dominican Republic

The soul measured the distance and jumped, with a facility it had not known it had, landing on the pillow like a thing of air or like a strange animal that could move noiselessly and invisibly.

"Why, of course he had a beautiful soul," the priest said.

"'Beautiful' doesn't begin to describe it," the mother-in-law asserted.

The soul turned to look at her and saw that as she spoke she was signaling to her daughter with her eyes. They contained both a command and a scolding, as if to say, "Start crying again, you idiot. Do you want the priest to say you were happy your husband died?" The daughter understood the signal and broke out into tearful wailing.

"Nobody ever had such a beautiful soul! Damian, how much I loved you!"

The soul could not stand any more: It wanted to know for certain, without losing another moment, whether or not it was truly beautiful, and it wanted to get away from those hypocrites. It leaped in the direction of the bathroom, where there was a full-length mirror, calculating the distance so as to fall noiselessly on the rug. It did not know it was weightless as well as invisible. It was delighted to find that nobody noticed it and ran quickly to look at itself in front of the mirror.

But good God, what had happened? In the first place, it had been accustomed, during more than sixty years, to look out through the eyes of Don Damian, and those were over five feet from the ground; also, it was accustomed to seeing his lively face, his clear eyes, his shining gray hair, the arrogance that puffed out his chest and lifted his head, the expensive clothes in which he dressed. What it saw now was nothing at all like that, but a strange figure hardly a foot tall, pale, cloud-gray, with no definite form. Where it should have had two legs and two feet like the body of Don Damian, it was a hideous cluster of tentacles like those of an octopus, but irregular, some shorter than others, some thinner, and all of them seemingly made of dirty smoke, of some impalpable mud that looked transparent but was not; they were limp and drooping and powerless, and stupendously ugly. The soul of Don Damian felt lost. Nevertheless, it got up the courage to look higher. It had no waist. In fact, it had no body, no neck, nothing: Where the tentacles joined there was merely a sort of ear sticking out on one side, looking like a bit of rotten apple peel, and a clump of rough hairs on the other side, some twisted, some straight. But that was not the worst, and neither was the strange grayish-yellow light it gave off: The worst was the fact that its mouth was a shapeless cavity like a hole poked in a rotten fruit, a horrible and sickening thing . . . and in the depths of this hole an eye shone, its only eye, staring out of the shadows with an expression of terror and treachery! Yet the women and the priest in the next room, around the bed in which Don Damian's corpse lay, had said he had a beautiful soul! . . .

The soul, paralyzed in front of its true image, knew it was lost. It had been used to hiding in its refuge in the tall body of Don Damian; it had been used to everything, including the obnoxious smell of the intestines, the heat of the stomach, the annoyance of chills and fevers. Then it heard the doctor's greeting and the mother-in-law's voice crying: "Oh, Doctor, what a tragedy it is!"

"Come, now, let's get a grip on ourselves."

The soul peeped into the dead man's room. The women were gathered around the bed, and the priest was praying at its foot. The soul measured the distance and jumped, with a facility it had not known it had, landing on the pillow like a thing of air or like a strange animal that could move noiselessly and invisibly. Don Damian's mouth was still partly open. It was cold as ice, but that was not important. The soul tumbled inside and began to thrust its tentacles into place. It was still settling in when it heard the doctor say to the mother-in-law: "Just one moment, please.". . .

The soul was back in its body again, and only three tentacles still groped for the old veins they had inhabited for so many years. . . .

The doctor . . . took Don Damian's forearm and began to chafe it with his hand. The soul felt the warmth of life surrounding it, penetrating it, filling the veins it had abandoned to escape from burning up. At the same moment, the doctor jabbed the needle into a vein in the arm, untied the ligature above the elbow, and began to push the plunger. Little by little, in soft surges, the warmth of life rose to Don Damian's skin. . . .

from *The Eye of the Heart: Short Stories from Latin America,*
edited by Barbara Howes, pp. 318–22.

∞

Her Soul Descending Out of Sight
A Hawaiian Myth of Love and Death
retold by Alexander Eliot, American author

In the darkness Hiku tracked Kewelu's gleaming soul . . .

In Hawaii, the House of Kalakaua traced its ancestry back to
Princess Kewelu, a maiden of the white sea strand. She loved Hiku
of the forest; and he left his mountain fastness to live with the
maiden in her coastal home. Garlanded with flowers, they played
up and down the beach; but Hiku grew weary of such a soft life
and wandered away, back into the rugged mountain region which
was his home.

His bride, in tears, tried hard to follow him; but the vines clung
round Kewelu as the forest thickened, and soon she could neither
go on nor return. Imprisoned among the vines, she began to struggle, turning and twisting desperately. Her efforts only served to
wind her ever more tightly in the sinuous embrace of the creepers
of the forest. Bound tight and strangled, she died. Her soul descended out of sight.

Hiku's father told him what had occurred. Filled with remorse,
Hiku searched far and wide until he found a hole leading along a
ladder of hanging vines, taking nothing with him into the bowels
of the underworld except an empty coconut shell.

In the darkness Hiku tracked Kewelu's gleaming soul, stalking it
just as carefully as he would the shiest forest creature. And the
moment that Kewelu's soul paused to look around, he snapped his
shell shut on it, catching the soul inside like a butterfly. Then
swiftly he swarmed back up the vine into the air again.

Kneeling beside the beautiful corpse, Hiku opened his coconut
shell a crack and clamped it over Kewelu's big toe. Her soul, startled, blundered into the toe. Hiku gently massaged her foot, her
soul spread there, like a new warmth. He rubbed his ankle, her
calf, her knee, and so on. Her soul spread further and deeper into
the body. At last it reached home in her heart. Kewelu breathed
again. She opened her eyes and looked at him. Her soul looked out
of her eyes.

from *Myths*, p. 252.

A Child Asks About the Soul
Robert Coles, American professor of psychiatry and author

It's too big for you to figure out. My dad tells me that when I ask him about God and where heaven is and if there's a soul.

"When I wake up early, and our dog really wants to go out, and he leaps on my bed, and I know he won't let me go back to sleep, I just know it—he'll lick my face, and he'll whine, and he'll lean against me hard, real hard—and when I give up and take him out, and I just stand there, and it's still dark, and you can hear your dog sniffing, it's that quiet: It's then I know there's someone up there, maybe God, maybe lots of people, too, the souls of all the dead folks. It's too big for you to figure out. My dad tells me that when I ask him about God and where heaven is and if there's a soul. He says there is *definitely* a soul, but it's not 'physical,' so I shouldn't keep asking him, 'Where is it?'

"He's right; you can ask too many questions! That's me—always trying to find out answers to everything! I wish you *could* find them. In the last year or so, I've sort of slowed down asking! I just look up there and say, 'Maybe!' I was walking our dog in the park, and it was real quiet, and you just wonder if there aren't people out there—*souls* out there—and they must want to talk with someone. I guess they talk with each other. But how? Where are they? Dad says he thinks when you die, you soul dies with you. But then, it's not a soul, it's your mind he's talking about, isn't it? It's probably best just to forget everything except what you have to do today: and the same thing with tomorrow. The only thing is, when you go to Hebrew school and *schul* [synagogue], they tell you God is with us, the Jews, and your soul is His gift to you, that's what the rabbi told us kids when he visited our classroom, and I was going to ask him where in your body God puts the soul He gives you, but I decided that I'd be getting myself into real trouble, because the Hebrew school teacher says I ask too many questions, and I should learn Hebrew and read from Torah and stop trying to be a 'philosopher king.' Well, what's that? Yes, I asked. The teacher didn't think it was funny, my question [as he and I did!]. He said, 'No more questions!' If I'd raised my hand like that, when the rabbi came to visit our class, I think the teacher would have taken that [black-board] point of his and charged me with it, like in the Middle Ages, when the knights went after each other with swords or spears."

from *The Spiritual Life of Children*, pp. 140–41

Her Pilgrim Soul
Alan Brennert, American science fiction writer

Well, despite her memories of a . . . previous existence, she's spent all her life, subjectively, in that hologram. And the older she gets, the more she re-members.

She was aging, it seemed, at a rate of about five months every hour; ten years each day. At eight o'clock in the morning she had been a frightened, lonely five-year-old girl; by eight that evening, she was a more mature, outgoing ten-year-old. Kevin called in sick to the dean's office, had his classes suspended indefinitely, and over the next twelve hours watched as Nola literally grew up before his eyes. The degree of detail—as her hair grew longer, then shorter, then long again; as her body slightly but perceptibly elon-gated, at just the right rate of speed for a normal child's growth—was astonishing. The minutiae involved, from the subtle changes in weight distribution to the larger growth in bone structure, were staggering to contemplate—they required thousands of different "processes" running at once; even her garments would change from hour to hour, from dress clothes to play, all of it still quite old-fashioned. Kevin spent all day listening carefully to this shy, beguiling apparition as it went from kindergarten to elementary school, from five to six to seven years old, speech becoming in-creasingly more sophisticated, reactions exactly appropriate for a girl of whatever age she was at that moment—by the time she reached six, she had outgrown the ball, so Kevin had fashioned a holographic doll for her; at seven, a jump-rope; and at eight, a set of jacks.

That evening, Daniel returned from Rotch Library with his re-search on the "big green house" Nola had described twelve hours—or was it five years?—earlier.

"There *is* a Granville family living in that area," Daniel said, sotto voce, as they watched Nola sitting cross-legged in the holo display, playing jacks. "The house she described . . . It's been in the family since the turn of the century. The current owners don't have a daughter named Nola, but . . . " He hesitated. "The woman I talked to *did* recall a great-aunt of hers by that name . . . something of a black sheep, apparently; the family never talked much about her."

Kevin put a hand to his mouth, restraining a manic laugh. This was becoming more baroque by the minute. "Does anybody know where this . . . 'great-aunt' *is?*"

Daniel hesitated again. "She died. Quite a while back; no one knew the exact date, and county records for the area don't reveal anything, either."

Kevin didn't reply. He got up from his work station, moved over to where Nola was playing with her jacks. There was a faraway look in her eyes, but as soon as she glimpsed Kevin, her face lit up with a wide smile. "Hi, Kevin." She had the shy, guileless look of a young girl with her first crush.

"Hi, Nola." Her smitten look was not lost on him. "You, uh, want me to make you some more toys? You must be getting tired of the jacks."

"That's okay," she said, standing. "I don't need any."

"Don't you get kind of . . . bored, Nola?" Daniel asked.

She shrugged lightly. "Sometimes. But when I do, I just . . . go somewhere else."

Kevin and Daniel exchanged puzzled looks.

"In my head," she explained. "Like just now, I was out by the drained lake. Remembering the time Daddy took us out for a picnic, and I walked into the water up to my knees, and"—her face clouded over—"Daddy paddled me. Hard." She winced. "I didn't want to remember that part."

"So when you think about places . . . people . . . things . . . it's like you're almost there?" Kevin asked.

"Yeah," she said, then added, with a shy smile. "But I like being here, with you, better."

Kevin couldn't help but smile back. Daniel looked at him and thought. My God, he's actually blushing! "Nola?" he said, filling the awkward silence. "You remember when it was your Daddy took you to the lake? What year?"

Again that endearingly sober look as she concentrated. "I think it was . . . nineteen and seventeen. Or maybe sixteen. Yeah," she said more confidently, "that's right. Nineteen and sixteen."

Kevin and Daniel stared at each other, dumbfounded.

Later, in Kevin's private office adjacent to the lab, Daniel sat slumped in a chair as Kevin paced. "Maybe," Daniel suggested, "we should call in Hinerman, over in AI Alley."

"No," Kevin said quickly. "He'd turn this into a sideshow. And even if she *is* an AI program—which I don't believe for a minute—how does she *see* us? Hinerman would be as incapable of explaining that as we are."

Daniel shook his head. "She's totally aware of her surroundings—even her *form*—yet seems perfectly comfortable with them. As though it were the most natural thing in the world."

"Well, despite her memories of a . . . previous existence, she's spent all her life, subjectively, in that hologram. And the older she gets, the more she remembers. It's almost as though she's existing on two different levels of consciousness—one a remembered past that expands as she ages, the other her real-time presence here, with us."

Daniel hesitated. "Look," he said, tentatively, "I know this is going to sound pretty bizarre, but. . . ." Daniel screwed up his nerve under Kevin's even gaze. "Do you suppose that somehow . . . in some way, a . . . soul . . . a human *soul* has been reincarnated, inside that computer?"

Kevin sighed indulgently. "Daniel, I'm not even sure I believe in the human soul, much less in reincarnation."

"Why? Why is the idea of a soul any less believable than that of any of a dozen subatomic particles? We can't prove *they* exist, either."

"Yes, but that's *different*. We *can* posit their existence by the behavior of other, observable phenomena."

Daniel was silent a moment, then stood, went to the door, and opened it. He nodded in the direction of the lab. "There's your phenomenon in there, Doc," he said. "Go observe."

from *Her Pilgrim Soul,* pp. 208–11.

Meditation on a Line from Saint Teresa
Raymond Carver, American author, 1939–1988

Words lead to deeds. . . . They prepare the soul, make it ready, and move it to tenderness.

There is a line of prose from the writings of Saint Teresa which seemed more and more appropriate as I thought toward this occasion, so I want to offer a meditation on that sentence. It was used as an epigraph to a recent collection of poems by Tess Gallagher, my dear friend and companion who is here with me today, and I take the line from the context of her epigraph.

Saint Teresa, that extraordinary woman who lived 373 years ago, said: "Words lead to deeds. . . . They prepare the soul, make it ready, and move it to tenderness."

There is clarity and beauty in that thought expressed in just this way. I'll say it again, because there is also something a little foreign in this sentiment coming to our attention at this remove, in a time certainly less openly supportive of the important connection between what we say and what we do: "Words lead to deeds. . . . They prepare the soul, make it ready, and move it to tenderness."

There is something more than a little mysterious, not to say— forgive me—even mystical about these particular words and the way Saint Teresa used them, with full weight and belief. True enough, we realize they appear almost as echoes of some former, more considered time. Especially the mention of the word "soul," a word we don't encounter much these days outside of church and perhaps in the "soul" section of the record store.

"Tenderness"—that's another word we don't hear much these days, and certainly not on such a public, joyful occasion as this. Think about it: When was the last time you used the word or heard it used? It's in as short supply as that other word, "soul."

There is a wonderfully described character named Moiseika in Chekhov's story "Ward No. 6" who, although he has been consigned to the madhouse wing of the hospital, has picked up the habit of a certain kind of tenderness. Chekhov writes: "Moiseika likes to make himself useful. He gives his companions water, and covers them up when they are asleep; he promises each of them to bring him back a kopeck, and to make him a new cap; he feeds with a spoon his neighbor on the left, who is paralyzed."

Even though the word tenderness isn't used, we feel its presence in these details, even when Chekhov goes on to enter a disclaimer by way of this commentary on Moiseika's behavior: "He acts in this way, not from compassion nor from any considerations of a humane kind, but through imitation, unconsciously dominated by Gromov, his neighbor on the right hand."

In a provocative alchemy, Chekhov combines words and deeds to cause us to reconsider the origin and nature of tenderness. Where does it come from? As a deed, does it still move the heart, even when abstracted from humane motives?

Somehow, the image of the isolate man performing gentle acts without expectation or even self-knowledge stays before us as an odd beauty we have been brought to witness. It may even reflect back upon our own lives with a questioning gaze.

There is another scene from "Ward No. 6" in which two characters, a disaffected doctor and an imperious postmaster, his elder, suddenly find themselves discussing the human soul.

"And you do not believe in the immortality of the soul?" the postmaster asks suddenly.

"No, honoured Mihail Averyanitch; I do not believe it, and have no grounds for believing it."

"I must own I doubt it, too," Mihail Averyanitch admits. "And yet I have a feeling as though I should never die. Oh, I think to myself: 'Old fogey, it is time you were dead!' But there is a little voice in my soul says: 'Don't believe it; you won't die.'"

The scene ends but the words linger as deeds. "A little voice in the soul" is born. Also the way we have perhaps dismissed certain concepts about life, about death, suddenly gives over unexpectedly to belief of an admittedly fragile but insistent nature.

Long after what I've said has passed from your minds, whether it be weeks or months, and all that remains is the sensation of having attended a public occasion, marking the end of one significant period of your lives and the beginning of another, try then, as you work out your individual destinies, to remember that words, the right true words, can have the power of deeds.

Remember, too, that little-used word that has just about dropped out of public and private usage: tenderness. It can't hurt. And that other word: soul—call it spirit if you want, if it makes it any easier to claim the territory. Don't forget either. Pay attention to the spirit of your words, your deeds. That's preparation enough. No more words.

from *No Heroics, Please*, pp. 223–25.

Continuity
Heber D. Curtis, American astrophysicist, 1872–1942

I personally find it impossible to regard Handel's "Largo," Keats's "Ode to a Grecian Urn," and the higher ethics as mere by-products of the chemical interaction of a collection of hydrocarbon molecules. With energy, matter, space, and time continuous, with nothing lost or wasted, are we ourselves the only manifestation that comes to an end, ceases, is annihilated at three score years and ten?

What we crudely call the spirit of man makes new compounds, plays with the laws of chemical action, guides the forces of the atom, changes the face of the earth, gives life to new forms and takes it away from millions of animals and plants. Here is a flame that controls its own flaming, a creative spirit which cannot reasonably be less than the continuity it controls. This thing, soul, mind, or spirit, cannot well be exception. In some way, as yet impossible to define, it too, must possess continuity.

from the *Los Angeles Times*, Dec. 31, 1926.

The Soul's Distinct Connection
Emily Dickinson, American poet, 1830–1886

The Soul's distinct connection
With immortality
Is best disclosed by Danger
Or quick Calamity—

As lightning on a Landscape
Exhibits Sheets of Place
Not yet suspected—but for a Flash—
And Click—and Suddenness.

from *The Complete Poems of Emily Dickinson*, pp. 455–56.

Epilogue

So is our task ended, and an anthology compiled plentiful as the floods fed by the unfailing waters of the hills, rich in examples as the seashore in grains of sand; may its reception meet with none of the obstructions that bar the stream of Asuka, and the joys it shall afford accumulate, as dust and pebbles gather together to form a high mountain, into a boulder of delight.

—Ki no Tsurayuki, tenth-century editor
of an anthology of Oriental poetry

Bibliography

Andrews, Valerie. *A Passion for This Earth*. San Francisco, HarperSanFrancisco, 1989.

Bachelard, Gaston. *The Poetics of Space*. Translated by Maria Jolas. Boston: Beacon Press, 1969.

Bair, Lowell, trans. *Essential Works of Descartes*. New York: Bantam Books, Inc., 1961.

Barnard, John. *The Complete Poems of John Keats*. London and New York: Penguin Books, 1988.

Barrett, William. *Death of the Soul: From Descartes to the Computer*. New York: Doubleday Publishing Group, Inc., 1986.

Baulieu, Etienne-Emile, with Mort Rosenblum. *The Abortion Pill*. New York: Simon & Schuster, 1991.

Berman, Phillip L. *The Search for Meaning*. New York: Ballantine, 1990.

The Best of Ralph Waldo Emerson. Walter J. Black, Inc. Roslyn, NY, for The Classics Club, 1969.

Bettelheim, Bruno. *Freud and Man's Soul*. New York: Alfred A. Knopf, Inc., 1982.

Blavatsky, H. B. *The Key to Theosophy*. Pasadena, CA: Theosophical University Press, 1987.

Bly, Robert, trans. *Times Alone: Selected Poems of Antonio Machado*. Middletown, CT: Wesleyan University Press, 1983.

Bly, Robert, edited and with commentaries. *The Winged Life: The Poetic Voice of Henry David Thoreau*. San Francisco: Sierra Club Books, 1986.

Brennert, Alan. *Her Pilgrim Soul*. New York: A Tor Book, 1990.

Brinton, Scott, ed. *Poems of War Resistance*. New York: Grossman Publishers, 1960.

Bronowski, J. B., ed. *William Blake: A Selection of Poems and Letters*. Harmondsworth, Middlesex, England and New York: Penguin Books, 1958.

Brown, Joseph Epes, ed. *The Sacred Pipe: Black Elk's Account of the Seven Rites of the Oglala Sioux*. Norman and London: University of Oklahoma Press, 1953.

Browning, Elizabeth Barrett. *Selected Poems*. Baltimore: The Johns Hopkins University Press, 1992.

Campbell, Joseph. *The Way of the Animal Powers*. Vol. I, Part 2. New York: HarperCollins, 1990.

Carus, Carl Gustav. *Psyche: On the Development of the Soul*. Dallas: Spring Publications, 1989.

Carver, Raymond. *No Heroics, Please: Raymond Carver Uncollected Writings*. New York: Vintage Books, 1992.

Chagnon, Napoleon A. *Yąnomamö: The Fierce People*. Detroit and New York: University of Michigan Press/ Holt, Rinehart and Winston, 1968.

Charles, Ray, and David Ritz. *Brother Ray: Ray Charles' Own Story*. New York: Da Capo Press, 1978. Updated version, 1992.

Cleaver, Eldridge. *Soul on Ice*. New York: McGraw-Hill, 1991.

Coles, Robert. *The Spiritual Life of Children*. Boston: Houghton Mifflin, 1990.

Critchlow, Keith, "The Soul as Sphere and Androgyne," *Parabola* magazine, vol. III, no. 4.

de Voogd, Nina, trans. *The Passionate Nomad: The Diary of Isabelle Eberhardt.* Boston: Beacon Press, 1987.

Deren, Maya. *Divine Horsemen: The Living Gods of Haiti.* New York: McPherson and Company, 1953.

Downing, Christine. *Psyche's Sisters.* New York: HarperCollins Publishers, 1988.

Eliade, Mircea, ed. *Essential Sacred Writings from Around the World.* San Francisco: HarperSanFrancisco, 1992.

Eliot, Alexander. *Myths.* New York: McGraw-Hill, 1976.

Ferguson, Sheila. *Soul Food.* New York: Grove Press, 1989.

Fox, Matthew, *Meditations with Meister Eckhart,* Santa Fe, NM: Bear & Co., 1983.

Frankl, Viktor E. *Man's Search for Meaning.* Translated by Ilse Lasch. New York: Beacon Press, 1992.

French, R. M., trans. *The Way of a Pilgrim.* Foreword by Huston Smith. San Francisco: HarperSanFrancisco, 1991.

Goethe, Johann Wolfgang von. *Faust.* Translated by Alice Raphael. New York: The Heritage Press, 1930.

Goodrick-Clarke, Nicholas, trans. *Paracelsus: Essential Readings.* London: Crucible, 1990.

The Gospel of Sri Ramakrishna, trans. by Swami Nikhilananda. New York: Ramakrishna-Vivekananda Center, 1942.

Griffin, Jonathan, trans. *Selected Poems: Fernando Pessoa.* London: Penguin Books, 1974.

Griffin, Susan. *Rape: The Politics of Consciousness.* 3d revised and updated ed. San Francisco: Harper & Row, 1986.

Guralnick, Peter. *Sweet Soul Music: Rhythm and Blues and the Southern Dream of Freedom.* New York: Harper & Row, 1986.

Head, Joseph, and S. L. Cranston, eds. *Reincarnation: An East-West Anthology.* Wheaton, Madras, London: Quest Books, 1961.

Higgins, Perry, trans. *Love Poems: From Spain and South America.* San Francisco: City Lights, 1986.

Hillman, James. *Re-Visioning Psychology.* San Francisco: Harper & Row, 1975.

Hillman, James, ed. *Facing the Gods.* Dallas: Spring Publications, 1980.

Hillman, James. *The Thought of the Heart and the Soul of the World.* Dallas: Spring Publications, 1992.

Hillman, James, and Michael Ventura. *We've Had a Hundred Years of Psychotherapy: And the World's Getting Worse.* San Francisco: HarperSanFrancisco, 1992.

Howes, Barbara, ed. *The Eye of the Heart: Short Stories from Latin America.* New York: Bard Books, 1973.

Hubbard, Elbert. *Elbert Hubbard's Scrapbook.* New York: W. M. Wise & Company, 1923.

Huxley, Aldous. *The Perennial Philosophy.* New York: Perennial Library, Harper & Row, 1970.

Jayne, Sears, trans. *Commentary on Plato's Symposium on Love,* by Marsilio Ficino. Dallas: Spring Publications, 1987.

Johnson, Fred H. Jr., trans. *No Souvenirs,* by Mircea Eliade. New York: Harper & Row, 1977.

Johnson, Thomas H., ed. *The Complete Poems of Emily Dickinson.* Boston and Toronto: Little, Brown, 1967.

Jones, Alan. *Soul Making: The Desert Way of Spirituality.* New York: Harper & Row, 1985.

Jowett, Benjamin, trans. *The Dialogues of Plato.* Oxford: Oxford University Press, 1928.

Joyce, James. *A Portrait of the Artist as a Young Man.* New York: Penguin Signet Book, 1964.

Jung, C. G. *Modern Man in Search of a Soul.* New York: Harcourt Brace & Company, 1933.

The Kabir Book: Forty-Four of the Ecstatic Poems of Kabir. Versions by Robert Bly. New York: Beacon Press, 1977.

Kandinsky, Wassily. *Concerning the Spiritual in Art.* New York: Dover Publications, Inc., 1977.

Kazantzakis, Nikos. *The Saviors of God.* Translated and with an introduction by Kimon Friar. New York: Touchstone, 1960.

King James Version. Cambridge, MA: Cambridge University Press. Many editions.

Keen, Sam. *Fire in the Belly.* New York: Bantam, 1991.

Kerouac, Jack. *On the Road.* New York: Penguin Books, 1983.

Kerrane, Kevin, and Richard Grossinger, eds. *Baseball I Gave You All the Best Years of My Life.* Richmond: North Atlantic Books, 1976.

Kidder, Tracy. *The Soul of a New Machine.* New York: Little, Brown and Company, 1981.

Kundera, Milan. *The Unbearable Lightness of Being.* New York: Harper & Row, 1984.

Lawlor, Robert. *Voices of the First Day.* Rochester, VT: Inner Traditions, 1992.

Lawrence, D. H. *The Complete Poems of D. H. Lawrence.* With an introduction by Kenneth Rexroth. New York: Viking Press, 1964 and 1971.

The Letters of Abelard and Heloise. Translated by Betty Radice. New York: Penguin Classics, 1974.

Lowenstein, Tom, trans. *Eskimo Poems from Canada and Greenland.*

Pittsburgh: University of Pittsburgh Press, 1973.

Marcus, Greil. *Mystery Train.* New York: E. P. Dutton, 1975.

Meditations with Hildegard of Bingen. Versions by Gabriele Uhlein. Santa Fe: Bear & Company, 1982.

Meditations with Julian of Norwich. Edited by Brendan Doyle. Santa Fe: Bear & Company, 1983.

Melville, Herman. *Moby Dick.* New York: Modern Library, 1982.

Moore, Thomas. *Care of the Soul.* New York: HarperCollins, 1991.

Moore, Thomas. *The Planets Within.* Hudson, NY: Lindisfarne Press, 1982.

Murphy, Francis, ed. *Walt Whitman: The Complete Poems.* Harmondsworth, Middlesex, England and New York: Penguin Books, 1975.

Nance, John. *The Gentle Tasaday.* New York and London: Harcourt Brace Jovanovich, 1975.

Nathanson-Elkin, Sue. *Soul Crisis.* New York: Dutton, 1990.

Needleman, Jacob. *Lost Christianity.* New York: Element Books, 1993.

Neruda, Pablo. *Twenty Love Poems and a Song of Despair.* Translated by W. S. Merwin. New York and London: Penguin Books, 1969.

Otto, Rudolf. *The Idea of the Holy.* Translated by John W. Harvey. London: Oxford University Press, 1973.

Pegis, Anton C., ed. *The Summa Theologica* by St. Thomas Aquinas. New York: Modern Library, 1948.

Piggott, Stuart. *The Druids.* London: Penguin, 1979.

Plato. *The Phaedo: The Trial and Death of Socrates.* Translated from the Greek with introductory analyses by Benjamin Jowett. New York: Oxford University Press, 1963.

Plotinus. *The Enneads.* Translated by Stephen McKenna. Burdett, NY: Larson Publications, 1992.

The Poems of St. John of the Cross. English versions and introduction by Willis Barnstone. New York: New Directions, 1972.

Pouillon, Fernand. *The Stones of the Abbey.* Translated by Edward Gillott. New York: Harcourt, Brace & World, Inc., 1970.

Raffel, Burton, trans. *Beowulf.* New York: The New American Library, 1963.

Ranke-Heinemann, Uta. *Eunuchs for the Kingdom of Heaven.* Translated by Peter Heinegg. New York: Doubleday Dell Publishing Group, Inc., 1990.

Raymo, Chet. *The Soul of the Night.* Englewood Cliffs, NJ: Prentice-Hall, 1985.

Read, Herbert, *Collected Poems.* London: Faber & Faber, Ltd., 1981.

Sabine, George H., and Stanley B. Smith, trans. *De Republica* (On the Commonwealth), by Cicero. New York: Macmillan College Publishing, 1976.

Saint Teresa of Avila. *The Interior Castle.* Translated and edited by E. Allison Peers. New York: Image Books, 1961.

Santayana, George. *Three Philosophical Poets.* Cambridge, MA: Harvard University Press, 1910.

Sardello, Robert. *Facing the World with Soul.* Hudson, NY: Lindisfarne Press, 1991.

Sarton, May. *Journal of a Solitude.* New York and London: W. W. Norton & Company, 1977.

Schuster, M. Lincoln, ed. *A Treasury of the World's Greatest Letters.* New York: Simon & Schuster, 1940.

Shelley, Mary Wollstonecraft. *Frankenstein.* New York: Dell, 1965.

Shore, Eliezer. "The Soul of Community," *Parabola* magazine, vol. XVII, no. 1.

Singer, June. *A Gnostic Book of Hours: Keys to Inner Wisdom.* San Francisco: HarperSanFrancisco, 1992.

Singer, June. *Seeing Through the Visible World: Jung, Gnosis, and Chaos.* San Francisco: HarperSanFrancisco, 1991.

Smith, Huston. *The World's Religions.* San Francisco: HarperSanFrancisco, 1992.

Smith, Paul Jordan. "The Physician," *Parabola* magazine, vol. III, no. 1.

Steiner, Rudolf. *Metamorphoses of the Soul.* vol. 2, 2d ed. London: Anthroposophic Press, 1990.

Stevenson, Robert Louis. *Strange Case of Dr. Jekyll and Mr. Hyde.* New York: The Heritage Press, 1952.

Swan, James, ed. *The Power of Place.* Wheaton, Madras, London: Quest Books, 1991.

Swenson, May, and Leif Sjöbert, trans. *Windows and Stones: Selected Poems,* by Tomas Transtromer. Pittsburgh: University of Pittsburgh Press, 1972.

Thompson, Keith. *Waiting for Tyler,* an original essay, 1993.

Thompson, William Irwin. *The Time Falling Bodies Take to Light.* New York: St. Martin's Press, 1981.

Todd, Loreto. *Tortoise the Trickster and Other Folktales from Cameroon.* London, Henley, and Boston: Routledge & Kegan Paul, 1979.

Tompkins, Peter, and Christopher Bird. *The Secret Life of Plants.* New York: Harper & Row, 1973.

Tompkins, Ptolemy. *This Tree Grows Out of Hell.* San Francisco: HarperSanFrancisco, 1990.

Underhill, Evelyn. *Mysticism.* Cleveland and New York: The World Publishing Company, 1970.

Van Over, Raymond, ed. *Sun Songs: Creation Myths from Around the World.* New York: New American Library, 1980.

Verdet, Jean-Pierre. *The Sky: Mystery, Magic, and Myth.* Translated from the French by Anthony Zielonka. New York: Harry N. Abrams, 1992.

von Franz, Marie-Louise, *Patterns of Creativity Mirrored in Creation Myths,* Boston: Shambhala Publications, Inc., 1972.

Walker, Alice. *Living by the Word: Selected Writings 1973–1987.* New York: Harvest/Harcourt Brace Jovanovich, 1988.

Wheelwright, Philip, trans. *Aristotle: The Way of Philosophy.* New York: Macmillan College Publishing, 1960.

Willa Cather: 24 Stories. Selected and with an introduction by Sharon O'Brien. Nebraska: University of Nebraska Press, 1987.

Wolkstein, Diane. *The First Love Stories.* New York: HarperCollins, 1992.

Yates, Francis A. *The Art of Memory.* Chicago: The University of Chicago Press, 1966.

Yeats, W. B. *The Poems of W. B. Yeats: A New Edition.* New York: Macmillan Publishing Company, 1961.

Young, Al. *Bodies & Soul.* Berkeley, CA: Creative Arts Book Company, 1981.

Zielonka, Anthony, trans. *The Slave Trader,* by Edouard Corbiére. From *The Sky, Mystery, Magic, and Myth.* New York: Harry N. Abrams, 1992.

Zukav, Gary. "Evolution and Business" (chapter). A forthcoming book.

Zweig, Paul. *The Adventurer.* Princeton, NJ: Princeton University Press, 1974.

This constitutes a continuation of the copyright page.

PART 2: THE SEAT OF THE SOUL

PART 3: HEART AND SOUL

PART 5: SOUL WORK

PART 7: SOUL AND DESTINY

A lengthy and comprehensive effort has been made to locate all copyright holders and to clear reprint permission rights. If any acknowledgments have been omitted, or any rights overlooked, it is unintentional. If the publishers are notified, any omissions will be rectified in future editions of this book.